First World War

and Army of Occupation

War Diary

France, Belgium and Germany

33 DIVISION
100 Infantry Brigade
Worcestershire Regiment
2nd Battalion
1 January 1916 - 31 May 1919

WO95/2430/2

The Naval & Military Press Ltd
www.nmarchive.com
Published in association with The National Archives

Published by

The Naval & Military Press Ltd

Unit 10 Ridgewood Industrial Park,

Uckfield, East Sussex,

TN22 5QE England

Tel: +44 (0) 1825 749494

www.naval-military-press.com

www.nmarchive.com

Contents

Document type	Place/Title	Date From	Date To
Heading	WO95/2430/2 2 Battalion Worcestershire Regiment		
Heading	100th Bde 33rd Div 2/Worcester Rgt Jan Vol XVIII		
War Diary		01/01/1916	22/02/1916
Heading	33rd Divn 100th Bde 2 Worcester Regt Vol XX		
War Diary		22/02/1916	30/04/1916
War Diary	In The Field	01/05/1916	31/05/1916
War Diary	Jarden-Des Sports Annezine	01/06/1916	30/06/1916
Heading	100th Inf. Bde. 33rd Div. War Diary 2nd Battn. The Worcestershire Regiment. July 1916		
War Diary	In The Field	01/07/1916	31/07/1916
Heading	Report On Operations of 14th July by O.C. "C" Company		
Miscellaneous	The 2nd Battalion The Worcestershire Regiment At High Wood, Somme 1916		
Heading	100th Brigade. 33rd Division 2nd Battalion Worcestershire Regiment August 1916		
War Diary	In The Field	01/08/1916	31/03/1917
Miscellaneous	100 Inf. Bde	09/03/1917	09/03/1917
Map	Scheme 1		
Diagram etc			
Miscellaneous	Scheme 2	23/02/1917	23/02/1917
Miscellaneous	Scheme I All Reference To Attached Diagram		
Map	Scheme 2		
Miscellaneous			
Miscellaneous	C Form. Messages And Signals		
War Diary	In The Field	01/04/1917	30/09/1917
Miscellaneous	The Second Worcestershire Regiment. In The Action On The Menin Road, September 25th-27th, 1917 by Lieutenant-Colonel H.E. Gogarty. Commanding Landed to Section by Capt Stacke 8.1.26.		
Miscellaneous	The Second Worcestershire Regiment.		
War Diary	In The Field	01/10/1917	31/03/1918
Heading	100th Brigade. 33rd Division 2nd Battalion Worcestershire Regiment April 1918 Report On Operations Attached		
War Diary	Ypres	01/04/1918	04/04/1918
War Diary	Brandhoek	05/04/1918	06/04/1918
War Diary	Izel-Les-Hameau	07/04/1918	10/04/1918
War Diary	Caestre-Neuve Eglise	11/04/1918	11/04/1918
War Diary	Neuve Eglise	11/04/1918	14/04/1918
War Diary	Hill 70th N E	15/04/1918	15/04/1918
War Diary	Hill 70th N W Neuve Eglise	16/04/1918	17/04/1918
War Diary	Montdes Cats	18/04/1918	19/04/1918
War Diary	Noordpeene	20/04/1918	25/04/1918
War Diary	St. Marie Capell	26/04/1918	30/04/1918
Operation(al) Order(s)	IX Corps Special Order No 3	11/04/1918	11/04/1918
Miscellaneous	Report On the part taken by the 2nd Worcestershire Regiment in the defence of neuve eglise April 11th to April 14th, 1918		
War Diary	Heuringhem	01/05/1918	03/05/1918

War Diary	NE of Steenvoorde	04/05/1918	05/05/1918
War Diary	Sheet 27 L.15.c.8.8	06/05/1918	08/05/1918
War Diary	NE Busseboom 28/9.16.b.4.4	09/05/1918	12/05/1918
War Diary	W of Brandhoek 28/9.10.a.5.1	13/05/1918	23/05/1918
War Diary	W of Houtkerque Sheet 27 D.30.d.99	24/05/1918	27/05/1918
War Diary	E of Houtkerque 27/D30.d.99	28/05/1918	29/05/1918
War Diary	Dirty Bucket Corner	30/05/1918	31/05/1918
War Diary	A-30b 1.4 (Sheet 28)	01/06/1918	06/06/1918
War Diary	Ravine H 23.d.6.8 (Sheet 28)	07/06/1918	10/06/1918
War Diary	Havre H7c75.00 (Sheet 28)	11/06/1918	15/06/1918
War Diary	In The Line H.18.d.4.2	16/06/1918	25/06/1918
War Diary		26/06/1918	25/07/1918
War Diary	Kuollys Farm H7c 75.00 Sheet 28 NW	26/07/1918	30/07/1918
War Diary	H 30.a.7.8 Sheet 28 N.W.	31/07/1918	31/07/1918
War Diary	H.30.a.7.7.1 Sheet 28 N.W.	01/08/1918	09/08/1918
War Diary	Knollys Farm H7c 75.00 (Sheet 28 N.W.)	10/08/1918	14/08/1918
War Diary	Hqd. 1.5 Sheet 28 N.W.	15/08/1918	17/08/1918
War Diary	Tunnelling Camp	18/08/1918	21/08/1918
War Diary	Le Marais Serques	22/08/1918	28/08/1918
War Diary	Sus-St-Leger	29/08/1918	17/09/1918
War Diary	Lechelle Sheet 57	18/08/1918	20/08/1918
War Diary	57c SE	20/08/1918	30/08/1918
Miscellaneous	Report On Operations In Which The 2nd Bn. Worcestershire Regt. With Part.	21/09/1930	21/09/1930
Diagram etc	Legende		
Miscellaneous	Casualties to the Bn were as follows:-		
War Diary		01/10/1918	31/01/1919
War Diary	Martin Eglise	13/02/1919	26/02/1919
War Diary	Martin Eglise	01/02/1919	31/03/1919
War Diary	Cinder City Le Havre	01/04/1919	30/04/1919
War Diary	Le Havre	01/05/1919	31/05/1919

WO/95/2430/2

2 Battalion Worcestershire Regiment

2

100/33

100th Bde 33rd Div.

7/ Worcester Regt

Jan

Vol XVIII

Jan 16
May 19

S.A.

Vol 2. Page 9.

Instructions regarding War Diaries and Intelligence Summaries are contained in F. S. Regs., Part II. and the Staff Manual respectively. Title Pages will be prepared in manuscript.

WAR DIARY
or
~~INTELLIGENCE SUMMARY~~

(Erase heading not required.)

Army Form C. 2118

Place	Date	Hour	Summary of Events and Information	Remarks and references to Appendices
	1-1-16		The Battalion marched from ANNEZIN at 7.30.A.M to the trenches in B.1. sub-section GIVENCHY, relieved 21ST ROYAL FUSILIERS. Relief commenced at PONT FIXE at 10.30.A.M. and was completed at 12.30.p.m.. A very cold bleak day. The Battalion was disposed as follows:- 'D' Coy RIGHT FRONT, 'C' Coy, LEFT FRONT, 'A' Coy PONT FIXE. 'B' Coy 3 Platoons PONT FIXE and 1 Platoon SIDBURY HILL. The trenches were in a bad state. ORCHARD REDOUBT was over knee deep in mud SOUTH. Between 1.0.P.M to 3.0.P.M a carrying party was bringing Gas Cylinders down CHEYNE WALK from FRONT LINE. They must have been spotted by Germans as their guns started shelling CHEYNE WALK, and Cylinders had to be put under cover till after dark. The only work that could be done was cleaning trenches. The Battalion on our LEFT 6TH BUFFS. 12TH DIVISION. Battalion on our RIGHT, A. & S. HIGHLANDERS, 98TH BRIGADE.	Map BETHUNE 1/40,000
	2-1-16		A quiet night. At 9.30.A.M. Enemy commenced sending MINEWERFERS into our RIGHT FRONT Platoon and mine head on Canal Bank and damaged it badly burying 3 Miners and killing a Sergeant and one Man of ours and wounding 2 Men. About 10.45.A.M TRENCH MORTARS were particularly heavy, comming from SOUTH bank of CANAL. The RIGHT FRONT Platoon moved about 100 yards to the LEFT. The whole of the trench occupied by this Platoon was very badly damaged soon afterwards. The whole of our FRONT LINE was heavily shelled by light guns commencing about 10.45.A.M. damaging the wire and trenches slightly of our LEFT FRONT Coy. About 12. Noon shelling almost ceased for about half an hour. About 12.30.P.M it recommenced and kept up till 2.0.p.m. CHEYNE WALK and Battalion Head Quarters received particular attention. BAKER STREET was completely knocked in. PONT FIXE was shelled intermittently from 9.0.A.M to 2.0.P.M. All our communication by telephone was cut for some time and messages had to be sent by orderlies. Working parties on communication trenches had to cease work and stand to arms under cover as much as possible. Our guns were called upon to shell the location of TRENCH MORTAR Battery but did not seem to effect it. After dark it became very quiet and remained so for the remainder of the evening. Casualties 4 Men killed 2 Men wounded. At dusk our	

1875 Wt. W593/826 1,000,000 4/15 J.B.C. & A. A.D.S.S./Forms/C. 2118.

Vol. 2. Page. 10.

Instructions regarding War Diaries and Intelligence Summaries are contained in F. S. Regs., Part II. and the Staff Manual respectively. Title Pages will be prepared in manuscript.

WAR DIARY
or
~~INTELLIGENCE SUMMARY~~
(Erase heading not required.)

Army Form C. 2118

Place	Date	Hour	Summary of Events and Information	Remarks and references to Appendices
	2-1-16		Chaplain. CAPTAIN. J. R. STEWART, when officiating at Burial Service at WOBURN ABBEY. was killed by shell. He is a great loss to the Battalion!	Map. BETHUNE 1/40000
	3-1-16		Intermittent shelling of PONT FIXE by guns of light calibre during the whole night. No damage was done. Quite all along our front line. Very quiet day up till about 3.0pm when heavy shelling of CHEYNE WALK Battalion Head Quarters and PONT FIXE commenced. Front line was also shelled by Field Guns. The whole section was heavily shelled from 3.0pm to 4.0pm which died down and finally ceased about 4.15pm. Working parties were employed all night on right front line, BAKER ST. and CHEYNE WALK repairing damage done by shelling yesterday. Listening posts were sent out during the night close up to the German wire, no sounds of enemy were heard. Their flares seemed to be sent up from their 3rd line. About 6.30pm our guard on PONT FIXE bridge reported a lamp signalling from direction of enemy's trenches south of canal and twice read the words "JOHN BULL". At intervals during the night the enemy opened bursts of rapid fire on our front line trenches, evidently with the object of catching us repairing our trenches. Casualties. 1 man wounded 1 man shell shock.	
	4-1-16		Except for bursts of rapid fire the night was quiet. At 6.30am our relief by 16th Middlesex Regt commenced and was completed without incident. About 10.30am PONT FIXE was shelled soon after we had got clear of the trenches. Battalion marched to billets in ANNEQUIN (north). In the afternoon and evening we had to furnish working and carrying parties up to 200 men. No casualties today. Draft of 79 N.C.O's and men joined us today from 5th Battalion.	
	5-1-16		Billeted in ANNEQUIN. Had to furnish 280 men on working and carrying parties. About 2.30pm a German aeroplane came over our line but was driven back by our Anti air craft guns.	
	6-1-16		Billeted in ANNEQUIN. Furnished working parties up to 475 men.	
	7-1-16		Took over trenches in A 2 sub section. Relief commenced 3.0pm and was completed at 5.30pm. Enemy sent a number of trench mortars into our trenches around the Brickstacks between 6.0pm and 10.0pm. A few light shells were sent over in direction of church and village. Dispositions A Coy. Right front D Coy Left front B and C Companies PONT FIXE and HARLEY ST. Battalion on our right 16th K.R.R and 16th Middlesex.	Map Bethune 1/40000 sq. A15 d. 6.0.
	8-1-16		The night was generally quiet except for a few shots from hostile snipers. Between 7.45am and 8.15am our front line and HOLLOW were shelled by Field Guns and our second line and communication trenches with larger shells. HARLEY ST and PONT FIXE also shelled. Two shells hit house where B Coy's officers were billeted one going right in and destroying the kit of Capt. J. H. WATSON. Intermittent shelling the whole morning of the whole sub. section, LOVERS REDOUBT and PUDDING COTTAGES were shelled by 4.2. No damage done. Quite 50 per cent of the shells were blind. A mine was exploded by us near sap 6 at 4.30am which is believed to have been very successful. There was no hostile retaliation. Our Lewis guns opened fire when the mine was exploded. Patrols were sent round eastern	

1875 Wt. W593/826 1,000,000 4/15 J.B.C. & A. A.D.S.S./Forms/C. 2118.

Vol 2. Page 11.

Instructions regarding War Diaries and Intelligence Summaries are contained in F. S. Regs., Part II. and the Staff Manual respectively. Title Pages will be prepared in manuscript.

WAR DIARY
or
~~INTELLIGENCE SUMMARY~~

(Erase heading not required.)

Army Form C. 2118

Place	Date	Hour	Summary of Events and Information	Remarks and references to Appendices
	8-1-16		lip of new crater and found no signs of the enemy. Work carried out: parapet revetted on east face of Brickstack Keep. Trenches deepened in neighbourhood of Keep. Work commenced: new dugouts, pumping water from mine shaft, cleaning and repairing HUNTER ST. During the afternoon one of our aeroplanes kept flying very low over our trenches, and the Germans fired some thousands of rounds of ammunition at it from machine guns and rifles but it escaped unhurt. A few trench mortars were fired into the Brickstacks.	Map Bethune 1/40000
	9-1-16		During the night heavy gun firing was heard about 2.30 am. several miles north in the direction of RICHEBOURG or NEUVE CHAPPELLE. It lasted over an hour and then quietened down. Our particular front was quiet during the night. About 11.0 am enemy commenced shelling Battalion Head Quarters and the whole of the CUINCHY village line, PONT FIXE and HARLEY ST. Several trench mortars fell around the Brickstack Keep and that vicinity, which also came in for a certain amount of light shells. Sniping was kept up by our sentries during the night, and our Lewis Guns were active along the canal bank and railway. We put out fresh wire to right front of craters of new mine. Casualties two men wounded. B. Coy relieved A Coy on Right front, C Coy relieved D Coy on left front.	
	10-1-16		A few trench mortars were fired in and around the brickstacks during the night, doing no damage. Our sentries kept up a sniping fire on the enemy's line during the night. The HOLLOW was shelled with light Field guns during the morning. Battalion Head Quarters and PONT FIXE was shelled with Field guns from 11.0 am till 12 noon and then heavy shells. One shell penetrated the cellar at Battalion Head Quarters, destroying the documents in our office and wounding (shell shock) the Orderly Room Clerk, Sergt Sugg and one runner. Head Quarters had to vacate the building for about half an hour. Several of the shells were blind fortunately. PONT FIXE on both sides the canal was shelled with 4.2 Howitzers. Patrols reconnoitred round eastern crater and found no signs of enemy.	
	11-1-16		Trench mortar bombs were sent into the brickstack at intervals during the night. During the night we threw some bombs into the crater East of JERUSALEM HILL and in reply the Germans threw three bombs back. Our sentries kept up rifle fire on the German trenches during the night. Enemy's sniping very feeble. The usual shelling of PONT FIXE and HARLEY ST commenced about 10.0 am and kept up during the day. In the afternoon Battalion Head Quarters was again shelled by 4.2 howitzers, the house being hit again twice. Our patrols went round advanced crater on Railway Embankment and found no signs of the enemy. A Coy relieved B in Right front line. D Coy relieved C in left front-line.	
	12-1-16		Fairly quiet night. A few light shells came over village line during the night and some trench mortars in and around the brickstacks. The usual shelling began about 10.0 am and kept up till 1.0 pm. The HOLLOW and CABBAGE PATCH REDOUBT [torn] e shelled by light Field guns.	

1875 Wt. W593/826 1,000,000 4/15 J.B.C. & A. A.D.S.S./Forr

Vol 2. Page 12.

Instructions regarding War Diaries and Intelligence Summaries are contained in F. S. Regs., Part II. and the Staff Manual respectively. Title Pages will be prepared in manuscript.

WAR DIARY
or
~~INTELLIGENCE SUMMARY~~
(Erase heading not required.)

Army Form C. 2118

Place	Date	Hour	Summary of Events and Information	Remarks and references to Appendices
	12-1-16		During the afternoon PONT FIXE and HARLEY ST were again shelled. Two German aeroplanes were flying over German lines, but made no attempt to cross ours. We also had two aeroplanes up and the enemy opened rifle and machine gun fire on them from their trenches. We immediately called on our gunners to retaliate on the German trenches where the fire was coming from. Work done – Revetting lip of crater and making new trench to crater, other trenches widened and deepened and some dugouts reclaimed. C.Q.M.S. J. Wells was killed by a shell in HARLEY ST.	Map Bethune 1/40000
	13-1-16		Hostile snipers were more active than usual during the night. Our Lewis Gun fired on the trenches at "Stand to" in the morning and evening. A few trench mortars were sent in and around the brickstacks during the night doing no damage. During the morning the HOLLOW, PONT FIXE, HARLEY ST and the village line were shelled intermittently. In the afternoon it commenced again but not to such an extent. Some heavy shells were dropped into PONT FIXE about 4.30 pm. B Coy relieved A Coy in Right front. C. Coy relieved D in Left front. A Coy to SUPPORT, D Coy to PONT FIXE.	
	14-1-16		A fairly quiet night. Some sniping and trench mortaring during the night doing no damage. Shelling began about 10.30 am and continued till about 12.30 pm. PONT FIXE HARLEY ST PUDDING LANE and Battalion Head Quarters on which there were two direct hits. PUDDING LANE COTTAGES and that vicinity was shelled with 4.2 Hows. between 11.0 am and 12 noon. A German working party was discovered on their wire during the night, we brought up a Lewis Gun and fired on them and they scattered. We sent out patrols at 2.30 am and 5.0 am along the Railway Embankment and found no signs of the enemy. Two of our aeroplanes were flying very low and were fired on by machine guns and rifles. We called on our gunners to retaliate on trenches where the firing came from which they did. The Battalion was relieved by the 1st Cameronians today. Relief commenced at 5. pm and was completed about 8. pm. After relief the Battalion marched to Billets in BETHUNE where they arrived about 11. pm.	
	15-1-16		Billeted in BETHUNE, men resting and cleaning arms equipment and clothing. Capt (Rev) H Ewbank is attached to the Battalion for duty.	
	16-1-16		Billeted in BETHUNE. Baths allotted to the Battalion. Every man had a hot bath and clean change of underclothing.	
	17-1-16		Billeted in BETHUNE. Working party of 50 men furnished from 9.0 am till 5.0 pm.	
	18-1-16		Billeted in BETHUNE. Working party of 50 men furnished from 9 am till 5.0 pm. A, B and D Companies assembled at ANNEZIN FOSSE for drill and instruction and smoke helmet practice.	
	19-1-16		Billeted in BETHUNE. Working party of officers and 200 men from 9.0 am till 5.0 pm.	

Vol 2. Page 13.

Instructions regarding War Diaries and Intelligence Summaries are contained in F. S. Regs., Part II. and the Staff Manual respectively. Title Pages will be prepared in manuscript.

WAR DIARY
or
~~INTELLIGENCE SUMMARY~~

(Erase heading not required.)

Army Form C. 2118

Place	Date	Hour	Summary of Events and Information	Remarks and references to Appendices
	20-1-16		Billeted in Bethune. The Battalion went for a Route march via ANNEZIN, FOUQUEREUIL, FOUQUÈRES and returning home about 1 0 pm.	Map Bethune 1/40000
	21-1-16		Billeted in BETHUNE.	
	22-1-16		Billeted in BETHUNE. The C.O. Adjutant and Company Commanders visited the trenches to be taken over on the 24th inst.	
	23-1-16		Billeted in BETHUNE. The Battalion attended Divine Service in the unfinished Chapel in RUE D'AIRE at 9.30 am. The Battalion moved to south ANNEQUIN at 1.30 pm to relieve the 21st Bn Royal Fusiliers which was completed about 4.30 pm. There was slight shelling on the way and companies made a detour to avoid it. There were no casualties.	
	24-1-16		The Battalion relieved the 2nd ARGYLE and SUTHERLAND HIGHLANDERS in Z2. Relief commenced at 4.30 pm and was completed about 7.30 pm. The 1st Queens Gds took over our billets. A few shells landed in the surroundings of billets during the morning. There were no casualties. Dispositions in the line. A Coy in reserve B Coy Right front. C Coy Centre front. D Coy left front. Battalion on the Right. 1st Queens, on the left 20th Bn Royal Fusiliers.	
	25-1-16		The trenches were in a fairly good condition. Work done, cleaning and improving firesteps. Enemy's snipers were fairly active. At 12.30 am our artillery dispersed a working party and at Dawn our snipers dispersed the same party properly. A German was seen wearing a Great coat and round cap, more about him was impossible to find out. A few bombs were thrown by our bombers in retaliation to the enemy. The night was fairly quiet.	
	26-1-16		Our trenches were shelled with shrapnel, and a few 4.2s landed beyond our reserve trenches. Two men were wounded by enemy's rifle grenades; we put out several wire balls and constructed some Loop Holes and knocked out an enemy's snipers Post. About 11 pm Brigade Head Quarters took over Battalion Head Quarters dugouts. The Battalion Head Quarters took over the Company in reserve Dugouts. This Company was moved into the 2nd Line about mid-night. The night passed quietly. Our artillery fired during the night.	
	27-1-16		The Kaisers birthday. Our artillery very active, also our snipers, and did a lot of execution, knocking out several snipers' posts with an Elephant gun. During the afternoon our Artillery (Howitzers) bombarded craters west of NINE POINT and the enemy's trenches making direct hits several times. Our Right front Company evacuated the line during the bombardment and re-occupied it afterwards. The artillery also reported that they had knocked out an enemy's trench mortar in front of our left front Company. About 6 sticks with tape attached was noticed in ~~their~~ Enemys parapet, probably to test the wind. About 6 am in the morning a heavy bombardment was heard on our left, probably near GIVENCHY, lasting 10 minutes. The enemy slightly shelled our 2nd Line.	
	28-1-16		A small mine was exploded by the enemy opposite junction of B and C Companies, A21 d 4½ 1½ about 40 yards from the parapet at about 10.0 am. There were no casualties and no damage was done to the front line. This started heavy shelling by both sides, which lasted more or less for all day till 4.30 pm. The enemy shelled our front line 2nd Line and Support Lines with shrapnel and Trench Mortars, paying particular attention to junctions of communication Trenches and Keeps. Our Artillery fired on their front line trenches and appeared to do considerable damage.	

1875 Wt. W593/826 1,000,000 4/15 J.B.C. &A. A.D.S.S./Forms/C. 2118.

Vol 2. Page 14.

Instructions regarding War Diaries and Intelligence Summaries are contained in F. S. Regs., Part II. and the Staff Manual respectively. Title Pages will be prepared in manuscript.

WAR DIARY
or
~~INTELLIGENCE SUMMARY~~
(Erase heading not required.)

Army Form C. 2118

Place	Date	Hour	Summary of Events and Information	Remarks and references to Appendices
	28-1-16		Considering the amount of shelling very little or no damage was done to our trenches, which was put right during the night, by a party of the pioneer Battalion. Our casualties throughout the day were 4 killed and 20 wounded. From 5.0pm onwards hourly reports were made to Brigade. Battalion Head Quarters moved about 6.0pm to advanced Battalion Head Quarters. During the day B Company's communication was cut. A Platoon of A Coy holding LEWIS KEEP was relieved at 10 pm and joined their Company in the 2nd Line. During the preliminary bombardment a German carrying a white flag walked along their parapet and was fired on.	Map. Béthune 1/40000
	29-1-16		A mine was blown up by the enemy at 1.10 am. Rapid fire and Artillery fire was opened. There was no damage done nor any casualties. The mine was within 25 yards in line with the mine blown up the previous morning. We occupied No1 Crater and bombed the enemy's front line from it, withdrawing at day break. Artillery on both sides were more or less in active, a few light shells were fired about mid. day by the enemy. Enemy's snipers were a little more active. Orders were received that the Battalion would be relieved at 2. pm by 1st Queens and to go into Reserve trenches in Support. At 2 pm orders were received that the Battalion would move back to billets in ANNEQUIN FOSSE at 4.30 pm. The Battalion moved by Companies at 4.30 pm and reached ANNEQUIN FOSSE at about 6. pm. There were two casualties during the day.	
	30-1-16		Billeted in ANNEQUIN FOSSE. Companies rested and had a clean up.	
	31-1-16		Billeted at ANNEQUIN FOSSE. At 4.15 pm the Battalion started to relieve the 1st Queens in Section Z2. The relief was completed by 7.15 pm. Companies were ordered to hold the line as follows. A Coy. Right front C Company Centre front, D Company Left front, and B Company Reserve. B Company found 80 men for fatigue before going to the trenches. The night was very quiet except for Rifle Grenades & trench mortars which were rather troublesome. Two men were killed in C Company with rifle grenades. L/Sergt. Matthews A Company and Corpl Dunne B. Company were promoted Sergeant in recognition of good work in the Field.	

G. C. Lambton
Lieut-Colonel
Commanding 2nd Bn. The Worcestershire Regt.

Vol. 2. Page. 15.

100/33

Instructions regarding War Diaries and Intelligence Summaries are contained in F. S. Regs., Part II. and the Staff Manual respectively. Title Pages will be prepared in manuscript.

WAR DIARY
or
~~INTELLIGENCE SUMMARY~~
(Erase heading not required.)

Army Form C. 2118

Place	Date	Hour	Summary of Events and Information	Remarks and references to Appendices
	1-2-16		Very quiet night. One or two Trench Mortars were fired into our Saps killing two men unfortunately. About 4.30 A.M. trench mortars again opened on our front line. Rifle Grenades were also fired at us killing two more men. Our guns were called upon to retaliate and this had the effect of silencing their mortars. Our Bombers threw some bombs into the Southern Craters, effect not known. A number of Wire balls were made and put out during the night. The day passed very quietly. Some trench mortars were fired into our line at intervals. Little or no shelling. Work done – New traverse put up in Boyau 21. Some Steel plate loopholes were fixed in Snipers Posts. Parapet in High STREET repaired, Saps deepened. Enemy were working on their wire during the night.	MAP BETHUNE 1/40,000
	2-2-16		A fairly quiet night. Some sniping and trench mortaring. A few trench mortars were fired into our lines during the day. Our guns retaliated. Our snipers, using Armour Piercing Ammunition and a Special Gun destroyed several snipers plates and no sniping by Germans has taken place since. A few light shell were fired into our RIGHT Coy doing no damage. Work done – Firesteps and Parapets repaired, wire balls made and put out. A Sap was dug from our front line in direction of recently formed crater and to about 15 yards from it. The patrol covering this reported hearing the hammering of stakes in the crater. After dusk the enemy became active with Trench Mortars, Rifle Grenades and Rifle Fire. At 12 Mid-night we sprang a Mine just NORTH of large crater in front of BOYAU 15. A very large quantity of earth was thrown up and although our FRONT LINE was cleared for about 200 yards six men were injured by falling debris. Our guns opened fire for 10 minutes after explosion the enemy did not retaliate.	

S. 5

1875 Wt. W593/826 1,000,000 4/15 J.B.C. & A. A.D.S.S./Forms/C. 2118.

Instructions regarding War Diaries and Intelligence Summaries are contained in F. S. Regs., Part II. and the Staff Manual respectively. Title Pages will be prepared in manuscript.

WAR DIARY
or
~~INTELLIGENCE SUMMARY~~
(Erase heading not required.)

Army Form C. 2118

Place	Date	Hour	Summary of Events and Information	Remarks and references to Appendices
	3-2-16		At 3.A.M. we sprang another Mine SOUTH of the same Crater. Our guns again fired for 10. minutes. Immediately this mine was exploded the enemy sent flares up from the Crater now situated between the two Craters formed, so that little or no damage could have been done in it, and at the same time opened Rifle fire and threw Bombs in front of it, consequently our attempt to occupy the WESTERN lip was frustrated. A portion of the enemy's wire was blown away by the mine explosion. Part of our Sap was also damaged, this was cleared afterwards. All was quiet at daybreak. During the morning some Trench Mortars were fired into our FRONT LINE. Our guns when informed retaliated and caused enemy to cease mortaring. Our Snipers were active during the day and kept hostile sniping well under. A few heavy shells dropped near WIMPOLE STREET and WILSONS WAY communication trench. During the afternoon our Trench Mortars kept sending bombs into the Crater occupied by Germans, and prevented them working. An attack on this crater by the 16th MIDDLESEX was ordered to take place tonight, but there was not sufficient time to organize it thoroughly. Work done. — Wire balls made and thrown over parapet. General repairs to trenches.	
	4-2-16		During the night our LEWIS GUN fired at intervals preventing any hostile parties working in front of their line. Our Sentries also fired periodically. It was 6.a.m before the bombers of the attacking party on Crater got into position for going forward. They at once advanced and threw about 50 Hand Grenades into Crater. Enemy retaliated with	

Vol. 2. Page. 17.

Instructions regarding War Diaries and Intelligence Summaries are contained in F. S. Regs., Part II. and the Staff Manual respectively. Title Pages will be prepared in manuscript.

WAR DIARY
or
~~INTELLIGENCE SUMMARY~~
(Erase heading not required.)

Army Form C. 2118

Place	Date	Hour	Summary of Events and Information	Remarks and references to Appendices
	4-2-16		bombs and as it was almost daybreak it was not considered advisible to continue the attack, as it would have been impossible to consolidate position in the daylight even if taken. Bombing parties were therefore withdrawn to our trenches. The Company of the 16th MIDDLESEX were taken out of the line as soon as possible after daybreak. A quiet day followed. Enemys snipers seemed to be non-existant. No TRENCH MORTARS were fired by Germans. Our TRENCH MORTARS kept up a fire on Crater to prevent enemy working in it. A WHITE FLAG was noticed in enemy's line opposite No. 1. MINE HEAD., Work done – General repairs to trenches. A new sap was begun towards another Mine Crater from our advanced post in a nearer Crater. Attack on Crater as ordered last night, was again ordered for tonight and arrangements begun soon after dusk. Preparations were completed and attack launched about 11.30.P.M. The Crater was strongly held and attack failed. The attacking Company was withdrawn to our trenches.	
	5-2-16		The night was very quiet after the attack failed, but it was a very restless night for the troops as they were standing to arms most of the night. One or two TRENCH MORTARS were fired over our trenches but no damage was done. During the morning our Snipers were active and kept enemys Snipers well under, and demolished one of their Sniping positions. A RED and WHITE screen in the corner of the GERMAN LEFT hand Crater was located, probably an Artillery screen. Enemy's Artillery was quiet today. Work done – Continued Sap from SOUTHERN Crater and repaired trenches generally. Another attack was ordered to be made on Crater tonight by a Company of the 2ND ROYAL WELCH FUSILIERS. Our FRONT LINE was moved to the flanks to allow the attackers to form up. At 9.45.P.M. they got over our parapet and	

1875 Wt. W593/826 1,000,000 4/15 J.B.C. & A. A.D.S.S./Forms/C. 2118.

Vol. 2. Page. 18.

Instructions regarding War Diaries and Intelligence Summaries are contained in F. S. Regs., Part II. and the Staff Manual respectively. Title Pages will be prepared in manuscript.

WAR DIARY
or
~~INTELLIGENCE SUMMARY~~
(Erase heading not required.)

Army Form C. 2118

Place	Date	Hour	Summary of Events and Information	Remarks and references to Appendices
	5-2-16		through our wire, and made straight for the Crater lip. In seven minutes the position was in our possession and the work of consolidating was commenced and carried on during the night.	
	6-2-16.		Our Artillery was called upon to retaliate against TRENCH MORTARS and some light shelling after enemy had found we had secured the Crater lips. It was only for a short time and all became quiet again. We continued Sap between the two SOUTHERN Craters and established a post there. Some wire balls were thrown out to strengthen wire in front of LEFT COYS trenches. About 9.A.M the enemy attempted a bombing counter attack to drive party from Crater lip. They were immediately driven back and our Artillery was called upon to fire on their trenches. All was again quiet in about half an hour. During the day the GERMANS fired a large number of TRENCH MORTAR BOMBS and some RIFLE GRENADES into our trenches. They also opened Artillery fire on our FRONT LINE and COMMUNICATION trenches during the morning. Again in the afternoon from 3.0.P.M. to 4.30.P.M. they were very active and shelled the whole of our trenches and BATTALION HEAD QUARTERS, one direct hit on C.O's. dug-out, which fortunately did no damage beyond making a small crater on the roof. Heavy shelling ceased about dusk but single shells were sent over about every three or four minutes, all night into the third line and near WIMPOLE STREET. Saps were improved during the night and general repairs to trenches carried out. Enemy were kept out of Crater by continuous bombing.	
	7-2-16		The night was disturbing owing to the continuous shells comming over and TRENCH MORTARS and Snipers were busy most of the night. The shelling ceased at 5.0.A.M and the morning broke quietly. About 9.0.A.M some TRENCH MORTARS came over and our guns retaliated. A few light shells were fired at our trenches during the	

1875 Wt. W593/826 1,000,000 4/15 J.B.C. & A. A.D.S.S./Forms/C. 2118.

· Vol. 2. Page. 19.

Instructions regarding War Diaries and Intelligence Summaries are contained in F. S. Regs., Part II. and the Staff Manual respectively. Title Pages will be prepared in manuscript.

WAR DIARY
or
~~INTELLIGENCE SUMMARY~~
(Erase heading not required.)

Army Form C. 2118

Place	Date	Hour	Summary of Events and Information	Remarks and references to Appendices
	7-2-16		morning. At 2.30 P.M. a heavy shelling of our whole section was begun and continued till 4.30 P.M. doing considerable damage to our Communication trenches and knocking some of our front parapets in. The Crater in advanced position was shelled by enemy. All our guns were called upon to retaliate which they did with effect. Relief by 1/5th SCOTTISH RIFLES commenced at 5.30 P.M. and finished about 8 P.M. After relief the Battalion marched to billets in BETHUNE, RUE D'AIRE area. Tea with rum, and Bread and Cheese was served at BEUVRY, this was much appreciated by the men who continued the march very cheerfully arriving in BETHUNE about 11.0 P.M. Major. A. WHITTY. D.S.O. Quartermaster joined Battalion today.	
	8-2-16		Billeted in BETHUNE. The day was spent resting and cleaning arms, equipment and clothing.	
	9-2-16		Billeted in BETHUNE. Working parties of 200 men furnished. Battalion Head Quarters, "C" and "D" Companies route march wearing Smoke Helmets for practice.	
	10-2-16		Billeted at BETHUNE. Hot baths at COLLEGE DES JUNNES FILLES allotted Battalion. Every man had a bath and clean change of underclothing.	
	11-2-16		Billeted in BETHUNE. 200 N.C.O's & Men for Working party, furnished classes of instruction in BOMBING, SCOUTING, LEWIS GUN, and STRETCHER BEARERS.	
	12-2-16		Billeted in BETHUNE. Classes of instruction in BOMBING, SCOUTING, LEWIS GUN, and STRETCHER BEARERS Remainder of men at disposal of Company Commanders for practising Raiding expedition on GERMAN trenches.	
	13-2-16		Billeted in BETHUNE. Battalion attended Divine Service in MUNICIPAL THEATRE at 11.0 A.M. Service conducted by the REV: H. EWBANK, attached to Battalion. Some Side-drums and Flutes having been drawn from ORDNANCE, a small Corps of Drums was formed and played for the first time marching Battalion to church. They also beat RETREAT in billeting area to the delight of the inhabitants.	
	14-2-16		The Brigade having been ordered to take over the trenches in SECTION A and SUB-SECTION B.1 Battalion moved up in support and was billeted in ANNEQUIN (North). Battalion left BETHUNE at 1.0 P.M. and arrived in fresh billets between 3.0 p.m and 4.0 P.M. It rained during march and	Map BETHUNE 1/40,000 A.21 & 51 to Aq. d[illegible]

1875 Wt. W593/826 1,000,000 4/15 J.B.C. & A. A.D.S.S./Forms/C. 2118.

Vol. 2. Page. 20

Instructions regarding War Diaries and Intelligence Summaries are contained in F. S. Regs., Part II. and the Staff Manual respectively. Title Pages will be prepared in manuscript.

WAR DIARY
or
~~INTELLIGENCE SUMMARY~~
(Erase heading not required.)

Army Form C. 2118

Place	Date	Hour	Summary of Events and Information	Remarks and references to Appendices
	14-2-16		for about an hour after arrival in billets. Working parties of about 200 men had to be furnished soon after arrival, and Mining Fatigues of 8 Hours Shifts working night and day detailed.	
	15-2-16		Billeted in ANNEQUIN (North). Working parties of about 400 men furnished.	
	16-2-16		Billeted in ANNEQUIN (North) Working parties of about 400 men furnished. Hot baths were allotted from 8.0 A.M. to 1.0 p.m. All available men bathed and had a change of Underclothing.	
	17-2-16		Billeted in ANNEQUIN (North). Working parties of 400 men were furnished. C.O. and Adjutant, and Coy Commanders reconnoitred the trenches in A.2. SUB-SECTION.	
	18-2-16		D. Coy relieved support Coy in A2. sub-section at 7.0am to allow the latter to furnish mining fatigues. Remainder of Battalion moved to trenches at 5.0pm to relieve 16th Middlesex in A2 subsection. Relief was carried out in wind and rain, and was completed at 8.10pm without casualties. Evening was very quiet. One or two shells were sent into PONT FIXE.	
	19-2-16		Our snipers having selected posts during daylight yesterday, were active during the night and at daybreak. Some German snipers were located on Railway Embankment and Brickstacks. During the night the enemy sent up some red lights north of canal. Our machine guns fired at intervals during the night. It was a bright moonlight night. Morning quiet except for some light shelling on Village line and communication trenches which did no harm. Our artillery retaliated and hostile shelling ceased. One of our aeroplanes was forced to descend just behind our line. The enemy immediately shelled the place of descent, getting a direct hit on the aeroplane. One man was wounded, the other was all right. Work done – Trenches repaired generally. Six snipers posts were made commanding both sides of canal. Saps No 14, 15 & 16 were worked on and extended towards objective during the night. Wire strengthened.	
	20.2.16		Some rifle Grenades were fired into our trenches during the night, also one or two trench mortars. Our artillery was called on and the enemy ceased. Sniping was active on both sides, but we seemed to get the ascendancy. At dawn our snipers shot two Germans. A FRENCH flag was put up in a tree just in front of the German trenches. At 8.35am the enemy exploded a mine about 70 yards in front of the Right Coy's trench (A.22 a.0.4) which damaged our mine galleries and buried 4 miners. No damage was done to our trenches and we had no casualties. This was undoubtedly a pure defensive mine intended to destroy our mine gallery. The crater was within bombing distance of our advanced post in crater blown on 2.1.16 No artillery barrage was attempted by either side and the enemy made no endeavours to occupy lip on side.	

1875 Wt. W593/826 1,000,000 4/15 J.B.C. & A. A.D.S.S./Forms/C. 2118.

Vol. 2. Page 21.

Instructions regarding War Diaries and Intelligence Summaries are contained in F. S. Regs., Part II. and the Staff Manual respectively. Title Pages will be prepared in manuscript.

WAR DIARY
or
~~INTELLIGENCE SUMMARY~~

(Erase heading not required.)

Army Form C. 2118

Place	Date	Hour	Summary of Events and Information	Remarks and references to Appendices
	20.2.16		The remainder of the day was quiet. One or two shells were fired in the direction of PONT FIXE. Two aeroplanes were forced to descend about a mile behind our line, having been hit by rifle bullets fired from German front line. It would appear that their front line is very strongly held from the amount of rifle fire directed at these planes. Work done – Saps extended ten to fifteen feet, work on trenches revetting and cleaning continued, fire positions improved and another sniper post constructed. About 6.30pm a bombing attack on craters was made by Right front Coy (Capt. Watson) assisted by a platoon from D. Coy. This attack was driven back by bombs and rifle fire from enemy's positions in crater and front line. Instructions were received that another determined attempt must be made to secure these two craters lips 8-1-1916 and 20.2.16 during the night. Wind being favourable for a hostile gas attack, smoke helmets were ordered to be worn during the night.	
	21-2-16		O.C. B Coy organized another attack directed first at 20.2.16 crater. At 12.30am the lip of the crater was occupied and parties told off to consolidate there. After half an hours work it was found that crater 8.1.16 could be reached by sapping from crater 20.2.1916. This work was commenced and about 20 yards dug before morning. The enemy were apparently aware of some work going on and kept up rifle fire and bombing. Our guns were called on to fire 12 rounds which kept hostile fire down a little. One man was killed and two men wounded during these operations. At dawn it was found we were still about 40 yards from the lip of the 8.1.16 crater. It was impossible to continue the work during the day. Morning broke quietly, with no unusual effort on the part of the Germans to investigate the nights activity on our front. At 10.45am the enemy fired some large Trench Mortars into our Centre and Right Coy, and towards Cabbage Patch Redoubt. Our snipers were active and caused enemy much annoyance. One German was hit near a brickstack and our Elephant gun made a large hole in an iron truck from which a sniper was located. It may have accounted for the sniper as he ceased firing. Our observers noticed an enemy's working party behind their lines. Artillery were informed and dispersed them with a few rounds. Some light shells were fired at our Left Coy on Railway Embankment and followed this up with one or two heavies on bridge. At dusk work was begun lengthening sap towards crater 8.1.16 covered by bombers. Work done – Usual trench cleaning and repairing. Wire in front of the BULGE strengthened. Saps of Centre Coy extended 15 yards. 2nd Lieut Taylor rejoined from Base.	
	22-2-16		Sapping to lip of Crater 8-1-1916 continued and reached a point about 8 yards from lip. We now command the crater with bombing. A patrol was sent out from Left Coy and reached about 30 yards from the enemy's trenches where they lay and listened in a shell hole. The Germans could be distinctly heard talking and laughing and seemed pretty cheerful. It snowed during the day. Not much activity by either side. One or two light shells were fired into our section and our artillery fired at enemy's post on the Canal bank.	

1875 Wt. W593/826 1,000,000 4/15 J.B.C. & A. A.D.S.S./Forms/C. 2118.

2/33

33rd DIVn

2 Worcester Regt

Vol XX

5.20

Vol 2. Page 22.

Instructions regarding War Diaries and Intelligence Summaries are contained in F. S. Regs., Part II. and the Staff Manual respectively. Title Pages will be prepared in manuscript.

WAR DIARY
or
~~INTELLIGENCE SUMMARY~~
(Erase heading not required.)

Army Form C. 2118

Place	Date	Hour	Summary of Events and Information	Remarks and references to Appendices
	22.2.16		Sniping activity very much reduced and we have certainly got the upper hand. We put out some wire during the night. Parapets of front trenches improved and strengthened. Snipers places erected in the BULGE. Relieved by 16th Middlesex. Relief commenced at 5.30pm and was completed at 8.10pm. Mining fatigues of 8 hours shifts furnished.	
	23.2.16		Billeted in ANNEQUIN NORTH. Mining and working parties were furnished. Snow on the ground.	
	24.2.16		Billeted in ANNEQUIN NORTH. Mining fatigues and working parties were furnished. Test Gas alarm. Snow.	
	25.2.16		Working parties furnished. The Battalion relieved the 16th Middlesex in A2 Subsection. Trenches very dry and frozen. Relief completed by 8.0pm. 16th Middlesex go back to ANNEZIN and leave Brigade. 1/6th Scottish Rifles take over our billets in ANNEQUIN. K.R.R. on our left and Queens on the Right. Queens sent out a patrol to NEW YEARS CRATER. Very quiet night.	
	26.2.16		Frost and more snow in the night. Thaw set in during the morning and made the trenches fairly wet in places. Some trench mortars were sent over near the Brickstacks, but good retaliation by one of our Trench mortars had the effect of quietening the enemy. Precautions were used against Gas. A lot of very good wiring was done by C Coy. on the left. The Queens attempted to take a Bosche prisoner on the right crater by the "Y" Sap but failed. C. Coy sent out a patrol, which was fired on as they got over the parapet. A quiet night.	
	27.2.16		Trenches beginning to get wet as the thaw still continued. Enemy's trench mortars fired a lot during the morning and damaged some of our saps. One man of D Coy was killed and one wounded. Artillery did not retaliate at all well. Trench mortars fired again in the afternoon. Patrols sent out by all three Companies. Wire was put out and work done in the trenches. A quiet day. C. Company had two men wounded by Howitzer Shell firing down the Canal.	
	28.2.16		Trench mortars were fired on Right Coy during the morning and did a considerable amount of damage and wounded four men. One Coy of the 1/6th Scottish Rifles relieved B Coy in the morning, and B Coy returned to billets in ANNEQUIN NORTH and supplied the necessary permanent fatigues. The Battalion was relieved by 1/6th Scottish Rifles. Relief was completed at 8.30pm. The Battalion moved to billets in ANNEQUIN NORTH. Casualties 1 man killed.	
	29.2.16		One and half Coys left in ANNEQUIN NORTH for permanent fatigues. Remainder of the Battalion marched to	

1875 Wt. W593/826 1,000,000 4/15 J.B.C. & A. A.D.S.S./Forms/C. 2118.

Vol. 2. Page 23.

Instructions regarding War Diaries and Intelligence Summaries are contained in F. S. Regs., Part II. and the Staff Manual respectively. Title Pages will be prepared in manuscript.

WAR DIARY
or
~~INTELLIGENCE SUMMARY~~

(Erase heading not required.)

Army Form C. 2118

Place	Date	Hour	Summary of Events and Information	Remarks and references to Appendices
	29-2-16		billets at OBLIGHEM. 1st Cameronians take over billets in ANNEQUIN at 1.30pm. The billets were scattered and not good at OBLIGHEM. Drums met Battalion at TOBACCO FACTORY. The Battalion was placed under orders of the 19th Brigade.	

G. C. Lambton
Lieut.-Colonel
Commanding 2nd Bn. The Worcestershire Regt.

1875 Wt. W593/826 J.B.C. & A. A.D.S.S./Forms/C. 2118.

Vol. 2. Page. 24

Instructions regarding War Diaries and Intelligence Summaries are contained in F. S. Regs., Part II. and the Staff Manual respectively. Title Pages will be prepared in manuscript.

WAR DIARY
or
~~INTELLIGENCE SUMMARY~~
(Erase heading not required.)

Army Form C. 2118

Place	Date	Hour	Summary of Events and Information	Remarks and references to Appendices
	1-3-16		Inspection by Coy Commanders. "A" Coy and half of "C" Coy marched in from ANNEQUIN. N. The Drums beat Retreat at 5.30. p.m.	MAP. BETHUNE 1/40.000
	2-3-16		Working parties were sent to BETHUNE. Coys were at the disposal of Coy Commanders for Handling of Arms and Musketry practise.	
	3-3-16		The Commanding Officer inspected "C" Coy in marching order. The remainder of Battalion were at the disposal of Coy Commanders for Handling of Arms and Musketry practise. The Battalion Football team beat the 1st QUEENS at ANNEZIN by 6 goals to 1.	
	4-3-16		The C. O. inspected "D" Coy in marching order. The Battalion were allotted the Hot Baths at the ECOLE DES JEUNNES FILLES. BETHUNE during the morning and afternoon. Snow fell during the morning, but thawed again in the afternoon.	
	5-3-16		The Battalion attend Church in the yard of Chateau at 11. a.m. R. C's attended Mass in VENDIN CHURCH. The Commanding Officer and Company Commanders inspected the LE TOURAY LINE of breastworks, which were found in fairly good condition but required improvements.	
	6-3-16		The C. O. inspected "A" Coy in Marching Order in the morning. Wiring, Sapping and Bombing Classes were held and Lectures under Coy Commanders during the afternoon.	
	7-3-16		A party of 115 Officers, N. C. O's & Men marched to a FLAMMENWERFER display held at ESSARS. The C. O., Adjutant and Coy Commanders reconnoitred the line in Z. 1. Sub-section in the morning.	
	8-3-16		The Battalion marched into billets at BEUVRY and relieved the 16th K. R. R's.	

1875 Wt. W593/826 1,000,000 4/15 J.B.C. & A. A.D.S.S./Forms/C. 2118.

Instructions regarding War Diaries and Intelligence Summaries are contained in F. S. Regs., Part II. and the Staff Manual respectively. Title pages will be prepared in manuscript.

WAR DIARY
or
~~INTELLIGENCE SUMMARY.~~
(Erase heading not required.)

Army Form C. 2118.

Place	Date	Hour	Summary of Events and Information	Remarks and references to Appendices
	9-3-16		The Battalion relieved the 4th KINGS LIVERPOOLS in Z.1. Sub-section (AUCHY). Relief was completed by 9.30.P.M. The distribution of Coys was as follows:- "A" Coy. Right Front; "B" Coy Centre Front, "C" Coy Left Front. "D" Coy. Reserve Coy in FACTORY TRENCH. A quiet night was passed.	Map. BETHUNE 1/40.000.
	10-3-16		The Front Line was in a very good condition, but the Second Line was muddy, also parts of the Communication Trenches. A very quiet day. During the night Machine Guns played along the parapet opposite "B" and "C" Coys and prevented them wiring. "A" Coy put out some wire.	
	11-3-16		Everything was quiet on our Front, but there was a good deal of shelling on our Right near HOHENZOLLERN REDOUBT. "D" Coy sent up a Platoon to reinforce "C" Coy as their line was very weakly held. The Bombers were sent to "A" Coy as a considerable amount of bombing went on, on our Right. "A" Coy sent out patrols and put out wire.	
	12-3-16		Commanding Officers conference was held at Brigade Headquarters at 10. a.m. The Officers of the 1/6th SCOTTISH RIFLES reconnoitred the line during the morning. A Machine Gun loophole was shelled satisfactorily by our Howitzers, and the 18 Pounders did some wire cutting. About 5.P.M. a considerable amount of shelling and bombing started on our Right but was apparently only ~~[illegible]~~ (G.S.) a false alarm	
	13-3-16		The Battalion was relieved by the 1/6th SCOTTISH RIFLES. Relief was completed by 9. a.m.	

Vol. 2. Page. 26.

Instructions regarding War Diaries and Intelligence Summaries are contained in F. S. Regs., Part II. and the Staff Manual respectively. Title pages will be prepared in manuscript.

WAR DIARY
or
~~INTELLIGENCE SUMMARY.~~
(Erase heading not required.)

Army Form C. 2118.

Place	Date	Hour	Summary of Events and Information	Remarks and references to Appendices
	13-3-16		and the Battalion moved into billets in ANNEQUIN. S.	MAP BETHUNE 1/40000
	14-3-16		Very heavy fatigues were furnished by the Battalion. The men not on fatigue spent the day cleaning equipment and clothing.	
	15-3-16		Similar fatigue parties were again furnished. The Foot-baths were allotted the Battalion. Lieut ROBERTS and draft of 13 N.C.O's + Men joined the Battalion today.	
	16-3-16		Fatigue parties went on all day. The baths at ANNEQUIN. N. were allotted to the Battalion and every man had a hot bath and change of clothing. AUCHY Right Sector was reconnoitred.	
	17-3-16		The Battalion relieved the 1/6th SCOTTISH RIFLES in AUCHY Right Sector. Relief was completed by 8.30. P.M. "A" Coy Right Front, "B" Coy Centre Front, "D" Coy Left Coy, "C" Coy, Reserve Coy. A quiet night was passed.	
	18-3-16		There was very little activity during the day. About 5. P.M. the GERMANS started shelling the Battalion on our Right (E. SURREYS) and dropped a good many shells into our Right Coy, and also around Battalion Head Quarters. There were several LACHRIMATORY shells, and gas goggles were put on. Our guns were slow in retaliating. The bombardment stopped about 7.30. P.M. and we heard that the Germans had blown up two mines in front of the E. SURREYS. and did not get back until 7. a.m next morning.	

T2134. Wt. W708-776. 500000. 4/15. Sir J. C. & S.

Vol. 2. Page 24.

Instructions regarding War Diaries and Intelligence Summaries are contained in F. S. Regs., Part II. and the Staff Manual respectively. Title pages will be prepared in manuscript.

WAR DIARY
or
~~INTELLIGENCE SUMMARY.~~
(*Erase heading not required.*)

Army Form C. 2118.

Place	Date	Hour	Summary of Events and Information	Remarks and references to Appendices
	19-3-16.		Work repairing Right Coys line went on during the day as their trench was blown in, in several places. There was very little activity of any sort during the day.	MAP. BETHUNE 1/40000
	20-3-16		German Rifle Grenades did our Right Coy considerable damage, and our Centre Coy retaliated with their Rifle Grenade Battery. Our TRENCH MORTARS also fired a few rounds into the Crater.	
	21-3-16		"D" Coy was relieved in the afternoon by a Company of the 1/6th SCOTTISH RIFLES in order to carry out permanent working parties in ANNEQUIN. S.. "A" and "B" Coys relief was completed at 7.30.p.m "C" Coy stayed in reserve to 1/6th Scottish Rifles as their Fighting Strength was only about 200 Men.	
	22-3-16		Permanent working parties were furnished by day and night. The Foot-baths were at the disposal of "D" Coy. Divisional rest cancelled. The 1st QUEENS carried out a successful raid on the GERMAN trenches near MINE POINT.	
	23-3-16		Permanent working parties were furnished by day and night. "D" Coy relieved "C" Coy as Reserve Coy to 1/6th SCOTTISH RIFLES in AUCHY RIGHT SECTOR. Test Gas Alarm at 10.35.P.M. all Coys reported by 10.50.P.M. and the alarm was satisfactory.	
	24-3-16		Permanent working parties were furnished by day and night. The 1/6th SCOTTISH RIFLES were relieved by the 5th SCOTTISH RIFLES and "D" Coy returned to billets in ANNEQUIN. S. by 12 Mid-night.	

Vol. 2. Page. 28.

Instructions regarding War Diaries and Intelligence Summaries are contained in F. S. Regs., Part II. and the Staff Manual respectively. Title pages will be prepared in manuscript.

WAR DIARY
or
~~INTELLIGENCE SUMMARY.~~
(Erase heading not required.)

6 Army Form C. 2118.

Place	Date	Hour	Summary of Events and Information	Remarks and references to Appendices
	25-3-16		The Battalion was relieved by the 20th ROYAL FUSILIERS at 1. P.M. and marched off by Platoons and formed up as Battalion EAST of BETHUNE in order "D" "A" "B" and "C" Coys. The Drums played the Battalion into billets at RUE D'AIRE.	MAP. BETHUNE 1/40000.
	26-3-16		The Battalion marched to Church in the MUNICIPAL THEATRE at 9.30. A.M.	
	27-3-16		Bombing and Lewis Gun Classes were opened under Brigade arrangements at MONTHORENCY BARRACKS. Battalion Bombing, Lewis Gun, Wiring and Sapping Classes were started.	
	28-3-16		The Baths at the ECOLE DES JEUNNES FILLES were allotted the Battalion. "C" Coy practised night wiring.	
	29-3-16		Coys were at the disposal of Company Commanders during the morning, and from 2. P.M. to 3. P.M. in the afternoon. "D" Coy practised night wiring.	
	30-3-16		The Battalion went for a route march during the morning via ANNEZIN, VENDIN and OBLIGHEM returning to billets about 12.30. P.M.	
	31-3-16		Courses continued at the Brigade, and under Battalion arrangements during the morning. The Drums beat Retreat in the GRAND PLACE. BETHUNE at 5.30. P.M.	

G. C. Lambton Lieut Colonel
Commanding 2nd Bn The Worcestershire Regiment.

T2134. Wt. W708–776. 500000. 4/15. Sir J. C. & S.

Vol. 2. Page 29.

2 Worcesters

Instructions regarding War Diaries and Intelligence Summaries are contained in F. S. Regs., Part II. and the Staff Manual respectively. Title pages will be prepared in manuscript.

WAR DIARY
or
~~INTELLIGENCE SUMMARY.~~
(Erase heading not required.)

Army Form C. 2118.

S. 21

Place	Date	Hour	Summary of Events and Information	Remarks and references to Appendices
	1.4.16		The same courses during the morning. Coys practised night wiring and patrolling from 8 P.M. to 10. P.M. on open space near "C" Coy's Head Qrs.	BETHUNE. MAP 1/40000.
	2.4.16		The Battalion assembled for Church Parade at 10.30 A.M. The Battalion assembled in column of route at 6. P.M. and marched to ANNEQUIN. N. via LA BASSEE Road and relieved the 16th K.R.R's who took over the trenches in CUINCHY Right Sub-section. The usual permanent fatigues were furnished during the time we were in ANNEQUIN. N.	
	3.4.16		Inspection of Kit etc. under Company Commanders. A Brigade Bombing Course commenced at Brigade Head Qrs, also a Battalion Class was started under Lieut. Hopkins.	
	4.4.16		Companies on working parties. All men available working on protective defenses in ANNEQUIN. N.	
	5.4.16		"B" and "C" Coys and 1/6th SCOTTISH RIFLES relieved the 16th K.R.R's in CUINCHY Right Sub-section. "B" Coy was in Support and "C" Coy, CENTRE FRONT Coy.	
	6.4.16		The Coys in the trenches were heavily Trench Mortared but very little damage was done.	
	7.4.16		"B" and "C" Coys were relieved by 2 Coys of the 17th K.R.R's who were attached to the Brigade for instructional purposes.	
	9.4.16		The Battalion relieved the 1/6th SCOTTISH RIFLES in CUINCHY Right. "A" Coy Left Front Coy; "D" Coy Right Front Coy; "C" Coy in TOWER RESERVE Trench: "B" Coy remained in ANNEQUIN. N.	

Vol. 2. Page. 30.

Instructions regarding War Diaries and Intelligence Summaries are contained in F. S. Regs., Part II. and the Staff Manual respectively. Title pages will be prepared in manuscript.

WAR DIARY
or
~~INTELLIGENCE SUMMARY.~~
(Erase heading not required.)

Army Form C. 2118.

Place	Date	Hour	Summary of Events and Information	Remarks and references to Appendices
	8-4-16		Two Coys of 17th K.R.R's remained in the line, one as Centre Coy, and one as Support Coy. There was a lot of work to be done in the line when we took over, but most of the trenches were in a good condition. It was very quiet during the night and patrols were sent out; who reported nothing of importance.	
	9-4-16		"A" Coy was heavily Trench Mortared during the morning, and it took the HOWITZERS 20 Minutes to get on to them, however very little damage was done. A mine went up in front of the ROYAL WELSH FUSILIERS on our right, but did little damage to their trenches. "C" Coy relieved the Reserve Coy of the 17th K.R.R. at 5.30.P.M. and "B" Coy their Centre Coy at 6.30.P.M.	
	10-4-16		A very quiet day with little activity on either side.	
	11-4-16		The Battalion was relieved by the 17th K.R.R's. and moved to billets in ANNEQUIN. N. Relief was completed by 9.30.P.M. The usual working parties were furnished, and "C" Coy was relieved at 10.30.A.M. in order to furnish them.	
	12-4-16		Billeted in ANNEQUIN. N. One Company, "Standing to", and one Company on Mining Fatigues.	
	13-4-16		Billeted in ANNEQUIN. N. Companies practise Rapid Loading and Charging Magazines.	
	14-4-16		16th SCOTTISH RIFLES, "A" and "D" Coy's relieved the 17th K.R.R's in CUINCHY Right Sub-section.	

T2134. Wt. W708–776. 500000. 4/15. Sir J. C. & S.

Vol. 2. Page. 31.

Instructions regarding War Diaries and Intelligence Summaries are contained in F. S. Regs., Part II. and the Staff Manual respectively. Title pages will be prepared in manuscript.

WAR DIARY
or
~~INTELLIGENCE~~ SUMMARY.
(Erase heading not required.)

Army Form C. 2118.

Place	Date	Hour	Summary of Events and Information	Remarks and references to Appendices
	14-4-16		"D" Coy was Right Front Coy, and "A" Coy Reserve Coy. These two Companies were attached to 1/6th SCOTTISH RIFLES.	
	15-4-16		The Battery behind the billets in ANNEQUIN. N. was shelled by 4·5 shells from 8 to 8.30. A.M. and from 2 to 2.30. P.M.. No damage was done to the Battery or to Billets, but several men were slightly wounded – no one in the Battalion was wounded.	
	16-4-16		A quiet day in billets. "A" Coy relieved "D" Coy in Front Line, and "D" Coy took over Reserve position.	
	17-4-16		A showery day. "C" Coy worked on the sandbag shelters in WALKER ROAD, and the usual permanent fatigues were furnished.	
	18-4-16		The Battalion less "A" and "D" Coys was relieved in ANNEQUIN. N. by the 2nd Bn ROYAL WELSH FUSILIERS, and marched back to billets in RUE D'AIRE. "A" and "D" Coys and the 1/6th SCOTTISH RIFLES were relieved by the 5th SCOTTISH RIFLES at 7 P.M. and marched to RUE D'AIRE independently. Hot tea was ready for these Coy's about 10.30. P.M. and they reached billets at 12 Midnight.	
	19-4-16		The day was spent in cleaning arms, equipment etc,. The room next the Chapel in RUE D'AIRE was hired as a Recreation Room, and was also found very useful for lectures.	

Instructions regarding War Diaries and Intelligence Summaries are contained in F. S. Regs., Part II. and the Staff Manual respectively. Title pages will be prepared in manuscript.

WAR DIARY
or
~~INTELLIGENCE SUMMARY.~~
(Erase heading not required.)

Army Form C. 2118.

Place	Date	Hour	Summary of Events and Information	Remarks and references to Appendices
	20-4-16		Coys paraded on their own parade grounds for drill, handling of arms, and lectures.	
	21-4-16		The Battalion was allotted the Baths in the ECOLE DES JEUNNES FILLES, and every man was able to get a change of clothing.	
	22-4-16		The Battalion gave a Concert in the Chapel, RUE D'AIRE.	
	23-4-16		Church Parade was held in the Chapel, RUE D'AIRE. During the afternoon, all Officers and 2 N.C.O's per Coy reconnoitred the LE TOURAY Line, from the CANAL to LE PREOL.	
	24-4-16		The Battalion assembled for a Brigade Route March at 9 A.M. with full 1st Line Transport. General STRICKLAND (Temporary G.O.C. 33rd Division) met the Battalion near MONT BERENCHON, and watched them march past. He reported very favourably on the march discipline. Feet inspection in the afternoon under Coy arrangements.	
	25-4-16		C.O. and Coy Commanders visited AUCHY Right Sub-section.	
	26-4-16		The Battalion relieved the 1/4th SUFFOLKS in AUCHY Right Sub-section. The QUEENS on our Left and H.L.I (12th DIV) on our Right. Coys were disposed as follows. "D" - Left: "B" - Centre: "C" - Right: "A" - Support. Relief was completed about 10. P.M.. There was a lot of heavy shelling on our Right, but our own front was quiet.	
	27-4-16		Gas was reported at 5.30.A.M. and the RESERVE Coy and BN. HD. QRS wore gas helmets from 5.30.A.M.	

Vol. 2. Page. 33.

Instructions regarding War Diaries and Intelligence Summaries are contained in F. S. Regs., Part II. and the Staff Manual respectively. Title pages will be prepared in manuscript.

WAR DIARY
or
~~INTELLIGENCE SUMMARY.~~
(Erase heading not required.)

Army Form C. 2118.

Place	Date	Hour	Summary of Events and Information	Remarks and references to Appendices
	27-4-16		to 7.A.M.. The was a second attack at 8.A.M. which was more stringent and lasted half an hour. The first gas discharged was mixed with smoke, the second was pure gas and the air remained clear. Both gas attacks were delivered on the 16th DIV: near LOOS and VERMELLES and the Bn felt the effects of the gas used in these attacks. CAPT. F.H. LAURENCE and 1 Man went to hospital gassed, they walked into a gas pocket in RAILWAY ALLEY. There was a good deal of shelling on our Right during the day, but our own Coys were not shelled. The enemy were active on our front with Rifle Grenades, our Coys retaliated.	
	28-4-16		A quiet day with occasional shelling on the right, particularly near the QUARRY. At about 8.P.M. gas gongs were sounded, and gas was reported. All Coys were warned and put on Smoke Helmets. The Brigade reported that gas was being used NORTH of the CANAL, and also near HULLUCK. We felt no effects of these attacks, and the Coys took off their helmets after about an hour. The enemy were again very active with Rifle Grenades and the RIGHT Coy had several casualties.	
	29-4-16		A very quiet fine day. A FOKKER was brought down on our right about 11.A.M. No activity except Rifle Grenades which inflicted several casualties on our RIGHT and CENTRE Coys. It was impossible to get any more NEWTON Grenades, as the supply had run dry.	

T2134. Wt. W708–776. 500000. 4/15. Sir J. C. & S.

Vol. 2. Page 34.

Instructions regarding War Diaries and Intelligence Summaries are contained in F. S. Regs., Part II. and the Staff Manual respectively. Title pages will be prepared in manuscript.

WAR DIARY

or

~~INTELLIGENCE SUMMARY.~~

(*Erase heading not required.*)

Army Form C. 2118.

Place	Date	Hour	Summary of Events and Information	Remarks and references to Appendices
	30-4-16		A quiet day. We were relieved in the evening by the 1/6th SCOTTISH RIFLES and moved into advanced billets in ANNEQUIN. S.. The relief was completed by 10. P.M.. "A" Coy moved out during the afternoon in order to furnish the permanent working parties. "D" Coy our LEFT FRONT Coy was relieved by the 16th K. R. R's. as they took over the line up to the RAILWAY.	

[signature] Major
Commanding 2nd Bn The Worcestershire Regt.

T2134. Wt. W708–776. 500000. 4/15. Sir J. C. & S.

Page 35

Instructions regarding War Diaries and Intelligence Summaries are contained in F. S. Regs., Part II. and the Staff Manual respectively. Title pages will be prepared in manuscript.

XXXIV

2 Worcester Regt Vol XXXIII

Army Form C. 2118.

S. 22

WAR DIARY

or

~~INTELLIGENCE SUMMARY.~~

(Erase heading not required.)

Place	Date	Hour	Summary of Events and Information	Remarks and references to Appendices
	May			
In the Field	1st		Working parties in ANNEQUIN (South). At 8pm we were ordered to send up a Company in support of the Scottish Rifles. 'A' Company moved up into Factory Trench at about 10-30pm.	BETHUNE Map 1/40,000.
	2nd		A quiet day in billets. A gas alarm was sounded about 2am on the morning of the 3rd, The Battalion stood to, but no Gas was scented and the Battalion stood down after a short time.	
	3rd		In billets at ANNEQUIN	
	4th		Working parties were furnished. ANNEQUIN (NORTH) was shelled with very heavy Shells in the afternoon, but very little damage was done. One shell hole was about 12 Feet deep and appeared to have been made by an armour-piercing shell. The Battn relieved the 1/6th Scottish Rifles in AUCHY right Sub-section. "D" Coy relieved their Reserve Coy at 2-30pm, and the remainder of the Battn: relieved in the evening. The relief was completed about 10pm. A very quiet night followed. We found that the gap on the left had been filled in with Cheveaux des frize and loose wire put behind the other three gaps.	
	5th.		The Commanding Officer proceeded on Leave and Major L. M. Stevens took over the command of the Battalion. A quiet day except for a few rifle Grenades on our Right Front Company.	
	6th.		No activity except for a few Rifle Grenades, Wire was put out by our front Coys.	

T2134. Wt. W708-776. 500000. 4/15. Sir J. C. & S.

Instructions regarding War Diaries and Intelligence Summaries are contained in F. S. Regs., Part II. and the Staff Manual respectively. Title pages will be prepared in manuscript.

WAR DIARY

~~or~~

~~INTELLIGENCE SUMMARY.~~

(~~Erase heading not required.~~)

Army Form C. 2118.

Place	Date	Hour	Summary of Events and Information	Remarks and references to Appendices
	MAY			
	6th		Patrols were sent out also.	
	7th.		A very hot sunny day, The Germans were very inactive by day, but rifle Grenades and Machine Guns bothered the front Line at night. Two horns for sounding a gas alarm were fixed up	
	8th		The Battn less "D" Coy were relieved by the 1/6th Scottish Rifles. "A" Coy were relieved in the afternoon, and took over the permanent working parties at 5pm. The relief of the remainder of the Battn was completed by about 10pm. Very heavy fatigue parties were furnished. The three Companys supplied practically all their men in 24 hours.	
	9th.		A quiet day in billets. Heavy working parties were furnished. Two Gas shells were sent over during the afternoon and fell near "B" Coys Head Quarters.	
	10th		We received orders to remain in ANNEQUIN. (South) for 6 days, and then go into the line for 2 days. ANNEQUIN FOSSE, NORTH & SOUTH ANNEQUIN were shelled indiscriminately. No ~~damage~~ damage was done	
	11th		Still in Billets at ANNEQUIN. "D" Company was relieved by "B" Coy. A very quiet day.	
	12th		——— " ——— A very quiet day.	
	13th		——— " ——— A very quiet day. Pte Baxter of "B" Coy was accidently killed	

Instructions regarding War Diaries and Intelligence Summaries are contained in F. S. Regs., Part II. and the Staff Manual respectively. Title pages will be prepared in manuscript.

WAR DIARY
or
INTELLIGENCE SUMMARY.
(*Erase heading not required.*)

Army Form C. 2118.

Place	Date	Hour	Summary of Events and Information	Remarks and references to Appendices
	1916 May 13th		by Private West, who shot him in the Stomach while cleaning his Rifle. The rifle was one of the new pattern without a cut-off	
	14th		In the evening the Battalion relieved the 1/6th Scottish Rifles, and one company of the 16th K.R.Rs in Cuinchy Right Subsection. The relief was completed at 10pm, a very quiet night followed. The Scottish Rifles had succeeded in practically putting a stop to the German Rifle Grenade Fire. During the relief there was a considerable straffe going on, on the right and ANNEQUIN was shelled.	
	15th		The C.O and Coy Commanders of the 2nd Royal Welch Fusiliers came up in the morning to reconnoitre the line. In the evening the 16th K.R.Rs made their raid near the BABY. Crater, This raid was not very successful.	
	16th		The Right and Center Coys were bothered with small Trench Mortars about 20 or 30 came over. In the evening the Battalion was relieved by the 2nd Royal Welch Fusiliers who came from Billets in Montmorency Barracks, and we marched to billets in RUE D'AIRE BETHUNE. The relief was completed by 10-15pm and the last Coy got to billets about 12-30 am.	
	17th		In Billets in Bethune. General Cleaning up and Inspections by Coy Commanders	
	18th		—— do —— Coys at the disposal of Coy Commanders for Drill, Musketry and Bayonet Fighting "B" & "D" Coys practise night wiring. Brigade Courses started.	

Instructions regarding War Diaries and Intelligence Summaries are contained in F. S. Regs., Part II. and the Staff Manual respectively. Title pages will be prepared in manuscript.

WAR DIARY

or

INTELLIGENCE SUMMARY.

(Erase heading not required.)

Army Form C. 2118.

Place	Date	Hour	Summary of Events and Information	Remarks and references to Appendices
	May 19th.		In billets in Bethune. Coys at the disposal of Coy Commanders, for Drill. Musketry + Bayonet Fighting	
	20th "		—— do —— The Battalion went a Route March to BOIS des DAMES. where we had Dinners The Battalion returned to billets about 3-30 pm. It was a very hot day but the men did not seem very tired when they returned to billets	
	21st "		In billets in Bethune. Divine Service was held in the Chapel RUE D'AIRE at 10-30 am.	
	22nd		—— do ——. Company's at the disposal of Coy Commanders for Drill Musketry etc. Some of the Heats for the Boxing Competition were fought off, but the remainder were postponed owing to the rain	
	23rd "		In billets in Bethune. The Battalion assembled for a Brigade Route March at 6 am and marched via OBLINGHEM. MONT-BERENCHON. GONNEHEM. and CHOQUES. The Battn returned to billets about 10.a.m. The remaining Heats for the Battalion Boxing Competition was fought off in the Afternoon.	
	24th "		In billets in Bethune. Physical Training before Breakfast, Company Drill. Musketry, Fire Discipline + Control, during the morning. In the evening night patrolling and wiring, an the use of Very Lights.	
	25th "		In billets in Bethune. Physical Training before Breakfast. "A" + "B" Companies. Coy Drill, Musketry + Handing arms. "C" + "D" Companies were inspected by the C.O. The Brigade Boxing Competition was held in the evening. The Light Weight Competition was Won by Dr Hamilton and the "Heavies" was won by Lce Cpl Cook. "C" Coy.	

Instructions regarding War Diaries and Intelligence Summaries are contained in F. S. Regs., Part II. and the Staff Manual respectively. Title pages will be prepared in manuscript.

WAR DIARY
INTELLIGENCE SUMMARY.
(Erase heading not required.)

Army Form C. 2118.

Place	Date	Hour	Summary of Events and Information	Remarks and references to Appendices
	1916 May 26th		In billets in BETHUNE. Physical Training before Breakfast. The Swimming Bath in BETHUNE was allotted the Battn. The C.O. inspected "A" & "B" Coys. Two working parties of 100 men each were found to work at the trenches near Oblingham Mill	
	27th		In billets in BETHUNE. The C.O and Coy Commanders inspected the line in CUINCHY RIGHT Sub-section and arranged for a relief with the 1st MIDDLESEX REGT. Orders were received that all reliefs were cancelled	
	28th		The C.O and 2 Coy Commanders inspected the village line of the 16th Division in front of Vermelles. The Bn received orders to bivouac in the Jardin des Sports at 3-30pm. The move was completed in about an hour. Small bivouac's were supplied for the men, and they were quite comfortable	
	29th		Two Coy Commanders inspected the line of the 15th Division. Physical Training before Breakfast. Coy Parades and digging parties during the day.	
	30th		C.O & 2 Coy Commanders reconnoitered the 1st & 16th Divisional Village Line. This line was not in a good state of repairs. Companies paraded for the usual Company Parades.	
	31st		The remaining 2 Coy Commanders reconnoitred the 1st & 16th Divisional Village lines. Company parades and Working Parties as usual	

[signature] Major
Commanding 2nd Bn The Worcestershire Regiment

Page 40
-"-

Instructions regarding War Diaries and Intelligence Summaries are contained in F. S. Regs., Part II. and the Staff Manual respectively. Title pages will be prepared in manuscript.

WAR DIARY
~~or~~
~~INTELLIGENCE SUMMARY.~~
(Erase heading not required.)

2 Worcester Regt
Vol 23

Army Form C. 2118.

Place	Date	Hour	Summary of Events and Information	Remarks and references to Appendices
	June			BETHUNE MAP 1/40,000
Jardin-des Sports ANNEZINE	1st		Physical Training before breakfast. Coys were at the disposal of Coy Commanders during the morning for Company Drill. Handling Arms & Musketry and Bayonet Fighting during the afternoon There was a lot of heavy gunning during the evening in the direction of SOUCHEY	
	2nd & 3rd		Physical Training before breakfast. Coys at the disposal of Coy Commanders during the morning for Handling Arm & Musketry. During the afternoon Bayonet Fighting	
	4th		The Battalion paraded for Church parade in the JARDIN-des-SPORTS.	
	5th & 6th		Physical Training before breakfast Companies at the disposal of Company Commanders during the morning & afternoon	
	7th		The C.O. & Company Commanders reconnoitred AUCHY right subsection preparatory to taking over the line on the 8th.	
	8th		Physical Training before breakfast. The Battn were allotted the swimming baths during the morning and afternoon. The battn paraded for the trenches at 5-30pm. Guides met them at CAMBRIN CHURCH at 8-30pm to guide them to AUCHY right subsection. The relief was completed about 11-30pm "A" Coy 2/6 Warwickshire Regt was attached to the battalion for instruction. Companies were disposed as under. "A" Coy Factory Trench. Right Front "B" Coy. Center Front Warwicks. Left Front "D" Coy. Reserve. "C" Coy A quiet night.	

Min Brm (2) (1) W.B.

S.23

Instructions regarding War Diaries and Intelligence Summaries are contained in F. S. Regs., Part II. and the Staff Manual respectively. Title pages will be prepared in manuscript.

WAR DIARY
or
INTELLIGENCE SUMMARY.
(Erase heading not required.)

Army Form C. 2118.

Place	Date	Hour	Summary of Events and Information	Remarks and references to Appendices
	June 9th		A very quiet day for most part, very little activity. The enemy was working hard in the small new crater opposite Sap 1. Our Artillery shelled it intermittently during the afternoon.	
	10th		During the early morning two of our mines were exploded. One near the EASTERN TWIN crater and one at G4. b.35.35. A quiet day on the whole. There was a little activity with Rifle Grenades. The artillery kept the new craters under intervals all day. Weather was cooler today, but there was thunder and heavy showers.	
	11th		A quiet day except for Rifle Grenades. A very showery day. 2nd Lieut H. K. Senior was killed by Rifle Grenade about mid-day	
	12th		A very wet day, and very quiet. The battn was relieved by the 9th H. L. I. and proceeded to billets in ANNEQUIN. (South). "C" Coy was relieved about 3-30pm. so as to furnish the mining fatigues. The remainder of the battn were relieved during the evening and relief was completed about 11-30pm.	
	13th		In billets at ANNEQUIN (South) Very heavy working parties were furnished. 2 platoons of "C" Coy went to BEUVRY to practise for proposed raid.	
	14th		Still in billets, the remaining 2 platoons of "C" Coy went to BEUVRY. Companies had a change of clothing at the Baths. But no baths were available owing to being out of order.	

T2134. Wt. W708-776. 500000. 4/15. Sir J. C. & S.

Instructions regarding War Diaries and Intelligence Summaries are contained in F. S. Regs., Part II. and the Staff Manual respectively. Title pages will be prepared in manuscript.

WAR DIARY

or

~~INTELLIGENCE SUMMARY.~~

(Erase heading not required.)

Army Form C. 2118.

Place	Date	Hour	Summary of Events and Information	Remarks and references to Appendices
	June 15th		Still in billets. Very heavy fatigues. The battn were allotted the Foot baths.	
	16th		The battn relieved the 9th H.L.I. in AUCHY right sub-section. Coys were disposed as follows:- Right Front "B" Coy. Center "A" Coy. Left Front "C" Coy. Supports "D" Coy. relief was completed about 10pm Captain Underhill joined the Battn today.	
	17th		About 1am the Division on our right made a raid. The enemy retaliated on the Brickstacks. A few rifle grenades & trench Mortars were fired at our front. A quiet day on the whole. The Battn took up a new position during the evening. The whole of the divisional front had been extended So the battn had to hold the whole of the Brigade front (i.e. the whole of the AUCHY sector.) "B" Coy on the right, then "A" Coy, then "C" Coy. and "D" Coy on the Left. The 1st Queens Regt held all the keeps along the Division Front. Battn Head Qrs moved to No2 siding in front of WIMPOLE STREET.	
	18th		A very quiet day except for a few rifle Grenades. The weather was very much better.	
	19th		The enemy shelled junctions of communication trenches for a short period during the morning also they were very active with rifle Grenades.	
	20th		A quiet morning, about 4-40pm the enemy blew a small mine on the southern lip of R.W.F. craters, no damage was done to our Galleries or our Saps. There was no casualties. The battn was relieved by the 9th H.L.I. this evening. "B" Coy. were relieved about 2-30pm. to take over fatigues which were much heavier. The relief was completed about 11-30pm. The same billets at ANNEQUIN were occupied.	

Instructions regarding War Diaries and Intelligence Summaries are contained in F. S. Regs., Part II. and the Staff Manual respectively. Title pages will be prepared in manuscript.

WAR DIARY
~~or~~
~~INTELLIGENCE SUMMARY.~~
(Erase heading not required.)

Army Form C. 2118.

Place	Date	Hour	Summary of Events and Information	Remarks and references to Appendices
	June			
	21st		Still in billets. There was a good deal of shelling during the night including a certain number of Gas shells	
	22nd		Still in Billets. A very quiet day. But heavy working parties were supplied. We blew up a mine about 12 midnight, and the batteries opened fire for 5 minutes, otherwise the night was quiet.	
	23rd		Working parties were supplied until 5pm. A quiet day in billets. A fine Hot day till 4-30p when a heavy thunder started. The Battn relieved the 9th H.L.I. in CUINCHY right sub-section "C" Coy relieved the left center Company 2-30pm. The relief of the remainder of the Battalion was completed by 9-15pm. except 2 platoon of "D" Coy who were employed on Mining fatigue. The companies were disposed as under "B" Coy. Right Coy. "A" Coy right center "C" Left Center. "D" Coy Left Coy. The trenches were very wet owing to the rain but the front line was in good condition. The night passed very quietly Patrols were sent out.	
	24th		A very quiet morning the trenches remained very wet on account of rain during the night. A series of small bombardment of the Hun wire started at 11-15am & 3pm, also at 1 & 5am on the 25th. The shelling in the morning was not Heavy & the Huns retaliated very little, but there was considerable retaliated at 1 & 5am especially around Bn. Hd Qrs. The Huns blew up a long shallow mine just in front of their own wire, nearly opposite Boyau 11 at 5pm during the night our Lewis Guns kept open any Hostile gaps, and traversed the new crater.	

Page 44

Instructions regarding War Diaries and Intelligence Summaries are contained in F. S. Regs., Part II. and the Staff Manual respectively. Title pages will be prepared in manuscript.

WAR DIARY
~~or~~
~~INTELLIGENCE SUMMARY.~~
(Erase heading not required.)

Army Form C. 2118.

Place	Date	Hour	Summary of Events and Information	Remarks and references to Appendices
		June 25th	After the early morning straffe everything was very quiet. The artillery cut the wire in front "A" Coy near the Railway. The Huns blew another long shallow mine just N of and touching the mine of the 24th. A barage was opened on our front line and HIGH St. "C" Coy Head Quarters was shelled with 4·2s. No damage was done. At 10-30pm our Artillery bombarded Railway Point for 10 minutes. The Huns retaliated on our front line & on the batteries. We received information that the 15th Division were going to loose Gas on their front during the night but this was cancelled.	
		26th	A quiet morning, a certain amount of shelling during the ~~morning~~ afternoon. The Huns blew a mine opposite the Right company of the 16th K.R.Rs but did no damage our line was shelled but no Heavily The battn was relieved by the 9th H.L.I., the relief was completed about 9pm. At 8-30pm it started to pour with rain, and continued all night so that the trenches were very wet. Several local bombardments during the night. Went to billets in ANNEQUIN (South)	
		27th	Working parties were furnished by "B" & "D" Coys. "A" & "C" were given a rest. The 9th H.L.I. raided MINE POINT very successfully, capturing about 42 prisoners. 2 machine Guns & blowing in 2 mines. They had about 3 or 4 casualties. The 15th Division let off Gas on our Right but no report has yet been received.	

Page 45.

[redacted]ions regarding War Diaries and Intelligence [redacted]maries are contained in F. S. Regs., Part II. and the Staff Manual respectively. Title pages will be prepared in manuscript.

WAR DIARY
or
INTELLIGENCE SUMMARY.
(Erase heading not required.)

Army Form C. 2118.

Place	Date	Hour	Summary of Events and Information	Remarks and references to Appendices
		June 28th	Very heavy rain during the morning. The Battn were alloted the baths at LE PREOL and the majority of the Battn were able to get a bath and change of clothing. "A" & "C" Coys went to BEUVRY. in order to rehearse on the model German trench there. There were several small Artillery Bombardments during the day. But ANNEQUIN was not shelled.	
		29th	The Battn relieved the 9th H L I. in CUINCHY right sub-section the relief was completed about 9 pm. Just after the relief was completed the Huns opened a fairly heavy barage on High St & Back St. between boyau 2 & 4 and continued for about 1½ hours. They did little damage to "B" Coy front, our Guns retaliated very effectively. The Huns also shelled the Royal Scots Fusiliers. And we heard that the Huns made a small raid on the Left Platoon of that Battn The raid was easily repulsed, and did very little damage. The 15th Divn made a raid about 1 am proceeded by Artillery Bombardment & mines, but the raid was not very successful. "D" Coy on the Left were lightly shelled but little damage was done.	
		30th	Artillery bombardments were carried out on different parts of the Hun Lines by day & the Huns did not retaliate at all severely & the day passed quietly. A small German mine was blown between R. W. F. crater and the German Line but did us no damage. A few miners were Gassed The night was fairly quiet & the companie were able to patrol	

J. F. Leman Captain for Major
Commanding 2nd Bn The Worcestershire Regiment

T2134. Wt. W708–776. 500000. 4/15. Sir J. C. & S.

100th Inf.Bde.
33rd Div.

WAR
DIARY

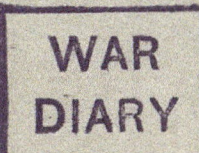

2nd BATTN. THE WORCESTERSHIRE REGIMENT.

J U L Y

1 9 1 6

Attached:-

Report on Operations
of 14th July by O.C.
"C" Company.

9/15 Worcester Regt.

100/33

33 July

Vol 24

S.24

Army Form C. 2118.

Instructions regarding War Diaries and Intelligence Summaries are contained in F. S. Regs., Part II. and the Staff Manual respectively. Title pages will be prepared in manuscript.

WAR DIARY ~~or~~ ~~INTELLIGENCE SUMMARY.~~

(Erase heading not required.)

Place	Date	Hour	Summary of Events and Information	Remarks and references to Appendices
In the Field	1st July		A quiet day with occasional bombardment. A and C Coys raided the German line near RAILWAY POINT. C Coy under Capt C.H. Capp were on the right and A Coy under Lieut R.W. Roberts on the left. Capt. J.F. Keenan was in command of the enterprise. At 12-15 a.m. an Artillery barrage opened, at 12-17 a.m. one mine went up at RAILWAY POINT and another at MINE POINT. The barrage was then lifted and the companies then advanced. The German second line was occupied and held in accordance with the pre-arranged scheme. There was a certain amount of opposition, especially on the right, and there were some lively bombing encounters near the Blocks. Eleven prisoners were captured. Several more were captured but were killed by the Artillery barrage or rifle fire. Four mine shafts were blown up and also two Machine Gun Emplacements, all the dug-outs in the area were bombed, and as these were full, considerable damage must have been inflicted. The trenches were damaged in every way possible. Our raiding party remained in the German line for 45 minutes, and then returned at the sound of a bugle. The Huns shelled our front line and communication trenches very heavily. Our casualties were two killed and about 15 in all badly wounded, although there were a lot more slight casualties. The Coys re-organized in OLD BOOTS trench and re-occupied their old position in our own front line. Our trenches were badly knocked about. The 16th K.R.R.s made an unsuccessful raid on our left.	BETHUNE N.W. 1/40,000
	2nd		A quiet day. We were relieved in the evening by the 4th Bn The King's Regt. The guides met the relieving Bn. at ANNEQUIN cross roads at 10-15 p.m. and the relief was complete at about midnight. The Bn. marched back to billets in BEUVRY and arrived at 3 a.m.	
	3rd		A quiet day in billets. General cleaning up, inspections under Coy. Comdrs. About 80 men were furnished as working parties.	

T2134. Wt. W708-776. 500000. 4/15. Sir J. C. & S.

Army Form C. 2118.

WAR DIARY

~~or~~

~~INTELLIGENCE~~ SUMMARY.

(*Erase heading not required.*)

Instructions regarding War Diaries and Intelligence Summaries are contained in F. S. Regs., Part II. and the Staff Manual respectively. Title pages will be prepared in manuscript.

Place	Date	Hour	Summary of Events and Information	Remarks and references to Appendices
In the Field	July 4th		The Raiding party were inspected by Major General H. J. S. Landon C.B. in the morning. The remainder of the day was spent in cleaning up.	
	5th		The Battn was inspected by Lieut General R B Haking during the morning. During the afternoon the deficiencies and some of the clothing which was very bad was made up.	
	6th		The Commanding Officer inspected the billets during the morning. Major L N Stevens left the Bn. to take the appointment of 2nd in Command of the 18th Lancashire Fusiliers. Orders were received to move at 2-20 pm. The Bn. left BEUVRY at 11-45 pm and marched to billets in BUSNETTES, arriving there about 3-45 a.m. The 12th Royal Scotts of the 39th Division relieved us in BEUVRY, but did not arrive until we had left. Capt. E. O. Underhill went sick.	
	7th.		A quiet day in billets at BUSNETTES. Major J. K. Pardoe arrived and took over command of the Battn. We received movement orders.	
	8th.		Physical training and running before breakfast. Coy inspections by Comdg. Officer during the morning. The Battn paraded for entrainment at 9 pm. and marched to LILLERS which was reached at 10 pm. The train left at 10-50 pm and reached SALEUX at 6 a.m. the following morning.	Map. AMIENS No 17 1/100,000
	9th.		The Battn marched off from the Station at 6-30 a.m. The transport following ¾ of an hour later. The Battn had a 9 mile march and reached billets in ST SAVEUR at about 10 a.m. The transport arrived an hour later and the men had time for dinner, when we received orders to move off at 3 pm. The billeting party went off at once and the Battn less transport left at 3. pm.	

T2134. Wt. W708—776. 500000. 4/15. Sir J. C. & S.

Army Form C. 2118.

Instructions regarding War Diaries and Intelligence Summaries are contained in F. S. Regs., Part II. and the Staff Manual respectively. Title pages will be prepared in manuscript.

WAR DIARY

~~or~~

~~INTELLIGENCE SUMMARY.~~

(Erase heading not required.)

Place	Date	Hour	Summary of Events and Information	Remarks and references to Appendices
	July			
In the Field	9th		We reached VECQUEMONT at 8.40 p.m. after a 10 mile march. The march was very hot, but the men marched very well and only 25 fell out. The billets were not very good, and very crowded.	
	10th		In billets at VECQUEMONT. The Battn had orders to move at 4 p.m. which was cancelled at the last moment.	
	11th		The Battn received orders at midnight to move and paraded at 6 a.m and marched 8 miles to MORLANCOURT reaching there at about 10 a.m. No men fell out. The billets were very crowded and dirty.	
	12th		The C.O. reconnoitred the line with the Brigadier General. Orders were received that the Battn would move about 9-30 p.m. Coy Comdrs held inspections of their coys during the day. The Battn paraded at 10 pm and marched about 5 miles to Bivouack near BECOURDEL-BECOURT. The whole Bn was bivouacked in a field just outside the village.	
	13th.		Still in bivouac. C.O. and Company Commanders reconnoitred the line near MAMETZ WOOD. The Bn. was ready to move at ½ hours notice.	
	14th		The Bn. stood to at 3 a.m. and was ready to move off. The Brigade assembled about 9 a.m and marched along the main road to FRICOURT where we bivouacked on either side of the road, close to several batteries. The Battalion left FRICOURT about 3 p.m and marched through MAMETZ village up to MAMETZ WOOD. The Bn. dug in near FLATIRON COPSE under a steep bank. There was a good deal of shelling went on during the night and the Huns sent over a number of lachrymatory shells.	
	15th		Coy. Comdrs: went up to reconnoitre a suitable reserve position for the Battalion. The Bn marched off in the mist about 5 a.m and passed BAZENTIN-LE-GRAND WOOD and finally formed up in reserve position between the BAZENTIN ROAD & HIGH WOOD with 'A' & 'B' Coys in Front line & 'C' & 'D' Coys in support.	

Instructions regarding War Diaries and Intelligence Summaries are contained in F. S. Regs., Part II. and the Staff Manual respectively. Title pages will be prepared in manuscript.

WAR DIARY

~~or~~

~~INTELLIGENCE SUMMARY.~~

(Erase heading not required.)

Army Form C. 2118.

Place	Date	Hour	Summary of Events and Information	Remarks and references to Appendices
	July.			
In the Field	15th.		Hd Qrs were established in a German dug-out. The 100th Infantry Bde: was ordered to attack the SWITCH LINE North of HIGH WOOD. The Glasgow Highlanders and 1st Queens (RWS) Regt were in the Front Line on the right and left respectively. The 16th KRRs were in support and the 2nd Worcesters in reserve. The 9th H.L.I. were held up by fire from HIGH WOOD and were unable to clear the wood. "C" coy was sent up to help them with D coy in support. "A" & "B" coys advanced across the open to the original jumping off trench of the 9th H.L.I. and then attempted to attack the SWITCH but the attack was held up by enfilading fire (Machine Gun) from HIGH WOOD. The Huns drove a number of the 7th Division out of HIGH WOOD & "A" & B coys formed a second line behind HIGH WOOD. "C" coy remained in the wood & D coy reinforced the 2nd line, as they had previously been at the edge of the wood. Later in the day the 7th Divn. retired from parts of the wood leaving "C" coys right flank entirely exposed so that they took up a position on the near edge of the wood. Heavy shelling continued all the day, but the Battn held their lines, 7th Divn. on the right & 21st Divn on the left. Capt L.G. Lawrence, Lieut B.C.C. Tipper, 2/Lt A.E. Prosser and 2/Lt C.F.W.H. Kevill-Davies were wounded.	
	16th.		The Battn was relieved at 3 a.m. by the 5th S.R. and the Bn returned to bivouacs near MAMETZ WOOD. The Bn rested during the day. Only one shell fell near the Bn and this did no damage.	
	17th		The Bn remained in bivouacs dug in the ground during the day as the Brigade was in Divisional reserve. About 9 pm we moved down the MAMETZ ROAD and relieved the 12th Bn Northumberland Fusiliers of the 21st Division, who were occupying the N. edge of MAMETZ WOOD. "B" "C" & "D" coys were in the Front Line and "A" in support. Bn. Hd. Qrs was in a deep dug-out in the centre of the wood.	

Instructions regarding War Diaries and Intelligence Summaries are contained in F. S. Regs., Part II. and the Staff Manual respectively. Title pages will be prepared in manuscript.

WAR DIARY

~~or~~

~~INTELLIGENCE SUMMARY.~~

(*Erase heading not required.*)

Army Form C. 2118.

Place	Date	Hour	Summary of Events and Information	Remarks and references to Appendices
	July			
In the Field	18th		The wood was shelled considerably with Gas Shells but little damage was done. We improved the positions, and moved up Head Quarters to the Front Line. The 9th H.L.I. occupied positions in our Front Line so that the Battn was ready to move at short notice. Very little shelling in the wood.	
	19th		Spent the day in position in MAMETZ WOOD. In the evening we were attached to the 19th Bde for their attack on HIGH WOOD. Two Battns attacked the wood from the front, one swept the wood and the fourth Bn was in reserve. The duty of the Bn was to push out to MARTINPUICH and HIGH WOOD road and protect the left flank of the attack. The Bn left MAMETZ WOOD about 9-30 pm and marched through BAZENTIN to the CEMETERY where "B" & "D" Coys took up the Front line position along the road without opposition; "C" Coy were in support & "A" in reserve. Hd. Qrs was in a shallow trench near the CEMETERY just off the road. The Huns shelled the road as the Bn marched up to their positions. "B" & "D" Coys sent out patrols. The 2nd Argyle & Sutherland Hrs. were on the right and the 1/4 Suffolks on the left.	
	20th		The Bombardment started in the early morning & was followed up by the attack of the 19th Bde. on the wood, about which we heard very little except that the Bde lost heavily. Our positions were shelled fairly heavily but no counter attack was attempted. At about 9-30 pm we received orders to vacate our positions and relieve the 20th Manchesters (7th Division) in the BAZENTIN position. The 100th Infy Bde were in Divisional reserve. "A" & "B" Coys occupied portions of our 2nd line between the CEMETERY & DELVILLE ROAD. 2 platoons of "D" Coy were in the strong point at the 5 Cross roads & "C" Coy and ½ of "D" behind BAZENTIN-LE-GRAND WOOD near Bn. Hd. Qrs. The Huns formed a Gas Shell barrage during the relief and several men were gassed. The Huns shelled a lot during the night especially on the front two Coys. 2/Lieut J. C. Miners was wounded.	

Instructions regarding War Diaries and Intelligence Summaries are contained in F. S. Regs., Part II. and the Staff Manual respectively. Title pages will be prepared in manuscript.

WAR DIARY

~~or~~

~~INTELLIGENCE SUMMARY.~~

(Erase heading not required.)

Army Form C. 2118.

Place	Date	Hour	Summary of Events and Information	Remarks and references to Appendices
	July			
In the Field	21st		A quiet day in the BAZENTIN position. The front coys were shelled during the day. The Bde was relieved in the evening by the 15th Divn. We were relieved about 10 pm by a strong Battn the 9th Royal Scotts. On relief the Bn. marched back by coys to bivouac at BECOURT. The Bn reached bivouac at 3 a.m. 2 Lieut O.V. Arnold wounded. Capt C H Pigg & 2nd Lieut A.W.E. Christie were gased.	
	22nd		We received a draft of 43 men of the Gloucester Regt. The Battn rested in bivouac during the day. The Division was in Corps reserve.	
	23rd		The Bn received orders to move and marched off at 8-30 a.m. and were bivouacked in a field about a mile from DERNANCOURT. with 1/QUEENS (R.W.S.) Regt & 100th Infy. Bde. Hd. Qrs. A draft of 28 arrived chiefly from 1st Battn. We received 45 tents.	
	24th		Still in bivouac. Parades under Coy Comdrs. The C.O. inspected "B" Coy. A draft of 74 arrived during the afternoon.	
	25th		Still in bivouac. Physical training before Breakfast. Coy parades & C.O.s inspection during the morning.	
	26th		Still in bivouac. Physical training before Breakfast. Coy parades and C.O.s inspection of "A" Coy. Bayonet fighting during the afternoon.	
	27th		The Bn assembled in mass in the field WEST of Camp for C.O.s parade. A Field General Court Martial was held at Bn. Hd. Qrs.	
	28th		Physical training before Breakfast. Company parades and C.O.s inspection of "C" Coy. A draft of 52 Ox and Bucks L.I. arrived in the evening.	
	29th		Still in Bivouac. Physical training before Breakfast. The C.O. inspected "D" Coy. The Battn assembled in mass in the field W of Camp at 11-30 a.m for Battn drill. The following awards were allotted to the Battn.: 10 Military Medals. A draft of 120 Other Ranks joined the Battn.	
	30th		The Bn paraded for Divine Service at 11-30 a.m under the Divnl Chaplain in the rear of Bde Hd Qrs. Major Landon C.B. presented ribbons of decorations awarded on the 29th in rear of the Camp.	

Instructions regarding War Diaries and Intelligence Summaries are contained in F. S. Regs., Part II. and the Staff Manual respectively. Title pages will be prepared in manuscript.

WAR DIARY

~~or~~

~~INTELLIGENCE~~ SUMMARY.

(*Erase heading not required.*)

Army Form C. 2118.

Place	Date	Hour	Summary of Events and Information	Remarks and references to Appendices
In the Field	July 31st		Physical training before breakfast. Companies were at the disposal of Company Commanders from 9. a.m till 12 noon. A concert was given by the "Shrapnells" in the evening.	

"

J.M. Pardoe

Major

Commanding 2nd. Bn. the Worcestershire Regiment

T2134. Wt. W708-776. 500000. 4/15. Sir J. C. & S.

Report on Operations of 14th July by O.C."C" Company.

The 2nd Battalion The Worcestershire Regiment
at High Wood, Somme 1916.

C.H. Pigg, O.C. C Company

The attack at dawn on 14th July saw a successful assault on the German main second line by which the two Bazentins and Longueval were captured, and Delville Wood was entered. Northwards from these the ground slopes gently up to a ridge of which High Wood is the centre and highest point. Beyond High Wood and to the west lies Martinpuich; to the east, Flers; and both these villages are protected by the ridge.

We were in good fettle; we had seen British and Indian cavalry go forward on the heels of the advance, and we knew that they had reached, some even said had ridden round, High Wood, and that our infantry outposts were in its southern end.

The night 14th-15th July was spent in the valley below Caterpillar Wood in old No Man's Land - in front of us a battery of R.F.A. fired all night long, and the ground near by showed part of the price paid for the recent advance. The German shelling was desultory as they were busy withdrawing their guns, and the men hollowed out sleeping places in the sides of the valley and took what rest they could on the chalky rubble without greatcoats. Most of us were astir at dawn stamping up and down to get warm, and we then learnt that "W" and "X" and "Y", the three other battalions in our brigade had been sent off to attack High Wood and the ridge to the east and west of it; our battalion, "Z" was in sppport, and we jested that we would billet the night in Martinpuich, a place which the British were not to enter for two long months.

9 H.L.I = W
16 K.R.R.C. = X
1 Queens = Y

At about 7 o'clock company commanders were called to headquarters, and ordered to go forward to reconnoitre.

Taking a runner apiece, we started, passing through the old German second line, of which scarcely a trace remained, and up the northern end of Bazentin le Grand wood. Here it almost seemed that we had left the region of war. Instead of a country of continuous shell holes we gazed upon green undulating pasture land, broken by an occasional hedge row, with a green and apparently untouched wood about a mile to the north-east.

Paralled to the ridge and rather more than a thousand yards in rear runs the road linking Bazentin to Longueval. This we crossed and shortly afterwards found what we sought in a stretch of meadow well covered from view by a rise in front of it. Here we waited in the sun sending back our runners to bring up the companies. After waiting some time we decided to walk back to meet them. As we recrossed the road above mentioned a patter of bullets fell round us from some distant machine gun. Near by was a small track where about 20 Germans had hollowed out a firing position. Three or four lay where they had fallen to our advancing troops, and we made a careful examination of one of them, a fine big fellow who lay on his back grasping his rifle. We had been annoyed by constantly reading in the papers of the poor physique and inadequate food and equipment of the enemy, and here was our man to disprove it. Perfectly equipped in every detail as the contents of his haversack showed, he had evidently suffered no lack of rations, whilst his uniform was new and his rifle of the latest pattern with the large magazine.

Soon afterwards the battalion came up, we recrossed the road and moved on. In a small shelter by the roadside lay a wounded German only too glad to be captured.

About 11 we moved forward again up the slope, and my company lay behind a hedge on the right of the battalion. Being now well in advance of our new line and not knowing how long we should remain in our present position, I sent out an N.C.O. and 3 men to the flank. We moved before they returned but when they did so they reported having approached within 400 yards of a German battery in action to the north of Longueval.

Near us were 11 dead horses and the graves of two men marking the point where our cavalry had been in action. At 11.30 we moved forward again and now lay in two lines of companies 500 yards in rear of the wood with a track on our right and headquarters in an enemy dugout just across the track.

My own Company, "C", was on the right of the leading line. We at once started to dig in; and there was now continuous indirect rifle and machine-gun fire from the enemy, with occasional shrapnel. Hereabouts lay the sword of an Indian cavalryman, but no trace of man or horse.

It was now one o'clock, and we knew nothing of the success or failure of the attack. "W" had assaulted the ridge to the West of the wood and part of the wood, "X" the wood itself, and "Y" the ridge to the East.

9th H.L.I = W.
16th KRRC = X

High wood was at this time in full leaf, and the undergrowth was thick so that it was not possible to see more than twenty yards ahead. In shape it is a quadrilateral with the Northern apex on the highest ground, and its longest side, from which we approached it, facing S.W. Unfenced tracks run round it, and many narrow rides through it. The length of the sides varies from 800 to 500 yards. A message now came down from the wood - "W" were in trouble and wanted support - I was ordered to take my Company into the wood and to report at "W" Headquarters.

We moved up in line from our scanty shelters, and turned into line of Platoons in file as we entered the wood. The dead lay thick on the track bordering the wood, and a few of the gallant "V's" who had pushed on after their successful work on the previous morning had dug in and held the Southern apex.

Manchester's

"Have we captured the whole of the wood?"

"Yes, and we are out the other side."

"Where are "W" Headquarters ?"

"Somewhere inside the wood."

This seemed satisfactory, and ordering the Platoons to lie down I took a runner and pushed forward to report. The journey was unpleasant; the undergrowth made movement slow, and the incessant crack of the bullets as they cut the trees all round us seemed to indicate that we did not hold all the wood.

We pushed on to the N.W. and reached a drive where men had tried to dig in and whereon many lay dead, cut down by machine guns. These were "W's" but none could tell me where their H.Q., were; some thought their Colonel was ahead of them, some that he was on the edge of the wood to which the drive ran. I sent the runner to the edge of the wood and pushed on alone. Thirty yards on there appeared a small wooden building for which I made, only to drop as a wicked chatter of machine guns leapt from it.

Crawling back I reached the drive again, and went back to bring up the Company. They were already on their way, and at their head was "P" leading with a bullet through his thigh. He was tied up and sent back, and the remainder were ordered to cross the drive and dig in on its forward edge which they succeeded in doing, linking up with the "W's" and the S.W. side of the wood. My runner returned and reported that he could not find "W" H.Q.; the Colonel was not on the S.W. side of the wood. A small patrol was sent out Northwards in rear of our drive to find touch with "X" on our right flank.

Company H.Q. dropped into the one of few shell-holes, conveniently placed in rear of the drive, and proceeded to send back information.

The situation briefly was this:- we had dug in close to the enemy on the enemy side of a drive which we could identify on the Map; we had lost an officer and many men; enemy rifle and machine-gun fire was very brisk; we were in touch with "W" on our left, but our right in the wood was in the air; pending further orders we intended to hold on where we were.

The Company Commander sat in his hole and thought. If he pushed forward unsupported he could gain nothing. Even if successful the Hun would rip him on either flank and we might then be driven clear of the whole wood. As he thought a Captain of

16th K.R.R.C. "X" crawled into the hole. He could give no information, had none of his company left, and was anxious to push forward, alone, if necessary; but from this he was dissuaded, and went to try and find some of his men. Followed shortly by a gunner officer who asked what he could do. He was asked to turn everything on to the German apex of the wood, and to try and get up some Stokes'

Lawrence

guns for the same purpose. Followed O.C. "D" Company strolling in gallant fashion along the drive strewn with dead and cut by machine-gun bullets. "D" Company he said, were waiting in support close up to the S.W. face of the wood - "A" and "B" led by the Colonel and Adjutant had attacked as on parade across the open on the West of the Wood, had been raked by machine guns but reached and helped to hold a line begun by the survivors of "W" close to the enemy line. They could not get forward.

He was asked to send up a patrol for use to our front. They came and crawled forward to try definitely to locate the enemy. In three minutes the N.C.O., in charge returned to say that G was shot - the patrol brought him back and laid him on the drive with a broken arm and a broken thigh. We tied him up and I went to the edge of the wood to find a doctor. One was found tying up the wounded on the S.W.face; and now occurred one of those incidents which bring everlasting credit to the R.A.M.C. This doctor was spent with fatigue; for two nights and three days he had been incessantly at work; it was a constant struggle for him to remain awake; but he entered the wood, spent twenty minutes bandaging and putting the wounded into a rifle splint, went out and fetched two orderlies and a stretcher and sent "G" down in safety, all without cover and under heavy fire.

Events now moved more quickly; O.C. "D" Company fell shot through the thigh on the edge of the wood; a heavy battery of ours opened fire and dropped its shells some forty yards to our front, very good shooting, but a trifle close to us; a message came from the Brigade to say we were to hold on to our present line; and a single seater flew low over the wood to try and locate us. We signalled to him but it is doubtful if we were seen. I had been shelled heavily many times, but what followed was my worst experience. An enemy field battery opened rapid fire on us from our left rear ~~flank~~, and continued for twenty minutes before being silenced by our guns. Up and down the face of the wood and along our drive they played. A man crawled into the

H.Q. hole groaning with his face in rags; shells burst at the foot of the trees on the hedge of our hole, and round us and over us in the wood.

It was too much for the "V's " on the face, and they retired from the face to the open where they were worse off than before, and whence their officers fetched them back. My own men crouched a little closer in their holes, and looked to the cleaning of their rifles, and prayed that the evening would advance.

The patrol sent out N. to find touch with "X" on our right flank now returned. They reported their inability to do so, and their words were borne out when twice during the next hour an enemy machine gun fired from the N.E. face along the drive which we held.

The long July day drew to a close, and a summons arrived for all officers to report to the S. apex of the wood. Here the senior officer present, a Major of the "V's" took command. We were ordered to withdraw for the night to the S.E.face, to hold on there, to reorganize at once, and to send out frequent patrols to our front during the night. We reorganized along the S.W.face - "W" on the left, ourselves, "Z" next, a few "X" and"V" on our right; 700 yards among some 200 men and 2 or 3 Lewis guns. We collected ammunition from the dead and distributed it, and bound up and sent down the wounded. The worst part of our day was over, but there was no sleep and once the enemy were reported advancing. We gave them two minutes rapid fire after withdrawing our patrols. An officer crawled in wounded in several places; he had spent the day in hiding near the enemy. At

Pte Alford midnight my batman appeared with a bottle of whiskey and some food. We shared it and were very glad of it as the nights were cold. This batman had a wonderful knack of turning up in the most awkward places and never failed me. At 3.0 a.m. a runner arrived with a written message "All troops will be clear of the wood by 3.30". We were loth to leave a spot we had hoped to take and keep, but we supposed our guns would bombard the wood at

3.30 and another attack would follow.

Quickly the word was passed along and we left by Battalions beginning from the right. As we went down the slopes through the enemy shells we passed countless machine gun teams digging themselves in before dawn. Three quarters of a mile back we passed through the new British line. Later we read in the papers that this line had been firmly consolidated, whilst we distracted the enemy's attention.

"Our advanced troops were then withdrawn."

-x-x-x-

100th Brigade.
33rd Division

2nd BATTALION

WORCESTERSHIRE REGIMENT

AUGUST 1 9 1 6

2/15 Worcestershire Regt.

Army Form C. 2118.

Instructions regarding War Diaries and Intelligence Summaries are contained in F. S. Regs., Part II. and the Staff Manual respectively. Title pages will be prepared in manuscript.

WAR DIARY

~~or~~

~~INTELLIGENCE~~ SUMMARY.

(*Erase heading not required.*)

Vol 25

Place	Date	Hour	Summary of Events and Information	Remarks and references to Appendices
In the Field	August 1st		In Camp near DERNANCOURT. The Battn assembled in column of route facing SOUTH on the road EAST of Camp at 5-30 a.m., Head of Bn. at Railway crossing, and practiced an attack up the valley. Lectures and inspections were held under Company arrangements in the afternoon. Bayonet fighting and recruit's drill took place after tea.	
	2nd		Companies paraded under Coy arrangements during the morning. Bayonet fighting and recruit's drill took place after tea.	Miss Little.
	3rd		Still in Camp. Owing to the heat breakfasts were ordered at 7 a.m. and Companies were at the disposal of company commanders for tactical exercises from 7-45 a.m. to 10-15 a.m. The Drums beat Retreat in the evening.	
	4th		The Battn assembled on the road at 5-30 a.m accompanied by the Cookers. We practised an attack with two companies in the front line and two in support. After the attack the Battn had breakfasts. An Outpost scheme was carried out during the morning. The Commanding Officer and two Coy Commanders reconnoitred the line of the 51st Division leaving camp about 11-15 a.m.	
	5th.		Companies were at the disposal of Coy Commanders for tactical exercises during the morning. In the evening Coys paraded for practice in Night Outposts, patrolling etc. Coy Sergt. Majors lectured the men of the new drafts from 5. to 6 p.m.	
	6th.		Still in Camp. Roman Catholics paraded for a celebration of Mass in a field behind the Camp. The Battn was given orders to move the following morning.	S. 25
	7th.		The Battn assembled on the road EAST of Camp at 1-30 a.m. and marched up to the trenches near HIGH WOOD relieving	

Army Form C. 2118.

WAR DIARY
~~or~~
~~INTELLIGENCE SUMMARY.~~
(Erase heading not required.)

Instructions regarding War Diaries and Intelligence Summaries are contained in F. S. Regs., Part II. and the Staff Manual respectively. Title pages will be prepared in manuscript.

Place	Date	Hour	Summary of Events and Information	Remarks and references to Appendices
In the Field	August 7th	contd:	The 6th SEAFORTHS (51st Division). The 34th Division were on our left. We had a busy day deepening the trenches which were very shallow.	
	8th.		Our 9.2 batteries bombarded WOODLANE TRENCH in the afternoon. At midnight a trench was started about 100 yards in front of our lines which was dug satisfactorily by 'A' coy on the left, but on the right 2/Lieut F.G. Worster was wounded while laying out the tape and very little work was done.	
	9th.		A further bombardment took place by the Artillery. Work was continued on the new trench on the right during the night. The whole trench was deepened to about 4 or 5 feet. This trench was afterwards called WORCESTER TRENCH.	
	10th.		There was heavy shelling during the day. The Battn. was relieved at 4 p.m by the 16th K.R.R.C. and took up a position (reserve) in MAMETZ WOOD. A quiet night followed.	
	11th.		A quiet day. Many working parties up to the front line were furnished by the Battalion.	
	12th		MAMETZ WOOD and vicinity was shelled intermittently during the day. The same heavy carrying parties were furnished by the Battn. The 1st MIDDLESEX reconnoitred our position preparatory to taking over the line.	
	13th.		The Battn. was relieved by the 1st Middlesex. Relief was completed by about 4.30 a.m. We marched to bivouacs near BECORDEL. The remainder of the day was spent in cleaning up.	
	14th.		Bayonet fighting was practiced before breakfast. The C.O. inspected 'A' coy in clean fatigue dress during the	

T2134. Wt. W708–776. 500000. 4/15. Sir J. C. & S.

Instructions regarding War Diaries and Intelligence Summaries are contained in F. S. Regs., Part II. and the Staff Manual respectively. Title pages will be prepared in manuscript.

WAR DIARY
or
INTELLIGENCE SUMMARY.
(Erase heading not required.)

Army Form C. 2118.

Place	Date	Hour	Summary of Events and Information	Remarks and references to Appendices
In the Field	August 14th	contd:	morning. The other three companies supplied heavy working parties on BAZENTIN Support line.	
	15th.		Bayonet fighting before breakfast. The C.O. inspected "B" coy in clean fatigue dress during the morning. The other companies paraded under coy commanders for handling of arms and Company drill. 150 men passed through the Gas Chamber at Divisional Headquarters in the morning. The sail-cloth baths were also allotted to the Battn, and every man was able to get a bath.	
	16th.		Still in bivouac near BECORDEL. Bayonet fighting parade in the morning. Several strong working parties were furnished by the Battn and worked on the reserve lines near BAZENTIN-LE-GRAND. "A" company paraded under their coy commander.	
	17th		The C.O. inspected "C" coy in clean fatigue dress. "D" coy paraded for wiring drill near FRICOURT in the morning and "B" coy in the afternoon. The O.C. 222nd Coy R.E. supervised the drill. All available men paraded for handling of arms during the morning. There were Brigade Sports at 6p.m NORTH of Camp. The Battn entered a relay team, a tug-of-war team, and there was also an officers tug-of-war.	
	18th.		Bayonet fighting parade in the early morning. The C.O. inspected "D" coy during the morning. "A", "B" and "C" coys paraded under coy commanders. The Battn was standing by ready to move at one hours notice from 2-45p.m.	
	19th		We received move orders about 8a.m, and 4 officers were sent on to POMMIERS REDOUBT to reconnoitre the position. The Battn marched off at 10a.m to POMMIERS REDOUBT where they halted on the road and afterwards marched on to MONTAUBAN TRENCH. The rations were issued and the men had dinner. At about 5p.m Coys marched up to the line and relieved the 6th K.R.R.C (41st Brigade)	

Instructions regarding War Diaries and Intelligence Summaries are contained in F. S. Regs., Part II. and the Staff Manual respectively. Title pages will be prepared in manuscript.

WAR DIARY

~~or~~

~~INTELLIGENCE SUMMARY.~~

(*Erase heading not required.*)

Army Form C. 2118.

Place	Date	Hour	Summary of Events and Information	Remarks and references to Appendices
In the Field	August 19th	contd:	in the trenches on the left of DELVILLE WOOD. "A" and "B" coys were in the front line, "D" in ORCHARD TRENCH and GREEN JACKET and "C" in CARLTON TRENCH close to Battn. Hd. Qrs. The relief took a long time as there was a lot of shelling on the left, and was not completed until after midnight. The 9th. H.L.I. were on our left.	
	20th		The front Companies sent out patrols during the night but were unable to do much work as the relief was not completed until very late. Parts of the line were in a very bad state indeed. A patrol sent out on the right was able to get into touch with the K.O.Y.L.I. of the 14th Division. The front companies were shelled during the day and on the right our own heavies dropped some shells near our trench by STRONG POINT.	
	21st.		Relief orders came in during the morning but were cancelled soon afterwards and we received orders for a small attack in conjunction with the GLASGOW HIGHLANDERS on the new German line, which an aeroplane had reported to have been considerably strengthened during the previous night. The Glasgow Highlanders attacked but did not take the trenches: our attack did not develop as there was such a short time in which to organise it.	
	22nd.		Relief orders came in during the day and Coy Commanders of the 16th K.R.R.C. reconnoitred the line. During the afternoon "A" and "B" coys who were in GREEN JACKET and CARLTON TRENCH relieved one coy of the 16th K.R.R.C. and one coy of the Glasgow Highlanders in the left sub-section. During the same night the remainder of the battalion in the right sub-section was relieved by the 16th. K.R.R.C. and in the left sub-section by the 1/QUEEN'S Regt. The Battn then marched back to MONTAUBAN TRENCH and arrived there at about 4.a.m.	

T2134. Wt. W708–776. 500000. 4/15. Sir J. C. & S.

Instructions regarding War Diaries and Intelligence Summaries are contained in F. S. Regs., Part II. and the Staff Manual respectively. Title pages will be prepared in manuscript.

WAR DIARY
~~or~~
~~INTELLIGENCE SUMMARY~~.
(Erase heading not required.)

Army Form C. 2118.

Place	Date	Hour	Summary of Events and Information	Remarks and references to Appendices
In the Field	August 23rd		The Battn rested during the day. Orders for an attack were received. Major Leman reconnoitred the line in the morning. There was a conference of Coy Commanders during the afternoon. The Brigade had been ordered to attack TEA TRENCH on the following day, 1/QUEENS on the left, 16th K.R.R.C. Centre and 2nd WORCESTERS on the right. The 9th H.L.I. were in Brigade reserve. After Conference "C" and "B" coys marched up to the line. "C" coy occupied the front line and "B" coy ORCHARD TRENCH. The 16th K.R.R.C. moved to the left. "A" coy moved to GREEN JACKET at 10 p.m. Head Qrs and "D" coy moved to CARLTON TRENCH at 3 a.m. The following officers joined for duty:- Lieut E. A. Aplen, Lieut. C. Lattey, Lieut. H. C. Ward, 2/Lt. B.G.Y. Hawkes, 2/Lt. H.S. Seccombe, 2/Lt. A. K. White, 2/Lt. H. C. Downes and 2/Lt. F. J. Henning.	
	24th.		The Battn relief was completed about 4 a.m. Coys. and Head Qrs. moved to battle position at 3-20 a.m. The preliminary bombardment opened at 3-45 p.m. The 14th. Division attacked at 5-45 p.m. from DELVILLE WOOD. The 100th Brigade attacked at 6-45 p.m. "C" coy was in the front line, "B" in the second and "A" in third (this coy was responsible for the right flank). "D" coy was reserve company. The attack proved a great success. The 2nd. objective was reached and consolidated, strong posts were formed, and touch was obtained with the Ox. & Bucks L.I. (14th Division) on our right and also with the K.R.R.C. on our left. About 20 prisoners were captured and the casualties were not heavy. The officer casualties were:- Capt W. Ferguson wounded, 2/Lt. T. N. Wilmot died of wounds, 2/Lt. L. R. Telling wounded, Lt. Ward wounded, Lt. C. Lattey wounded, Lt R. Y. Dunnett shell shock, 2/Lt B.G.Y. Hawkes wounded but at duty. Other ranks 141, killed wounded and missing.	
	25th		We received relief orders about 1 a.m and the relief of the Battn by the 1st MIDDLESEX was completed by about 7 a.m. Coys on relief returned to MONTAUBAN TRENCH and had hot tea and rations. The men rested as much as possible during the day. About 5 p.m we received further relief	

Instructions regarding War Diaries and Intelligence Summaries are contained in F. S. Regs., Part II. and the Staff Manual respectively. Title pages will be prepared in manuscript.

WAR DIARY
or
INTELLIGENCE SUMMARY.
(Erase heading not required.)

Army Form C. 2118.

Place	Date	Hour	Summary of Events and Information	Remarks and references to Appendices
In the Field	August 25th.	contd:	orders, and on the arrival of the 1/4 Suffolk Regt. (98th. Brigade) companies marched back independently to FRICOURT CEMETERY, where the Battn. assembled and the Drums marched us to BECOURS BIVOUAC (E.12.a). The men made use of shell boxes as bivouacs.	
	26th.		The day was spent in generally cleaning up, and the men got as much rest as possible.	
	27th.		The Battn. assembled for Divine Service NORTH of Camp at 10-20 a.m. The Brigadier addressed the Battn. during the morning and congratulated us on our good work in the attack. The Battn. received congratulatory letters from the Brigade and Division. A draft of 21 arrived. Lieut. F. H. F. Booth joined for duty.	
	28th.		Bayonet fighting parade before breakfast. The C.O. inspected "A" coy. "B", "C", and "D" coys were at the disposal of coy commanders. In the evening coys were lectured by coy commanders. General Landon addressed the Battn. in the evening and congratulated them on the good work done in the attack on TEA TRENCH.	
	29th.		Physical training and coy parades in the morning. The Divisional Band played selections in the evening near the camp. Move orders came in about 4 p.m. and later orders at 10 p.m. and 12 midnight.	
	30th.		The Battn. assembled at 7-50 a.m. and marched to billets at RIBEMONT. The billets were very crowded, as the whole of the Brigade were in the area. The other brigades of the Division also moved back from the line. During the march two men fell out.	
	31st.		The Battn. assembled at 8-10 a.m. and marched to billets in MOLLIENS. The G.O.C. 4th. Army watched the Battn. march past at QUERIEU and said that they marched very well. The billets in MOLLIENS were quite good. About 17 men fell out after a 10 mile march but the remainder of the Battn. marched in well.	

G W Pardoe Lieut. Colonel

Comdg 2nd. Bn. the Worcestershire Regt.

Instructions regarding War Diaries and Intelligence Summaries are contained in F. S. Regs., Part II. and the Staff Manual respectively. Title pages will be prepared in manuscript.

WAR DIARY
or
~~INTELLIGENCE SUMMARY.~~
(Erase heading not required.)

100/33 2nd Warwicks

Army Form C. 2118.

Vol 2

Place	Date	Hour	Summary of Events and Information	Remarks and references to Appendices
	1-9-16		The Battalion assembled at 9.30 A.M and marched from MOLLIENS to TALMAS (about six miles) reaching billets about 11.30 A.M. The Battalion had quite good billets and expected to stop at TALMAS for two nights, but movement orders were received late at night.	LENS MAP No. 11. 1/100.000
	2-9-16		The Battalion assembled at 9.45 A.M. and marched from TALMAS to RIBEACOURT (about 12 miles). We had dinners en-route. About 40 men fell out, but the majority joined up soon after arriving in billets. The billets were good and the Companies had plenty of room.	
	3-9-16		Sunday was spent in RIBEACOURT. The Battalion assembled for Divine Service at 11 A.M. and there was a lecture by the Commanding Officer for all Officers and N.C.O's in the afternoon.	
	4-9-16		The Battalion assembled at 9.50 A.M. and marched to NEAUX (about 12 miles). We arrived at NEAUX about 2.P.M. The billets were rather scattered. Packs were not carried on this march.	
	5-9-16		The Battalion assembled at 9 A.M. and marched to CROISSETTE (about 12 miles), reaching billets about 2.P.M. The billets were good. Packs were brought along on lorries.	
	6-9-16		The Battalion assembled at 9 A.M. and marched from CROISSETTE to GOUY a distance of about 10 miles as we passed through MAISNIL and TERNAS. Packs were carried but only two men fell out.	S.2b

Instructions regarding War Diaries and Intelligence Summaries are contained in F. S. Regs., Part II. and the Staff Manual respectively. Title pages will be prepared in manuscript.

WAR DIARY
or
~~INTELLIGENCE SUMMARY.~~
(Erase heading not required.)

Army Form C. 2118.

Place	Date	Hour	Summary of Events and Information	Remarks and references to Appendices
	7.9.16		The Battalion remained at GOUY. During the morning we went for a short route march via BUNEVILLE and MONT-EN-TERNOIS.	
	8.9.16		The Battalion assembled in column of route at 7 A.M. and marched to MONT-EN-TERNOIS where busses were waiting to convey us to HALLOY. The route was via FREVENT, BOUQUEMAISON and DOULLENS. The majority of the Battalion were billeted in huts. Head Quarters were in the village. The Transport proceeded by road.	
	9.9.16		The Battalion remained in billets at HALLOY. The Commanding Officer and Company Officers reconnoitred the line near FONQUEVILLERS. The Battalion assembled in the field adjoining the camp for inspections and handling of arms.	
	10.9.16		The Battalion assembled at 8.30 A.M. and marched from HALLOY to HUMBERCAMP and reached billets about 1 P.M. The billets were very crowded and not very good.	
	11.9.16		The Battalion assembled at 6.15 P.M. on the square adjoining Orderly Room and marched to positions in and around FONQUEVILLERS. "D" Coy was at the CHATEAU-DE-LA-HAIE. "B" and "C" Coys were in cellars and dugouts in FONQUEVILLERS and "A" Coy temporarily in a trench, as the company they were to relieve did not move out until the following night. The Transport moved to GAUDIEMPRE. The Battalion relieved the 9th H.L.I. as garrison of FONQUEVILLERS.	

T2134. Wt. W708—776. 500000. 4/15. Sir J. C. & S.

Instructions regarding War Diaries and Intelligence Summaries are contained in F. S. Regs., Part II. and the Staff Manual respectively. Title pages will be prepared in manuscript.

WAR DIARY

or

~~INTELLIGENCE SUMMARY.~~

(Erase heading not required.)

Army Form C. 2118.

Place	Date	Hour	Summary of Events and Information	Remarks and references to Appendices
	12-9-16		Two working parties of 1 Officer and 50 men each were supplied. "A" Company relieved a company of the LANCASHIRE FUSILIERS (52nd Brigade) and we became Battalion in reserve to the 1st QUEENS. The 100th BRIGADE took over from the 52nd BRIGADE (17th Division). Two Officers joined for duty.- 2nd LIEUT. R. B. W. VINTER and 2nd LIEUT. J. POWNALL.	
	13-9-16		Two working parties of 1 Officer and 50 men were supplied, also two parties of 3 Officers and 150 men each. The latter parties paraded at 9 p.m. and 9.30 p.m. respectively for work under the supervision of the R. E's. 2nd LIEUT. F. L. PARKER joined for duty.	
	14-9-16		Working parties were supplied during the day and heavy working parties supplied in the evening. Nine officers joined us for duty.- 2nd LIEUT. J. O. COULRIDGE. 2nd LIEUT. A. FITZ-HUGH 2nd LIEUT. L. T. FLUX. 2nd LIEUT. H. P. PHILLIPS. 2nd LIEUT. P. E. VIDLER. 2nd LIEUT. R. W. A. WATTS. and 2nd LIEUT. R. HARRISON.	
	15-9-16		Working parties were supplied during the day and at night.	
	16-9-16		Small working parties were furnished for Brigade. Parties worked on Garrison Defences. The baths were allotted to the Battalion.	
	17-9-16		Parties worked at Garrison defences, improving the main communication trenches through the village and also the drainage. Small brigade working parties were furnished.	

Army Form C. 2118.

Instructions regarding War Diaries and Intelligence Summaries are contained in F. S. Regs., Part II. and the Staff Manual respectively. Title pages will be prepared in manuscript.

WAR DIARY
or
~~INTELLIGENCE SUMMARY~~
(Erase heading not required.)

Place	Date	Hour	Summary of Events and Information	Remarks and references to Appendices
	18-9-16		Company Commanders reconnoitred the LEFT SECTOR of the line preparatory to relieving the 1st QUEENS REGT. Working parties were furnished.	
	19-9-16		Heavy working parties were furnished by the Battalion and worked on Brigade fatigues and also on the Defences of FONQUEVILLERS.	
	20-9-16		The Battalion relieved the 1st QUEENS REGT in the LEFT SECTOR during the evening. The 16th K.R.R's were on our left and the CAMERONIANS on our right. The bombing, sniping and observation posts were taken over by daylight, but the relief of Companies did not take place until 4.30 P.M. The Companies were disposed as follows:- "A" Coy. RIGHT FRONT - "B" Coy. LEFT FRONT - "C" Coy RIGHT SUPPORT and "D" Coy LEFT SUPPORT. The relief was completed without any difficulty, and there was little activity during the night. 2nd LIEUT. A.W. CALE was wounded.	
	21-9-16		The front line was shelled lightly during the morning and a few Minnenwerfers and rifle grenades were sent over during the day. One man was killed and another wounded by Trench Mortar. The Companies sent out Patrols during the whole night but no information of any importance was obtained. The trenches were in a bad state, and all available men were working in the front and	

Instructions regarding War Diaries and Intelligence Summaries are contained in F. S. Regs., Part II. and the Staff Manual respectively. Title pages will be prepared in manuscript.

WAR DIARY
or
~~INTELLIGENCE SUMMARY.~~
(Erase heading not required.)

Army Form C. 2118.

Place	Date	Hour	Summary of Events and Information	Remarks and references to Appendices
			Support trenches.	
	22.9.16		The enemy sent over a lot of shell in the direction of HEBUTERNE. Companies sent in reports to the effect that patrols had heard guns being brought up. There was very little activity in the front system of trenches, but many shells were sent over the village. The Companies worked at their trenches during the day, but there was a difficulty in obtaining floor-boards.	
	23.9.16		ST MARTINS LANE and parts of the front line was shelled with 4.2's and a few Gas Shells. ST MARTINS LANE was smashed in, in two places. "C" Coys worked on the damage done during the night.	
	24.9.16		We heard that the Brigade would probably be relieved shortly, but no definate information was received. "A" and "B" Coys in the Front Line on Right & Left respectively were relieved by "C" and "D" Coys, in the evening.	
	25.9.16		The C.O. and Officers of the 5th YORK and LANCS Regt. came up in the morning and reconnoitred our line. GENERAL PINNEY took over command of the 33rd Division from command of 35th Division.	
	26.9.16		We received more orders stating that the Battalion would be relieved on the	

T2134. Wt. W708—776. 500000. 4/15. Sir J. C. & S.

Instructions regarding War Diaries and Intelligence Summaries are contained in F. S. Regs., Part II. and the Staff Manual respectively. Title pages will be prepared in manuscript.

WAR DIARY

or

~~INTELLIGENCE SUMMARY.~~

(Erase heading not required.)

Army Form C. 2118.

Place	Date	Hour	Summary of Events and Information	Remarks and references to Appendices
			24th and arrangements were made with the 5th YORK and LANCS Regt as regards the relief. Very good news was received from the "SOMME", COMBLES was practically surrounded and THIEPVAL attacked in the afternoon. The "TANKS" were again of use. 2/Lieut. A.W.E. CHRISTIE fell down a dis-used well, when patrolling in NO MANS LAND and was killed, His body was recovered. Very little activity on our front.	
	27-9-16		The Battalion was relieved in the evening by the 5th YORK and LANCS, and moved back to billets at SOUASTRE	
	28-9-16		The Battalion paraded at 9 A.m. and marched via ST. ALMAND and GAUDIEMPRE to SOMBRIN. where we had good billets.	
	29-9-16		The Battalion assembled at 9 A.m. and marched about 4 miles in the rain to SUS-ST-LEGER. The billets were very good and we arrived about 11 A.m. The C.O. inspected the Coys in the afternoon.	
	30-9-16		The Battalion assembled at 8.30 A.m and marched about 4 miles to billets in LE SOUICH. The billets were exceptionally good. The Divisional General lectured on training in the afternoon at the PATRONAGE, BOUQUEMAISON.	

G. E. W. [illegible] Captain
Comdg. 2nd Bn. The Worcestershire Regt

100/33

2 Worc R

Vol 27

Army Form C. 2118.

Instructions regarding War Diaries and Intelligence Summaries are contained in F. S. Regs., Part II. and the Staff Manual respectively. Title pages will be prepared in manuscript.

WAR DIARY

or

~~INTELLIGENCE SUMMARY.~~

(Erase heading not required.)

Place	Date 1916	Hour	Summary of Events and Information (Sheet 1)	Remarks and references to Appendices
			October 1st	Lens Map No 11
			Sunday was spent in general cleaning up. The Battn assembled in the Court of the Chateau for Church parade.	
			Oct. 2nd	
			Capt. Ewbank left the Battn for the 1st Border Regt. Rev. Wright joined for duty. Physical training & coy. parades during morning & afternoon. Major Leman rejoined from 4th Army School & took over command of the battalion.	
			Oct. 3rd	
			Physical training & parades during the morning & afternoon. The battalion paraded for night operations near LUCHEUX WOOD. in the evening. Rain in the morning interfered with parades.	
			Oct. 4th	
			A wet morning. The battalion assembled for a short route march at 11 am & marched for about an hour. A draft of 68 men of the Gloucester Yeomanry arrived at about 5pm.	

See Sheet 2

Instructions regarding War Diaries and Intelligence Summaries are contained in F. S. Regs., Part II. and the Staff Manual respectively. Title pages will be prepared in manuscript.

WAR DIARY

or

~~INTELLIGENCE SUMMARY.~~

(Erase heading not required.)

Army Form C. 2118.

Place	Date	Hour	Sheet 2 — Summary of Events and Information	Remarks and references to Appendices
			Oct 5th/ Physical training before breakfast. The baths at BOUQUEMAISON, were allotted to the battalion & two companies were able to get baths, but no change of clothing. The remainder of the battalion carried on with company parades.	
			Oct 6th/ The remainder of the battalion was able to get baths & one company also got clothes. The companies carried on with parades during the morning & afternoon	
			Oct 7th/ The battalion assembled near the Church at 9 a.m. & carried out an attack through part of LUCHEAUX WOOD, getting back to billets at about 1pm. The C.O. returned from leave.	
			Oct 8th/ The battalion assembled for Church parade in the court-yard in front of Battn Hd Qr Mess. In the afternoon Major Leman lectured to all officers & N.C.O's on Drill, & in the evening we had a concert which was a great success.	

See Sheet 3

Instructions regarding War Diaries and Intelligence Summaries are contained in F. S. Regs., Part II. and the Staff Manual respectively. Title pages will be prepared in manuscript.

WAR DIARY
or
~~INTELLIGENCE SUMMARY.~~
(Erase heading not required.)

Army Form C. 2118.

Place	Date	Hour	Sheet 3 — Summary of Events and Information	Remarks and references to Appendices
			Oct 9th/ Physical training before breakfast. The Battn assembled near the Church at 9 am & carried out an attack against a skeleton enemy, on the open ground to the East of the village. In the evening the companies paraded for night marching and night digging. Capt Ferguson rejoined the battalion.	
			Oct. 10th/ Physical training & extended order drill in the morning, bayonet fighting and company drill in the afternoon	
			Oct 11th/ Physical Training. The Battn paraded on the ground E. of the village for practise in the attack & extended order drill. The C.O. reconnoitred the line at HEBUTERNE.	
			Oct. 12th/ Physical Training. Practise attacks through LUCHEUX WOOD during the morning. Night marching & digging in the evening	

See Sheet 4

Instructions regarding War Diaries and Intelligence Summaries are contained in F. S. Regs., Part II. and the Staff Manual respectively. Title pages will be prepared in manuscript.

WAR DIARY
or
INTELLIGENCE ~~SUMMARY~~.
(Erase heading not required.)

Army Form C. 2118.

Place	Date	Hour	Sheet 4 Summary of Events and Information	Remarks and references to Appendices
			Oct. 13th/ Physical training. The Battn paraded for open order work on the ground S. of LE SOWICH. Grouping practises. Drill in the afternoon.	
			Oct. 14th/ The Divisional Commander inspected the battn in the morning on the Transport field. Extended order drill & recruits musketry in the afternoon.	
			Oct. 15th/ Church parade was cancelled on account of the Chaplain going sick. Indifferent shots of all Coy's paraded from 9am to 12 noon for musketry on the range S. of LE SOWICH.	
			Oct. 16th/ The battn paraded on the ground E. of LE SOWICH for attack practise.	
			Oct. 17th/ Physical training. Coys at the disposal of Coy Commanders for musketry, extended order & wiring etc. "B" Coy paraded in the evening for a night bombing attack.	

See Sheet 5

T2134. Wt. W708—776. 500000. 4/15. Sir J. C. & S.

Instructions regarding War Diaries and Intelligence Summaries are contained in F. S. Regs., Part II. and the Staff Manual respectively. Title pages will be prepared in manuscript.

WAR DIARY
or
~~INTELLIGENCE SUMMARY.~~
(Erase heading not required.)

Army Form C. 2118.

Place	Date	Hour	Sheet 5 — Summary of Events and Information	Remarks and references to Appendices
			Oct 18th	
			A wet day. The route march was cancelled. The transport proceeded by road to TALMAS.	
			Oct. 19th	
			The Battn left LE SOUICH. at 8.30 am & marched to BOUQUEMAISON, where we embussed in French busses & bussed to LA NEUVILLE. via DOULLENS & AMIENS. The Battn debussed at LA NEUVILLE & marched to billets in CORBIE. The billets were quite comfortable. The transport arrived at about 9.30 pm. from TALMAS.	AMIENS Map. No 17
			Oct. 20th	
			The Battn marched out to some open ground West of LA NEUVILLE. and did Battn drill for about an hour.	
			Oct. 21st	
			The Battn assembled at 8.40 am and marched to billets in MEALTE. No one fell out and the men marched past the Divisional Commander very well. The billets were not good.	

See Sheet 6

Instructions regarding War Diaries and Intelligence Summaries are contained in F. S. Regs., Part II. and the Staff Manual respectively. Title pages will be prepared in manuscript.

WAR DIARY

or

~~INTELLIGENCE SUMMARY~~.

(Erase heading not required.)

Army Form C. 2118.

Place	Date	Hour	Sheet 6 — Summary of Events and Information	Remarks and references to Appendices

Oct. 22nd

The Battn assembled at 10.30 am and marched to MANSEL CAMP. Everyone was in tents & we were rather crowded.

Oct. 23rd

The C.O. & Coy Commanders reconnoitred part of the line during the morning, but were unable to see much owing to a thick mist. The Coy's paraded for physical drill & bayonet fighting during the morning and played football in the afternoon. The Divisional Band played in the evening. Move orders were received & issued but they were cancelled during the night.

Oct. 24th

A wet day. The companies paraded for inspections and parties were detailed to work under the Camp Commandant. Move orders were received in the evening

See Sheet 7

T2134. Wt. W708—776. 500000. 4/15. Sir J. C. & S.

Instructions regarding War Diaries and Intelligence Summaries are contained in F. S. Regs., Part II. and the Staff Manual respectively. Title pages will be prepared in manuscript.

WAR DIARY
or
~~INTELLIGENCE SUMMARY.~~
(Erase heading not required.)

Army Form C. 2118.

Sheet 7

Place	Date	Hour	Summary of Events and Information	Remarks and references to Appendices
			Oct 25th	
			The Battn less transport paraded at 10 am and moved with 200 yards between companies to BRIQUETERIE. Camp near MONTAUBAN. The paths were very muddy and the battn reached camp about 1pm. Everyone was in tents. The transport moved to a field near CARNOY. The camp was very wet and muddy but we were quite comfortable and were able to get blankets.	
			Oct 26th	
			A muddy day in camp. A working party of 50 men was supplied. The C.O. and Coy Commanders went up to reconnoitre the FLERS line in the morning.	
			Oct 27th	
			250 men were supplied for brigade fatigues during the day, these parties were used for carrying R.E. material from TRONES WOOD dump to a forward dump. A ration of rum was issued to these men in the evening. The remainder of the Battn were employed in general cleaning up and draining the camp. A very wet evening.	

See Sheet 8

Instructions regarding War Diaries and Intelligence Summaries are contained in F. S. Regs., Part II. and the Staff Manual respectively. Title pages will be prepared in manuscript.

WAR DIARY
or
~~INTELLIGENCE SUMMARY.~~
(Erase heading not required.)

Army Form C. 2118.

Sheet 8

Place	Date	Hour	Summary of Events and Information	Remarks and references to Appendices
			Oct 28th/ 250 men were supplied for brigade working parties and the remainder of the Battn were employed on general cleaning up & draining & also wood cutting etc. A windy but fine day.	
			Oct. 29th/ Working parties supplied. All remaining men worked at improvements to camp & surroundings. Move orders received.	
			Oct. 30th/ The CO reconnoitred the right brigade front in the morning & the Battn relieved the 5th Scottish Rifles in the evening in the left subsection of the right brigade. The relief took a long time on account of the very muddy state of the ground: it was completed at 2 a.m. A Coy was in the front line B Coy in support in the Gun Pits & C & D in Ox Trench near Bn H.Q. 2/Lts Vinter & Cornwall were wounded.	
			See Sheet 9	

T2134. Wt. W708—776. 500000. 4/15. Sir J. C. & S.

Instructions regarding War Diaries and Intelligence Summaries are contained in F. S. Regs., Part II. and the Staff Manual respectively. Title pages will be prepared in manuscript.

WAR DIARY

or

~~INTELLIGENCE SUMMARY.~~

(Erase heading not required.)

Army Form C. 2118.

Place	Date	Hour	Summary of Events and Information	Remarks and references to Appendices
			Sheet 9	
			Oct. 31st	
			A fairly quiet day. The men in the trenches were very uncomfortable as all the existing trenches were only 4 ft deep & nearly full of water. There was great difficulty in carrying up rations & supplies to the front coys.	
			G. I. L. Storey Captain for Lieut Colonel Comdg 2nd Bn The Worcestershire Regt	

T2134. Wt. W708—776. 500000. 4/15. Sir J. C. & S.

Instructions regarding War Diaries and Intelligence Summaries are contained in F. S. Regs., Part II. and the Staff Manual respectively. Title pages will be prepared in manuscript.

WAR DIARY
or
~~INTELLIGENCE SUMMARY.~~
(Erase heading not required.)

Army Form C. 2118.

2/15 Worcestershire Regt.

Vol 28

Place	Date	Hour	Summary of Events and Information	Remarks and references to Appendices
In the Field	1-11-16		Orders for an attack on HAZY TRENCH were received. "C" Coy moved up into position in "25" TRENCH early in the morning. CAPT. FERGUSON was killed by a sniper near the GUN PITS. The Companies were in their positions of assembly an hour before the attack. "A" and "B" Coys in the T head trench, and "C" Coy in the open behind the T head trench. "D" Coy remained in OXFORD trench near Battalion Head Quarters. The attack was launched about 3.30 P.M. in conjunction with an attack by the H.L.I. on the right. The attack was held up by Rifle and Machine Gun fire from the LEFT flank, and the Companies were forced to retire to their trenches. The Battalion had about 80 casualties. "D" Coys moved up in the evening to relieve "A" and "B" Coys and "C" Coy moved into the T head position. A and B Coys on relief returned to OXFORD trench. A Coy of the 16th K.R.R's were at the disposal of the Battalion and were used to carry up stores to the line.	ALBERT 1/40,000.
	2-11-16		A fairly quiet day but the men were very exhausted and wet from the effects of the attack and weather. Relief orders were received during the day, and the Battalion was relieved in the evening by the 16th K.R.R's. "A" and "B" Coys were relieved in the afternoon and moved into HOG'S BACK TRENCH. "C" and "D" Coys were relieved in the evening. The relief was not completed until the morning of the 3rd when all the	

S. 24

T2134. Wt. W708—776. 500000. 4/15. Sir J. C. & S.

Instructions regarding War Diaries and Intelligence Summaries are contained in F. S. Regs., Part II. and the Staff Manual respectively. Title pages will be prepared in manuscript.

WAR DIARY
or
~~INTELLIGENCE SUMMARY.~~
(Erase heading not required.)

Army Form C. 2118.

Place	Date	Hour	Summary of Events and Information	Remarks and references to Appendices
			Battalion had returned to HOG'S BACK TRENCH.	
	3-11-16		The Battalion remained in HOG'S BACK TRENCH during the day and cleaned up as much as possible. The 1st QUEENS made an attack during the evening which was unsuccessful. "B" Coy was attached to them, but was only used for carrying up rations.	
	4-11-16		The Battalion remained in HOG'S BACK. In the evening orders for an attack were received. The Commanding Officer went to the FRENCH Battalion Head Quarters during the afternoon to arrange about guides etc. The Battalion paraded outside HOG'S BACK TRENCH about 6.P.M. and marched in single file along the trench boards to FRENCH Regimental Head Quarters in SUNKEN ROAD. S.W. of MORVAL. Here the Battalion formed up and lay down. French Platoon Guides led the Battalion to their positions in single file through the French relay posts in the order D. C. B. A.. The Companies finally reached a position behind the FRENCH Front line, and dug in across the FRENCH end of MIRAGE and BARITSKA trench in four lines paralell to the French line in order D. C. B. A. A system of relay posts was established between Companies and Battalion Head Quarters which was with French Battalion Head Quarters in THUNDERER trench, and between Battalion Head Quarters and French Regimental Head Quarters. French and	

T2134. Wt. W708–776. 500000. 4/15. Sir J. C. & S.

Instructions regarding War Diaries and Intelligence Summaries are contained in F. S. Regs., Part II. and the Staff Manual respectively. Title pages will be prepared in manuscript.

WAR DIARY
or
~~INTELLIGENCE SUMMARY.~~
(Erase heading not required.)

Army Form C. 2118.

Place	Date	Hour	Summary of Events and Information	Remarks and references to Appendices
			English runners were used together at the relay posts. The Companies dug in, in their proper positions before daylight and were not troubled while at work. The trenches had been previously taped out by the R.E.	
	5-11-16		The companies remained as still as possible during the morning, and only had a few shells over. There was considerable artillery activity during the morning, and the attack was launched at 11.13 A.M. preceded by an artillery creeping barrage. The Battalion attacked along BARITSKA and MIRAGE trench which were found to be full of dead Germans, and then "right formed", and moved forward towards LE TRANSLOY, finally occupying a position just below the crest. Five Officers including three Company Commanders were killed during the first part of the attack, and LIEUT. BENNETT led the Battalion and did conspicuous good work. Heavy shell fire and Machine Guns opposed the attack. The Battalion consolidated the position as soon as it was gained, and the 16th K.R.R's came up on the left flank. 2nd LIEUT WATTS was sent out on the right flank to obtain touch with the FRENCH which he succeeded in doing, he was however wounded while on this patrol. The line consolidated was called BENNETT TRENCH. Green flares were lit in the front line at 1.15 and 3.P.M. and these were observed from Battalion Head Quarters. The	

Instructions regarding War Diaries and Intelligence Summaries are contained in F. S. Regs., Part II. and the Staff Manual respectively. Title pages will be prepared in manuscript.

WAR DIARY
or
~~INTELLIGENCE~~ SUMMARY.
(Erase heading not required.)

Army Form C. 2118.

Place	Date	Hour	Summary of Events and Information	Remarks and references to Appendices
			Runners did very good work during the whole of the operation in getting messages to and from the front line. The Battalion was relieved during the evening by the 5/6th SCOTTISH RIFLES and returned to HOGS BACK TRENCH through the FRENCH lines. The total casualties were 8 Officers and 102 other ranks. The Battalion moved straight on from HOGS BACK to GUILLEMONT where they arrived about 4 A.M.	
	6-11-16		The Battalion rested in shelters in GUILLIMONT during the morning and were relieved by the 1st WORCESTERSHIRE REGT in the afternoon. The Battalion then moved back to a camp in a very muddy field in the CITADEL near FRICOURT Cross roads.	
	7-11-16		A day spent in cleaning up and resting as far as possible in CITADEL camp. As much clothing as possible was issued, but there was very little opportunity of doing any washing.	
	8-11-16		Another day at the CITADEL. Company inspections were held.	
	9-11-16		The Brigadier General inspected the Battalion in the morning and read out a letter of congratulation from the French Regimental Commander of the 60th REGIMENT. The Transport moved by road to LA NEUVILLE enroute to LONGPRE.	
	10-11-16		The Battalion paraded at 8.30 A.M. and marched to BUIRE station. We entrained at 2 P.M. and detrained at AIRANES about 4.30 P.M. The Battalion march about 4 miles to billets	

T2134. Wt. W708—776. 500000. 4/15. Sir J. C. & S.

Instructions regarding War Diaries and Intelligence Summaries are contained in F. S. Regs., Part II. and the Staff Manual respectively. Title pages will be prepared in manuscript.

WAR DIARY
or
~~INTELLIGENCE SUMMARY.~~
(Erase heading not required.)

Army Form C. 2118.

Place	Date	Hour	Summary of Events and Information	Remarks and references to Appendices
			at LONGPRE in the ABBEVILLE district	
	11-11-16		The day was spent in general cleaning up and inspections.	
	12-11-16		Church Parade was held in the grounds of a private house during the morning, and the "Drums" played in the same ground in the afternoon.	
	13-11-16		Physical Training and Running before breakfast. Companies paraded for Handling of Arms and Squad Drill in the morning and for Classes and Lectures during the afternoon.	
	14-11-16		Physical Training and Running before breakfast. Handling of Arms and Squad Drill during the morning. Coys paraded for Bayonet Fighting in the afternoon.	
	15-11-16		Physical Training before breakfast. The Battalion paraded during the morning on the high ground WEST of the village. Companies parade for Bayonet Fighting in the afternoon.	
	16-11-16		Physical Training before breakfast. Companies paraded for Platoon Drill and Fire Control during the morning and Bayonet Fighting in the afternoon.	
	17-11-16		Physical Training before breakfast. The Battalion paraded for a Route March in the morning. Companies paraded at 5.P.M. and practised marching on a point at night.	
	18-11-16		Physical Training before breakfast. Companies paraded for Musketry and Extended Order Drill during the morning.	

Instructions regarding War Diaries and Intelligence Summaries are contained in F. S. Regs., Part II. and the Staff Manual respectively. Title pages will be prepared in manuscript.

WAR DIARY
or
~~INTELLIGENCE SUMMARY.~~
(Erase heading not required.)

Army Form C. 2118.

Place	Date	Hour	Summary of Events and Information	Remarks and references to Appendices
	19.11.16		Church Parade was held during the morning in the grounds of M. Griblin. The Divisional Band played from 3 to 4 P.M. in LONGPRE Market Place.	
	20.11.16		Physical Training before breakfast. Companies paraded for Squad Drill, Musketry, and Handling of Arms during the morning. Lectures during the afternoon.	
	21.11.16		Physical Training before breakfast. Companies practised "Moving to a starting point" and assault in waves, during the morning. Bayonet Fighting in the afternoon.	
	22.11.16		Physical Training and Running before breakfast. The Divisional General paid an official visit in the morning accompanied by Brigadier General Baird. Everything was satisfactory.	
	23.11.16		Physical Training before breakfast. Companies practised creeping under barrage and Out-posts during the morning. Bayonet Fighting in the afternoon.	
	24.11.16		Physical Training before breakfast. "C" Coy. - Musketry. Other Companies - Route march. Companies paraded at 5 P.M. and practised assault on trenches by night.	
	25.11.16		Physical Training before breakfast. Battalion and Company drill on ground N. of LONGPRE during the morning.	
	26.11.16		Church Parade was held during the morning in the grounds of M. Griblin. The 33rd Divl.	

T2134. Wt. W708—776. 500000. 4/15. Sir J. C. & S.

Instructions regarding War Diaries and Intelligence Summaries are contained in F. S. Regs., Part II. and the Staff Manual respectively. Title pages will be prepared in manuscript.

WAR DIARY
or
~~INTELLIGENCE SUMMARY.~~
(*Erase heading not required.*)

Army Form C. 2118.

Place	Date	Hour	Summary of Events and Information	Remarks and references to Appendices
			Supply Column String Band played from 2 to 4 P.M in the Market Square.	
	27-11-16		Physical Training before breakfast. "D" Company was at Musketry. The remaining Companies practised attack by Platoons and Companies during the morning. Bayonet Fighting in the afternoon.	
	28-11-16		Physical Training before breakfast. During the morning the Battalion practised Advancing, Strong Points, etc. Companies paraded for Bayonet Fighting in the afternoon.	
	29-11-16		Physical Training before breakfast. "A" Company was at Musketry. The remaining Companies practised Close and Extended order drill and use of Entrenching Tools. Bayonet Fighting in the afternoon.	
	30-11-16		Physical Training before breakfast. The Battalion paraded during the morning and practised a Battalion scheme which included, Officers reconnaisance, Communication, Signal Stations, and Aid Post etc. Companies paraded for Bayonet Fighting in the afternoon.	
			M K Pardoe Lieut Col Commanding 2nd Bn The Worcestershire Regiment	

T2134. Wt. W708–776. 500000. 4/15. Sir J. C. & S.

Instructions regarding War Diaries and Intelligence Summaries are contained in F. S. Regs., Part II. and the Staff Manual respectively. Title pages will be prepared in manuscript.

WAR DIARY
or
INTELLIGENCE SUMMARY.
(Erase heading not required.)

Army Form C. 2118.

100/33

2 Worcester Regt

Vol 29

Place	Date	Hour	Summary of Events and Information	Remarks and references to Appendices
In the Field	Dec 1st 1916		Physical Training before breakfast. "C" Coy Musketry. "A" Coy (50 men) on fatigue remainder Coy Drill. "B" & "D" digging trenches, practising advancing under barrage	
	Dec 2nd		Battn paraded at 8.45 am and marched to CONDY FOLIE. Divisional General presented Ribbons to recipients. In the afternoon men rubbed feet	
	Dec 3rd		The morning was spent in cleaning up by all Coy's. Battn paraded 2.45 pm and marched to LONGPRE Stn and entrained for MERICOURT arriving about 8 pm. The Battn then marched to MORLANCOURT	
	Dec 4th		The day was spent in having a thorough inspection of Gas Helmets, Ammunition etc, also cleaning up billets.	
	Dec 5th		The Battn assembled in column of route 9.30 am & marched to Camp 111 arriving about noon. The afternoon was spent in cleaning up	
	Dec 6th		The Battn assembled at 9.20 am & marched VIA BEL AIR to Camp 111 not from BRAY. We reached Camp 111 at 11.30 & were all billetted in French huts which were quite dry. The remainder of the day was spent in cleaning up. We took over from W. YORKS	

See Page 2

T2134. Wt. W708–776. 500000. 4/15. Sir J. C. & S.

Instructions regarding War Diaries and Intelligence Summaries are contained in F. S. Regs., Part II. and the Staff Manual respectively. Title pages will be prepared in manuscript.

WAR DIARY
or
INTELLIGENCE SUMMARY.
(Erase heading not required.)

Army Form C. 2118.

Place	Date	Hour	Summary of Events and Information	Remarks and references to Appendices
In the Field	Dec	7th	The Battn assembled in the morning & marched to Camp 16 on the other side of BRAY. The huts were not quite so good, but everyone was under cover. A Coy had a bomb accident in the morning. A French bomb exploded in a brazier & 18 men were wounded. The 1/Middlesex took over Camp 111. We took over from the Irish Guards.	
	Dec	8th	The Battn spent the morning in cleaning up & moved in the afternoon to Camp 20 which we took over from a Household Battalion. This camp was rather dirty. Our blankets did not arrive until late as the lorries did not turn up.	
	Dec	9th	The C.O. & Coy Commanders went up to reconnoitre the line early in the morning. The Battn paraded at 3pm & moved off by companies to the support position of the left brigade near LE PRIEZ FARM. We relieved the 2nd Battn 34th Regt (French) & completed the relief at about 9.30pm. The transport remained in MAUREPAS RAVINE & surplus personnel at Camp 20. The rations arrived early the following morning. HdQrs was in a German dug out & the companies in dug outs & trenches quite close.	

See Page 3.

Army Form C. 2118.

Instructions regarding War Diaries and Intelligence Summaries are contained in F. S. Regs., Part II. and the Staff Manual respectively. Title pages will be prepared in manuscript.

WAR DIARY
or
INTELLIGENCE SUMMARY.
(Erase heading not required.)

Place	Date	Hour	Summary of Events and Information	Remarks and references to Appendices
In the Field	Dec	10th	Very little movement was allowed by day. During the night the Battn supplied about 200 men for fatigues. There was a great difficulty in getting hot food up	
	Dec	11th	The Battn remained in the reserve position & supplied fatigues of about 300 men during the night. Orders came in at about 8 30 pm, that the Battn was going to relieve the 9/H.L.I on the 12th.	
	Dec	12th	The Coy Commanders reconnoitred the line early in the morning. The relief started at 6 30 pm & was not finished until 2 am, as "C" Coy got stuck in the mud for some time & 2/Lt Jones the Coy Commander was wounded. The Coys were disposed as follows:- "C" - Left Front "D" - Right Front "B" - Support "A" - Reserve in a trench just behind Battn HdQrs which was on the main BETHUNE ROAD. The Household Battn was on our left & the 16/K.R.R. on our right. There was a certain amount	

T2134. Wt. W708–776. 500000. 4/15. Sir J. C. & S.

See Page 4

Army Form C. 2118.

Instructions regarding War Diaries and Intelligence Summaries are contained in F. S. Regs., Part II. and the Staff Manual respectively. Title pages will be prepared in manuscript.

WAR DIARY
or
INTELLIGENCE SUMMARY.
(Erase heading not required.)

Place	Date	Hour	Summary of Events and Information	Remarks and references to Appendices
In the Field			of sniping during the night, but little shelling or M.G fire	
	Dec 13th		A quiet day. The Coy's improved their positions, as far as possible. "A" Coy was in a fairly good trench, but the front trenches were very muddy & wet	
	Dec 14th		The Coy Commanders of the 5th Scottish Rifles came up to reconnoitre the line early in the morning. The Battn was relieved in the evening by the 5th Scottish Rifles. The relief was not complete until about 1 am. We then marched back to MAUREPAS, where motor lorries took the Battn on to Camp 17 near SUZANNE. The Battn had a total of 85 trench feet	
	Dec 15th		The Battn rested & cleaned up during the day.	
	Dec 16th		General cleaning & inspections. The Battn was billetted in huts & had plenty of room. The surroundings of the camp were very muddy.	
	Dec 17th		Sunday was spent in cleaning up. The baths in SUZANNE were allotted to the Battn during the day. There were voluntary services in the 16/K.R.R.C lines.	
	Dec 18th		The Battn moved off by companies at 10 am, with half an hours interval between Coy's. We stopped for dinners near MAUREPAS & reached PEPIT BOIS lines at 2 pm, where guides of the 4/King's met the Coy's & led them to their respective positions. The	

See Page 5

Instructions regarding War Diaries and Intelligence Summaries are contained in F. S. Regs., Part II. and the Staff Manual respectively. Title pages will be prepared in manuscript.

WAR DIARY
or
INTELLIGENCE SUMMARY.
(Erase heading not required.)

Army Form C. 2118.

Place	Date	Hour	Summary of Events and Information	Remarks and references to Appendices
In the Field			Battn occupied the support position & were all in dug outs. A hard frost in the night.	
	Dec 19th		Spent in generally cleaning up the surroundings which were very dirty indeed. A standing fatigue to unload the Decauville train was supplied. A hard frost in the night	
	Dec 20th		About 200 men were furnished for carrying parties & took material to the Brigade Dump at AIGUILLE. There was a heavy bombardment on the night, but no shells fell near our lines	
	Dec 21st		The CO & Coy Commanders reconnoitred the line early in the morning. A quiet day in the reserve position	
	Dec 22nd		The Battn relieved the 9/HLI in the left sector of the line. The Coy's moved off at 3pm & the relief was completed at about 1am. The Coy's were disposed as follows:- "A" - Right Front "B" - Left Front "D" - Support "C" - Reserve	

See Page 6

Instructions regarding War Diaries and Intelligence Summaries are contained in F. S. Regs., Part II. and the Staff Manual respectively. Title pages will be prepared in manuscript.

WAR DIARY
or
INTELLIGENCE SUMMARY.
(Erase heading not required.)

Army Form C. 2118.

Place	Date	Hour	Summary of Events and Information	Remarks and references to Appendices
In the Field			The trenches were very wet & muddy & the Coy's took a long time relieving. The Germans fired salvoes during the night, near the end of AGILE .T, the Sunken Road & Battn HdQrs. The 16/K.R.R.C. were on our right & 98th Brigade on our left.	
	Dec 23rd		A quiet day. The Coy's held inter platoon reliefs during the evening.	
	Dec 24th		"D" Coy relieved "B" Coy on the left & "C" Coy relieved "A" Coy on the right. The left & support Coy's were able to get hot tea in our food containers & the right Coy cooked hot tea on solidified alcohol.	
	Dec 25th		There were several artillery strafes during the day & the Huns retaliated on our support lines. Three men of "B" Coy were killed in a dug out in the support line, no other damage was done. The wire from Bn HdQrs to the support company was shelled at intervals during the day.	
	Dec 26th		The Battn was relieved by the 14th H.L.I. in the evening (120th Brigade). 9/H.L.I. guides brought the relieving platoons as far as the BETHUNE ROAD & succeeded in losing three platoons temporarily. The relief took a long time owing to the very bad state of the trenches & was not completed until 1 am. The Coy's had hot tea at ANDOVER, changed their boots & went on to MAUREPAS, where busses	

T2134. Wt. W708—776. 500000. 4/15. Sir J. C. & S.

See Page 7

Instructions regarding War Diaries and Intelligence Summaries are contained in F. S. Regs., Part II. and the Staff Manual respectively. Title pages will be prepared in manuscript.

WAR DIARY
or
INTELLIGENCE SUMMARY.
(*Erase heading not required.*)

Army Form C. 2118.

Page 1

Place	Date	Hour	Summary of Events and Information	Remarks and references to Appendices
In the Field			met us & took us on to Camp 14 on the far side of BRAY. The accommodation was very limited & the camp in a muddy condition. The majority of the Battn was in by 8 am	
	Dec 27th		A quiet day spent in Camp 14. The men rested, but were unable to do much cleaning up on account of the very dirty & muddy state of the camp.	
	Dec 28th		The Transport moved off by road at 8 am. The Battn moved off at 12 noon & marched to EDGEHILL STATION where we entrained for LONGPRÉ. The Battn detrained very quickly at LONGPRÉ & marched to AILLY LE HAUT CLOCHER, where we arrived at 12 midnight. The billets were quite good & the village seemed clean.	
	Dec 29th		A quiet day spent in cleaning up as far as possible	
	Dec 30th		Thorough cleaning up & inspections. No parades were ordered.	
	Dec 31st		Church parade was held in the field at the E. End of the village. The senior Chaplain officiated. The "Drums" beat the Old Year out at 12 midnight	

M K Pardoe Lieut Col.
Comdg 2nd Battn The Worcestershire Regt.

T2134. Wt. W708—776. 500000. 4/15. Sir J. C. & S.

Instructions regarding War Diaries and Intelligence Summaries are contained in F. S. Regs., Part II. and the Staff Manual respectively. Title Pages will be prepared in manuscript.

WAR DIARY
or
INTELLIGENCE SUMMARY

(Erase heading not required.)

Army Form C. 2118.

100/33

2nd Worcestershire Regt.

Vol 30

S.30

Place	Date	Hour	Summary of Events and Information	Remarks and references to Appendices
In the Field	1-1-17		A Holiday. All the Companies had dinners, and the Sergeants had a mess dinner in the evening	
	2-1-17		The Battn paraded for physical Training, squad & extended order drill. The ground EAST. of the village was used for all parades.	
	3-1-17		Physical Training Battalion, Company & Platoon Drill	
	4-1-17		The Commanding Officer inspected Companies on the Parade Ground. Col: V.H. Pardoe went on leave & Major G.J.S. Stoney took over command of the Battn	
	5-1-17		The Battn paraded at 9.45 am, and marched to GORENFLOS, where a Brigade scheme was carried out, demonstrating inter-communication between Aeroplanes and Infantry.	
	6-1-17		The Coys paraded for drill on the parade ground. 2/Lt Gillespie joined the Battn. An inter-company football ~~match~~ competition was started	
	7-1-17		A voluntary service was held in the Concert Hall.	
	8-1-17		Coys paraded for physical training, handling of arms, platoon drill & bayonet fighting. 5 N.C.O's were put through a Course of Bayonet Fighting. The "Shrapnels" gave a concert in the Concert Hall at 6 pm.	
	9-1-17		Coys paraded for physical training, squad, extended order drill & bayonet fighting	
	10-1-17		The Battn assembled for a route march and marched along the ABBEVILLE road, Capt. Watson joined the Battn and was posted to "B" Coy	
	11-1-17		The Coys paraded for physical training, platoon & coy drill, also for night operations.	

See Page 2

2449 Wt. W14957/M90 750,000 1/16 J.B.C. & A. Forms/C.2118/12.

Page 2

Instructions regarding War Diaries and Intelligence Summaries are contained in F. S. Regs., Part II. and the Staff Manual respectively. Title Pages will be prepared in manuscript.

WAR DIARY
or
INTELLIGENCE SUMMARY

(Erase heading not required.)

Army Form C. 2118.

Place	Date	Hour	Summary of Events and Information	Remarks and references to Appendices
In the Field	12-1-17		The Battn assembled for a route march and marched along the main ABBEVILLE road, practising the Gas Alarm during the march. Coy commanders & N.C.O's representing Coy's attended a Gas demonstration in the use of the Small Box Respirator held at GORENFLOS. The "Sweeps" concert party gave a Concert in the Concert Hall several representatives of the Battn performed.	
	13-1-17		The C.O inspected Coy's in billets during the morning. The Divisional General presented medal ribbons to Capt. Watson M.C. and Sergt. Moore M.M. also to several men of the 16th K.R.R.C. Both battns paraded for the presentation.	
	14-1-17		Voluntary Services were held in the Concert Hall.	
	15-1-17		Coys paraded for physical training, handling of arms, & platoon drill. Night wiring classes were held in the evening. A Brigade cross-country run was held at BUSSUS-BUSSEL. Teams of 1 Officer and 20 men per Battn entered for this race, which was won by us. Pte Denning came in first.	
	16-1-17		The coy's paraded for physical training, squad & extended order drill. In the afternoon the first round of an inter platoon soccer association was played off.	
	17-1-17		A snowy day. The Battn parade was cancelled & the C.O inspected some of the billets. A Brigade bombing demonstration was held in the morning at GORENFLOS.	
	18-1-17		Physical training before breakfast. The Battn paraded for a route march at 9.30 am and marched along the ABBEVILLE road, Practise gas attacks were ordered during the march. The soccer competition was continued in the afternoon. The transport left AILLY in advance of the Battn at 8.30 am.	

See Page 3

Instructions regarding War Diaries and Intelligence Summaries are contained in F. S. Regs., Part II. and the Staff Manual respectively. Title Pages will be prepared in manuscript.

WAR DIARY
or
INTELLIGENCE SUMMARY

(Erase heading not required.)

Army Form C. 2118.

Place	Date	Hour	Summary of Events and Information	Remarks and references to Appendices
In the Field	19-1-17		Physical Training & coy parades during the morning. The inter-platoon soccer competition was continued in the afternoon & won by "D" Coy.	
	20-1-17		The Battn paraded at 7 am & marched to LONGPRÉ where they entrained for BRAY-TOURBIERES at 9.30 am. We reached BRAY at about 6.15 pm & marched to Camp 112. The Battn had eight huts & were quite comfortable.	
	21-1-17		A very cold & frosty day. The coy's went for short runs & spent the rest of the day cleaning up the Camp.	
	22-1-17		Two companies were employed on camp fatigues & improved the duck-board tracks, latrines etc. The other two companies paraded for short marches & running.	
	23-1-17		The Battn paraded at 11.30 am & marched by coy's at 200 yards interval to SUZANNE, where the Battn was bivouacked in a camp of tents & dug-outs taken over from the 4th Kings. The camp was very dirty & the accomodation not good.	
	24-1-17		The Battn was employed cleaning up the camp & surroundings & making latrines etc. The cold spell continued & there was a scarcity of fuel. A German aeroplane flew low over the camp.	
	25-1-17		The Battn was allotted baths at SUZANNE during the morning & afternoon. When not bathing the coy's were employed generally cleaning up the lines & doing camp fatigues. A very cold day.	
	26-1-17		The CO & Coy Commanders reconnoitred the line during the morning. The Battn was employed finding fatigues & doing work in the camp.	

See Page 4

Page 4

Instructions regarding War Diaries and Intelligence Summaries are contained in F. S. Regs., Part II. and the Staff Manual respectively. Title Pages will be prepared in manuscript.

WAR DIARY
or
INTELLIGENCE SUMMARY
(Erase heading not required.)

Army Form C. 2118.

Place	Date	Hour	Summary of Events and Information	Remarks and references to Appendices
In the Field	27/1/17		The Battn moved off from SUZANNE. The transport & "C" Coy left at 2.30 pm for "B" Echelon (near CURLU). The first company moved off at 6.15 pm for a position near HOWITZER WOOD. The Battn arrived at 9.15 pm & occupied some very good dug-outs just in front of HOWITZER WOOD on the Eastern slope of a valley. Nearly all the men had wire beds & we were all quite comfortable with plenty of wood	
	28-1-17		The companies were employed on a few small Brigade fatigues & in working on the general improvement of the lines under the Pioneers Sergt. A Cookhouse & incinerator were started. Voluntary services were held in a dug-out, which was afterwards made use of as a Divisional Drying Shed. A quiet, but very cold day	
	29-1-17		Two parties of 100 & 90 men were sent up to MIDDLE DUMP in the morning & other smaller Brigade & Battn fatigues were supplied by the coys. One party collected fire-wood. A F.G.C.M. was held at our "B" Echelon. A quiet day. The frost continued	
	30-1-17		Two parties of 100 & 200 respectively were supplied on brigade fatigues. The C.O and Coy Commanders reconnoitred the line in the morning	
	31-1-17		The Battn relieved the 9th H.L.I. in the left subsector of the line. Coys marched off at 6pm via MARY AVENUE & were disposed as follows:- C Right front A Left front B Support D Reserve Rations were issued & water-bottles filled before the Battn paraded.	

M. K. Pardoe Lieut Col.
Comdg 2nd Bn The Worcestershire Regt.

2449 Wt. W14957/M90 750,000 1/16 J.B.C. & A. Forms/C.2118/12.

Army Form C. 2118.

Instructions regarding War Diaries and Intelligence Summaries are contained in F. S. Regs., Part II. and the Staff Manual respectively. Title Pages will be prepared in manuscript.

WAR DIARY
or
INTELLIGENCE SUMMARY
(Erase heading not required.)

2 Worcester Rgt
Vol 31

S. 31

Place	Date	Hour	Summary of Events and Information	Remarks and references to Appendices
In the Field	1-2-17		A quiet day. The support companies did all the carrying work for the Coys in the front line & also supplied working parties to work on the left & right of the front coys. Heavy minnies fell near H.d.Qrs at about 8.30 pm.	
	2-2-17		The enemy shelled the Brigade on the left very heavily between 4 & 5 & did a certain amount of damage to our left Coy. It was afterwards reported that they had raided the Battn on the left unsuccessfully, and that one Hun prisoner had been captured. Our own Artillery retaliated & shells fell very short on the left Coy front but did not cause any casualties. Everything was fairly quiet during the day. At about 8.30 pm a Hun Minnie fired on our right Coy & did a certain amount of damage. Retaliation was obtained but a number of our own shells fell short & did considerable damage to our right T head Sap, causing 5 casualties. The Huns were active with rifle grenades during the night in both Coy fronts.	
	3-2-17		Our artillery bombarded between 10.15 am & 4 pm & did some effective shooting on the German lines. The Germans retaliated but did not do much damage. Our artillery fired again between 11 pm & 1 am. The Germans shelled the left of the right Battn during the night.	
	4-2-17		Our artillery were active during the day, but the Germans did not retaliate heavily.	
	5-2-17		Considerable artillery activity during the day. The Battn was relieved by the 9th H. L. I, the relief commenced at 5 pm & was completed by 9 pm. On relief the Battn occupied the support position.	

See Sheet 2

2449 Wt. W14957/M90 750,000 1/16 J.B.C. & A. Forms/C.2118/12.

Instructions regarding War Diaries and Intelligence Summaries are contained in F. S. Regs., Part II. and the Staff Manual respectively. Title Pages will be prepared in manuscript.

Sheet 2

WAR DIARY
or
INTELLIGENCE SUMMARY
(Erase heading not required.)

Army Form C. 2118.

Place	Date	Hour	Summary of Events and Information	Remarks and references to Appendices
In the Field	6-2-17		The Battn supplied heavy working parties. The Coys were disposed as follows:- "A" Coy - Left front in very bad shelters on the hill. "B" " - Right " " MAN TRENCH. This Coy had good dug-outs. "C" " - 2 platoons in QUARRY & 2 behind MAN T. "D" " - in reserve position	
	7-2-17		Very heavy working parties were furnished during the day. The 9th H.L.I. made a very good raid on the German lines near the PERONNE ROAD. The German retaliation was not heavy.	
	8-2-17		Working parties supplied in the morning. The Battn was relieved in the evening by the Cameronians, the relief taking a long time owing to congestion of traffic in MARY AVENUE. On relief the Battn occupied the reserve position to the 98th (Right Bde) relieving the 5th S. Rifles. This relief was not completed until about 3 am. The Battn was disposed as follows:- 2½ Coys & HdQrs at FRISE BEND. 1 Coy (B) HOWITZER WOOD ½ Coy (A) OMMIECOURT DEFENCES	
	9-2-17		The Battn supplied a permanent working party to work under the Tunnelling Coy.	
	10-2-17		The permanent working party was supplied. The Battn was relieved in the evening by the 2nd A&S Highlanders & marched back to billets in SUZANNE. The move was completed at 4 am. The billets were quite good.	

See Sheet 3.

2449 Wt. W14957/M90 750,000 1/16 J.B.C. & A. Forms/C.2118/12.

Sheet 3

Instructions regarding War Diaries and Intelligence Summaries are contained in F. S. Regs., Part II. and the Staff Manual respectively. Title Pages will be prepared in manuscript.

WAR DIARY
or
INTELLIGENCE SUMMARY

(Erase heading not required.)

Army Form C. 2118.

Place	Date	Hour	Summary of Events and Information	Remarks and references to Appendices
In the Field	11-2-17		Voluntary services were held on Sunday & the day was spent in general cleaning up and fatigue work	
	12-2-17		Two Companies practised the fighting platoon in the morning & two in the afternoon on the ground N of SUZANNE. Small fatigues were supplied for the Town Major etc.	
	13-2-17		Attack practises carried on again. Small fatigues furnished.	
	14-2-17		" " " " " " " "	
	15-2-17		"C" Coy rehearsed the attack in the morning. In the afternoon "D" Coy made a demonstration Coy attack using the French formation. The Brigadier & C.Os of the other Battns in the Brigade watched the demonstration, which was very satisfactory.	
	16-2-17		The Battn moved up VIA SUZANNE ECLUSIER - FRISE BEND - FEUILLERES - MONACU to the trenches in the right sector of the CLERY subsector relieving the 1/4th Suffolks of the 98th Brigade. The Coys marched off at ½ hours interval, the first Coy starting at 3.30 pm. The relief was completed by 10 pm. The trenches were in fair condition, but a thaw was setting in. The Coys were disposed as follows:- "A" - Left B - Centre C - Right D - Support	
	17-2-17		The artillery bombarded the German trenches opposite our lines & our saps were cleared and only sentries left in the front line during the hours of bombardment 9.30 am to 1.30 pm and 6.15 to 6.30 pm. The M.G.C. cooperated	

See Sheet 4

Sheet 4

Instructions regarding War Diaries and Intelligence Summaries are contained in F. S. Regs., Part II. and the Staff Manual respectively. Title Pages will be prepared in manuscript.

WAR DIARY
or
INTELLIGENCE SUMMARY
(Erase heading not required.)

Army Form C. 2118.

Place	Date	Hour	Summary of Events and Information	Remarks and references to Appendices
In the Field	18-2-17		A fairly quiet day. The artillery bombarded for a short time during the morning. The Coys were able to do work on the lines in the evening. "D" Coy sent working parties to help A Coy	
	19-2-17		A quiet day. The trenches began to get very muddy & required a lot of working on. The Coys in the line & also parties from D Coy worked on WURZEL & MOINEVILLE TRENCHES and also the front line between them in view of a possible raid.	
	20-2-17		The heavy artillery bombarded the German trenches opposite a part of our line & our saps were cleared. The Battn was relieved in the evening by the 9th H.L.I. in the right subsector and relieved the 1/Queens as the Bde reserve Battn. The relief started at about 6.30 pm, on relief HdQrs B. D & ½ C Coys returned to FRISE BEND. A Coy to HOWITZER WOOD and ½ C Coy to OMMIECOURT DEFENCES	
	21-2-17		A quiet day in the reserve position at FRISE BEND. Working parties were supplied & the remainder employed on generally cleaning up. 2/Lt C.A.N. Fox North Staffordshire Regt. attd 2nd Worc Regt appointed Adjutant 2nd Bn The Worcestershire Regt, from 3/3/16 vice Capt C.H. Ralston evacuated to England 3/3/16	
	22-2-17		The Battn supplied a few working parties during the day. The raid party practised in the morning under Major Stoney & 2/Lieut Durlacher. A misty day.	
	23-2-17		Working parties supplied. The raid party practised on the hill and had a rehearsal of the raid in conjunction with the R.E. torpedo & demolition parties.	

See Sheet 5

2449 Wt. W14957/M90 750,000 1/16 J.B.C. & A. Forms/C.2118/12.

Army Form C. 2118.

Instructions regarding War Diaries and Intelligence Summaries are contained in F. S. Regs., Part II. and the Staff Manual respectively. Title Pages will be prepared in manuscript.

Sheet 5

WAR DIARY
or
INTELLIGENCE SUMMARY
(Erase heading not required.)

Place	Date	Hour	Summary of Events and Information	Remarks and references to Appendices
In the Field	24-2-17		The Battn relieved the 9th H L I. in the right subsector. The 1/Queens took over our dispositions as Battn in Brigade reserve. The 16/K.R.R. were on our left and the III Corps on our right. The relief was quite satisfactory & completed by 10 pm. The coys were disposed as follows:- D - Left Front B - Centre " C - Right " A - Support 50 men of "A" Coy were left at "B" Echelon under 2/Lt Hopkins. The night was quiet.	
	25-2-17		The Coys worked on their lines & "A" Coy sent up parties to do special work during the night. There was very little activity during the day. Reports were received that the Germans had evacuated their line opposite us, and instructions sent to the effect that we were to push out strong patrols & if possible occupy the German line, holding a Coy in readiness to make for MONT ST. QUENTIN. This order was shortly cancelled. Arrangements for the raid were continued.	
	26-2-17		Arrangements for the raid were continued. The Coys relieved in the evening as follows:- "A" Coy relieved "D" Coy & left platoon of "B" Coy. B. C & D Coys raiding parties occupied the reserve position vacated by "A" Coy. Coys did as much work as possible during the night.	

See Sheet 6

Army Form C. 2118.

Instructions regarding War Diaries and Intelligence Summaries are contained in F. S. Regs., Part II. and the Staff Manual respectively. Title Pages will be prepared in manuscript.

Sheet 6

WAR DIARY
or
INTELLIGENCE SUMMARY
(Erase heading not required.)

Place	Date	Hour	Summary of Events and Information	Remarks and references to Appendices
In the Field	27-2-17		The Battn carried out two very satisfactory raids during the evening. The first one of 50 men under A Coy started at 8.43 pm. 2/Lt Pearce was wounded & 11 O.R. The raid was a great success & 7 prisoners of the 8th Coy 2nd Guard Grenadier Regt, 2nd Guard Division were captured. The Hun retaliation was not heavy. A second raid was carried out at 1. am 28th by a volunteer party of 150 men under 2/Lt Durlacher. This raid was also very successful. 2/Lt Ward & 2/Lt Durlacher & 35 O.R were wounded. 6 O.R were killed. 2/Lt Heyes was killed during the second raid. 15 prisoners were taken & a lot of damage done. The raid was carried out in accordance with the arranged scheme & everything was very successful	
	28-2-17		A quiet day. The Battn was relieved by the 9th H.L.I. & took over the dispositions of the support Battn. The relief was very satisfactory & completed by 8.15 pm. A Coy was in the second line ½ B. C & D Coys in MAUD AVENUE. ½ B in CLERY CHATEAU	

G. J. L. Stoney Major
Comdg 2nd Bn The Worcestershire Regiment.

2449 Wt. W14957/M90 750,000 1/16 J.B.C. & A. Forms/C.2118/12.

Sheet No 1

Instructions regarding War Diaries and Intelligence Summaries are contained in F. S. Regs., Part II. and the Staff Manual respectively. Title Pages will be prepared in manuscript.

WAR DIARY
or
INTELLIGENCE SUMMARY
(Erase heading not required.)

Worcester Regt
2 ~~Wilts~~
Vol 32

Army Form C. 2118.

Place	Date	Hour	Summary of Events and Information	Remarks and references to Appendices
In the Field	1/3/17		The battalion had a quiet day in the Support position & supplied about 150 men for work with the 11th Coy. R.E. The Brigadier General came round in the afternoon & interviewed the raiding party.	
	2/3/17		The Bn supplied about 150 men for working parties. The 1/Queens raid was cancelled, as it was impossible to cut the wire owing to bad visibility.	
	3/3/17		The Bn was relieved in the support position by the 2nd R.W.F, the relief being completed by about 8 pm. On relief Coys marched back independently to SUZANNE, and took over the same billets as previously.	
	4/3/17		Spent in General Cleaning up. Voluntary Church parades were held in the Cinema Hall.	
	5/3/17		Coys were at the disposal of Coy Commanders for general cleaning up & inspections, & as much clothing etc as possible was issued in order to lighten the transport for the move. The baths were allotted to the battalion & every man was able to get a wash & change.	
	6/3/17		The Battn paraded at 8am & marched with full transport from SUZANNE via BRAY to CORBIE. The march was about 15 miles, and only 2 men fell out although packs were carried, we had dinners en route, & reached billets at about 3 pm.	

2449 Wt. W14957/M90 750,000 1/16 J.B.C. & A. Forms/C.2118/12.

See Sheet No 2.

S 32

Sheet No 2.

Instructions regarding War Diaries and Intelligence Summaries are contained in F. S. Regs., Part II. and the Staff Manual respectively. Title Pages will be prepared in manuscript.

WAR DIARY
or
INTELLIGENCE SUMMARY

(Erase heading not required.)

Army Form C. 2118.

Place	Date	Hour	Summary of Events and Information	Remarks and references to Appendices
In the Field	7/3/17.		Spent in General Cleaning up & inspections. The billets were not good considering the distance behind the line.	
	8/3/17.		The C.O. inspected "B", "C", & "D" Coys in the morning. "A" Coy was struck off parades for classes of instruction.	
	9/3/17.		The Battalion assembled at 9am & marched to the parade ground East of LA NEOVILLE for Battalion drill. "A" Coy was available for classes from 10.30am onwards. The inter platoon soccer competition was started.	
	10/3/17.		The Battalion paraded at 9.45 am & marched to a field behind the Brigade Office, where the G.O.C. XVth Corps inspected the Bn & presented medals to 5 recipients who were awarded Military Medals for the raid. The G.O.C. 33rd Division inspected the Battalion in close column, after the Corps Commander's inspection.	
	11/3/17.		The battalion paraded 200 strong for Divine Service in the Cinema Hall. The Battalions were allotted during the morning.	
	12/3/17.		The Battalion assembled at 9am & marched to the parade ground for Battalion drill & organisation of fighting platoons. A party of 120 picked men of the battalion with the "Drums" under Captain Underhill formed a guard of honour at a presentation of medals to French Interpreters etc, by the Corps Commander. The presentation took place in the Market	

2449 Wt. W14957/M90 750,000 1/16 J.B.C. & A. Forms/C.2118/12.

See Sheet No 3.

Sheet No 3.

Instructions regarding War Diaries and Intelligence Summaries are contained in F. S. Regs., Part II. and the Staff Manual respectively. Title Pages will be prepared in manuscript.

WAR DIARY
or
INTELLIGENCE SUMMARY
(Erase heading not required.)

Army Form C. 2118.

Place	Date	Hour	Summary of Events and Information	Remarks and references to Appendices
In the Field			Square, & the 9/HLI and ourselves formed the guard. The Divisional Band was also present & the 'Drums' of both Battalions. The ceromony was very satisfactory & both battalions very smart.	
	13/3/17		Parades of platoon training & organisation were held during the morning. Coys paraded for drill in the afternoon & the C.O. instructed Officers & N.C.Os in map reading & tactical exercises.	
	14/3/17.		The Battalion paraded at 9am & marched to the parade ground where the new attack formations were practised.	
	15/3/17		Parades of Platoon training & organisation were held during the morning. Coys paraded for drill in the afternoon & the C.O. instructed all Officers & N.C.Os in map reading & tactical exercises. A F.G.C.M. on L/Cpl Austing was held at the Brigade.	
	16/3/17.		The battalion assembled for a route march at 9am & practised company marches between CORBIE & VILLERS BRETONNEUX. Major Stoney lectured to all Officers & platoon commanders during the afternoon.	
	17/3/17.		Platoon training & organisation in the morning. In the afternoon representatives from the battalion played in a brigade match against the Australians in Ameins.	
	18/3/17.		The Bn paraded for Church parade at 10.30 am & marched to a service which was held in the TIVOLI THEATRE.	
	19/3/17.		The morning was spent in battalion & Company training & exercises in the new attack formations. In the afternoon companies paraded for bayonet fighting.	

2449 Wt. W14957/M90 750,000 1/16 J.B.C. & A. Forms/C.2118/12.

See Sheet No 4

Sheet No 4.

Instructions regarding War Diaries and Intelligence Summaries are contained in F. S. Regs., Part II. and the Staff Manual respectively. Title Pages will be prepared in manuscript.

WAR DIARY
or
INTELLIGENCE SUMMARY
(Erase heading not required.)

Army Form C. 2118.

Place	Date	Hour	Summary of Events and Information	Remarks and references to Appendices
In the Field	20/3/17		Physical training before breakfast. The Battalion paraded at 9.30 am & marched via FOUILLY to a position on the AUBIGNY-VILLERS-BRETONNEUX road where the Bn deployed from column of route to Artillery formation, & after advancing a certain distance extended into the usual attack formation & advanced to the final objective. The Bn then closed & marched back to CORBIE.	
	21/3/17		The Bn assembled on the main at 9 am & marched up to the parade ground for battalion drill & platoon training & organisation. The range was allotted to the Battalion all day. Pte St Pier was awarded the Bronze medal for military valour (Italian).	
	22/3/17		The Coys were at the disposal of Coy commanders during the morning as the C. O. attended a Brigade tactical ride on the country S. E of CORBIE – FOUILLY. In the afternoon the Battalion paraded for drill, & all Officers & N.C.Os for instruction in map reading.	
	23/3/17		The Bn assembled at Bn H. Q at 9 am & marched, via LA NEUVILLE, on to the open ground S. E. of CORBIE, where attack formations were practised. The Bn attacked a ridge with two companies in the front line & one in support. In the afternoon Coys paraded for bayonet fighting.	

2449 Wt. W14957/M90 750,000 1/16 J.B.C. & A. Forms/C.2118/12.

See Sheet No 5

Sheet No 5.

Instructions regarding War Diaries and Intelligence Summaries are contained in F. S. Regs., Part II. and the Staff Manual respectively. Title Pages will be prepared in manuscript.

WAR DIARY
or
INTELLIGENCE SUMMARY
(Erase heading not required.)

Army Form C. 2118.

Place	Date	Hour	Summary of Events and Information	Remarks and references to Appendices
In the Field	24/3/17		Captain Durlacher & 2/Lieut Hopkins awarded M.C for good work in the raid. Sergt Grinnell the D.C.M and Sergt Connelly the M.M. The Bn furnished a guard of 5 Officers & 120 picked men to attend a presentation of medal ribbons by the Corps Commander on the parade ground East of CORBIE. The Corps Commander was unable to attend & the Div General presented the ribbons. The following had ribbons presented:– Capt Durlacher, 2/Lieut Hopkins, C.S.M Bragg, C.Q.M.S Lugg, Sergt Jones, Sergt Grinnell, Sergt Connelly, Pte St Pier. In the afternoon, massed bands & Drums played in the Square. The Divisional & K.R.R.C. bands in the Stand & the "Drums" of the Queens & ourselves with the pipers of the H.L.I. in the Square.	
	25/3/17		The Bn paraded for Divine Service in the field next to the football ground in the morning.	
	26/3/17		A draft of 2 Officers & 115 O.R joined at 2 am from the Base. A wet day, so parades were cancelled, & coys carried on in billets. The draft was inspected by the C.O.: A party of 8 Officers & 100 O.R. attended a lecture by Capt Huntingdon on Bayonet Fighting.	
	27/3/17		The Battalion with full 1st line transport marched via LA NEUVILLE to BONNAY & formed up in the Square. It then started to snow hard & the transport continued the route back to CORBIE by the upper road.	

See Sheet No 6.

2449 Wt. W14957/M90 750,000 1/16 J.B.C. & A. Forms/C.2118/12.

Sheet No 6.

WAR DIARY
or
INTELLIGENCE SUMMARY
(Erase heading not required.)

Army Form C. 2118.

Instructions regarding War Diaries and Intelligence Summaries are contained in F. S. Regs., Part II. and the Staff Manual respectively. Title Pages will be prepared in manuscript.

Place	Date	Hour	Summary of Events and Information	Remarks and references to Appendices
			The Battalion then carried out an outpost scheme on the high ground between HEILLY & VAUX-SUR-SOMME. "B" Coy formed a day outpost Coy & then the other 3 Coys formed night out-post Coys. The Bn then closed & marched back to CORBIE. In the afternoon the C.O., Coy Commanders, & Gas N.C.Os attended a gas demonstration on the LA NEOVILLE hills.	
	28/3/17		The Bn assembled at 9am & marched out to the parade ground for battalion drill & platoon training. The Armourer Sergt inspected rifles. Sergt Cubberley conducted a Range-finding class in the morning, & the Intelligence Officer conducted a Scouting class in the afternoon.	
	29/3/17		Platoon training & organisation. The range was allotted to Coys. "D" Coy was struck off for classes. Coys paraded under C.S.Ms in the afternoon & Officers & Platoon commanders went out for a tactical scheme with the C.O. In the evening the 1/Queens invited the Officers of the Battalion to an "At Home" in the Cinema Hall.	
	30/3/17		The Bn paraded at 9am & marched in the direction of VILLERS BRETONNEUX. An attack was carried out on CORBIE in accordance with the tactical scheme held the previous day. The Battalion paraded for ~~—~~ outposts in the evening, & formed an outpost line from HEILLY to VAUX-SUR-SOMME.	

See Sheet No 7.

2449 Wt. W14957/M90 750,000 1/16 J.B.C. & A. Forms/C.2118/12.

Sheet No 7

Instructions regarding War Diaries and Intelligence Summaries are contained in F. S. Regs., Part II. and the Staff Manual respectively. Title Pages will be prepared in manuscript.

WAR DIARY
or
INTELLIGENCE SUMMARY

(Erase heading not required.)

Army Form C. 2118.

Place	Date	Hour	Summary of Events and Information	Remarks and references to Appendices
			"B" Coy attacked & penetrated "A" Coy's line.	
In the Field	31/3/17		The Bn paraded for a route march at 9am, & marched via FOUILLOY-AUBIGNY. In the afternoon the battalion beat the 1/Queens 1-0 in a 'Soccer' match.	

M K Pardoe

Lieut-Colonel

Comdg: 2nd Bn The Worcestershire Regiment.

2449 Wt. W14957/M90 750,000 1/16 J.B.C. & A. Forms/C.2118/12.

BRIGADE OFFICE
No. B.M.7
MAR 1917
661
100th INFANTRY BRIGADE

HEADQUARTERS
No.
MAR 1917
33rd DIVISION

33 Div.
G. 20.

100 Inf. Bde.

The Corps Commander's remarks on the report on the raid carried out by the 2 Worc. R. on Feb. 27th/28th are -

"The operation appears to have been carefully planned and well worked out. It reflects great credit on all concerned."

E.R. Pierson Major
for Major, G.S.
33rd Division.

9/3/17.

B.of G.

I

SCHEME 1

For line of action & dispositions of each unit see diagram below

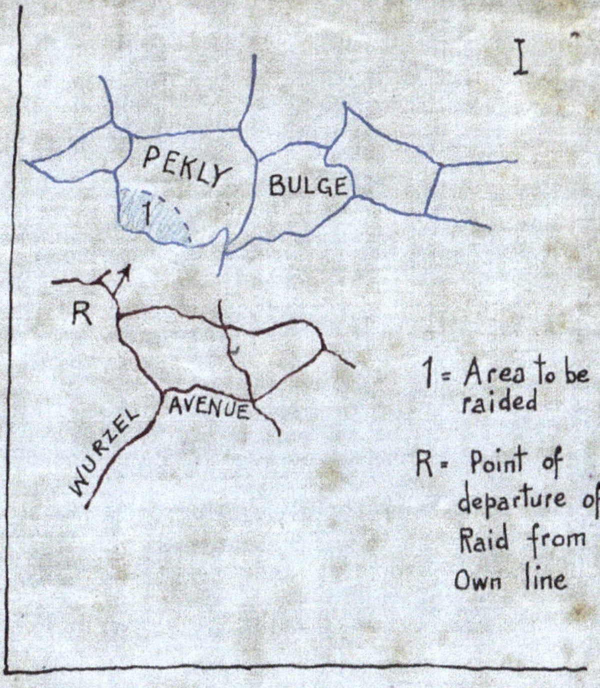

Key

O = Zero = time when Raid Party will be in position beyond own wire.

— Group {N.C.O. / 7 Bombers / 4 Bayonet Men

— Blocking Party {2 Bayonet Men / 2 Bombers / 1 Carrier / 2 Iron Cone men

— R.E. with demol. for dug outs

— O.C. column

— R.E. Party with Bangalore torpedoes under R.E. Officer & to lay tapes.

— Stretcher Bearer Party

— Collecting Station & Escort for Prisoners. etc & telephones.

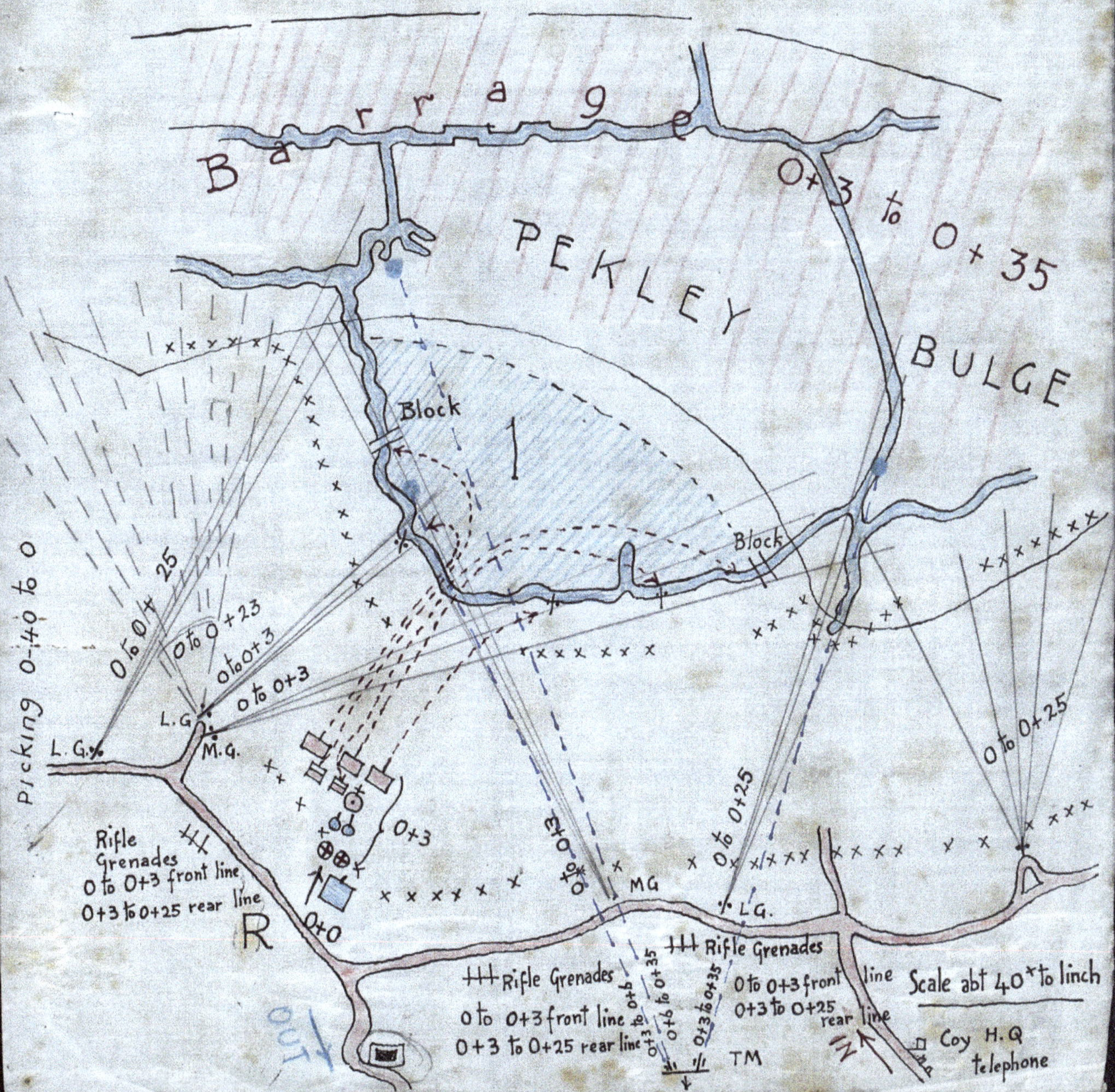

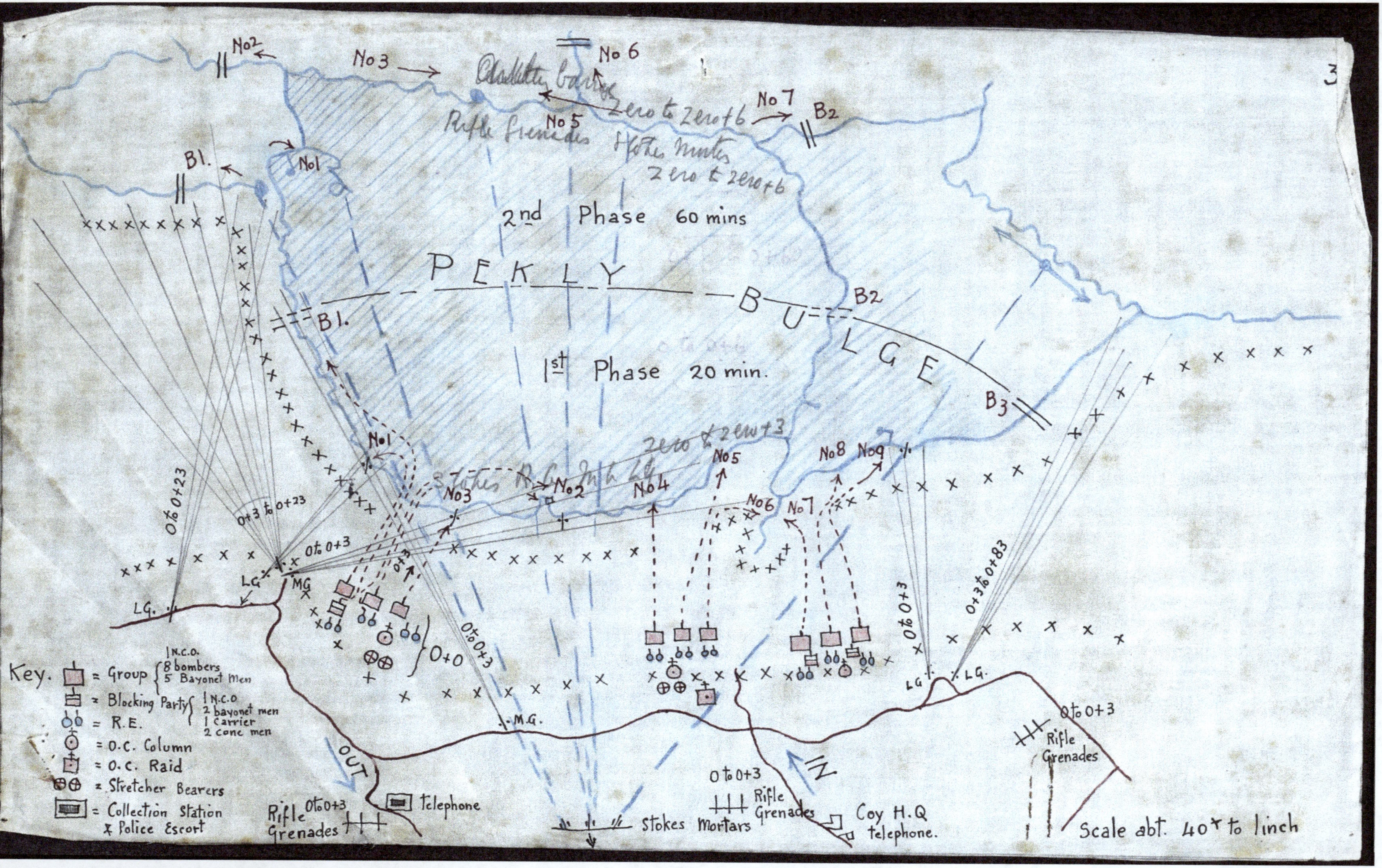
3
PEKLY BULGE
2nd Phase 60 mins
1st Phase 20 min.
No 1
No 2
No 3
No 4
No 5
No 6
No 7
No 8
No 9
B1.
B2
B3
LG.
MG
M.G.
0 to 0+23
0+3 to 0+23
0 to 0+3
0+0
0+3 to 0+83
zero to zero+6
zero to zero+3
Rifle Grenades
OUT
IN
Telephone
Stokes Mortars
Coy H.Q telephone.
Scale abt. 40x to 1inch
Key.
= Group { 1 N.C.O. 8 bombers 5 Bayonet men
= Blocking Party { 1 N.C.O. 2 bayonet men 1 Carrier 2 cone men
= R.E.
= O.C. Column
= O.C. Raid
= Stretcher Bearers
= Collection Station x Police Escort

SCHEME 2.

The Area to be raided is divided into two portions as indicated on diagram by 1st and 2nd phases.

The Raid Party will consist of 3 Columns, each under an Officer, and the whole party will be under the Command of one Officer.

Each Column will be divided into 3 groups, to each of which will be assigned a distinct and particular objective.

Each Group will be led by a full N.C.O. and will consist of 8 bombers, 5 bayonet men and 2 R.E. with demolition material for dugouts and machine gun emplacements; and will be given a distinct and particular objective, to reach which immediately, every effort will be made by them.

Columns will be numbered from the left 1, 2 and 3.

The Groups will be numbered also from the left 1 to 9.

Blocking Parties will consist of :-

2 Bayonet men.)
2 Bombers.) under the Command of an N.C.O.
1 Carrier.)
2 Cone men.)

One blocking party will be attached to No. 1 Group, one to No.7, and one to No. 9.

The O.C., Raid will follow in rear of No. 2 Column and will be accompanied by 2 runners and 2 telephone men by which means he will keep Bn. H.Qs. via Escort Station and Centre Coy. H.Q. informed as to how operations proceed. In addition an Artillery Officer will accompany the O.C., Raid, taking with him telephone in order to be in direct touch with his Artillery Bde.

The Artillery will be required to cut the enemy's wire as shewn by gaps on attached diagram (page 3) and also to cut enemy's parapet at points X (see diagram page 1).

They will also be required to lay barrages as shewn on diagram (page 1).

viz:- 0 to 0 plus 3 on pts. X X X T.M's. and Hows.

0 to 0 plus 23 on a1 a2 a3 a4

0 plus 23 to 0 plus 83 on a1 a3 a4

In/

Blocking Parties to work in close co-operation with the groups to which they are attached; they will maintain their blocks at all costs and will be the last to "come in". They will on no account enter the enemy's trench until their group has dealt with the enemy there.

Time of departure and "Come in" of Raid Party will be indicated by the watch. Officers and full N.C.Os. will each carry a watch, which they will synchronise beforehand.

The O.C., Raid Party will blow a whistle at 0 plus 23, i.e., - - - - - - - - - - - - to remind the groups that the time is up.

The Area to be raided will be lit up by Very Lights. Groups consisting of 1 N.C.O. and 1 man will be detailed to carry out this arrangement.

Trenches marked ← in and out → will be closed to all traffic other than those connected with raid from 0-30 to 30 minutes after conclusion of raid.

Prisoners, etc. will be brought back by bayonet men to point (see diagram) where they will be taken over by escort consisting of 1 Sergeant, 2 Corporals, 8 men, who will forward prisoners, etc., immediately to Bn. H.Qs.

R.E. with Bangalore Torpedoes will follow up the Raid Party and place in position torpedoes in enemy's line when required. These will be fired by R.E. immediately after the Raid Party has "come in".

A telephone message will be sent to Bn. H.Qs. by O.C., Raid Party as soon as party have entered enemy's line. Similarly, as soon as Raid Party are "all in" a message will be sent by 'phone to Bn. H.Qs. A line of telephone will be laid from pt. to Bn. H.Qs; as an alternative to that from the Centre Front Coy. H.Q. The former will be exclusively for the use of O.C., Raid.

R.E. will lay tapes from own front trench to enemy's trench along the path of Raid Party. These tapes will not be taken up on conclusion of raid.

At/

At 0-60 to 0 a patrol party will go out on right of Raid Zone, returning at 0-30.

At 0-30 to 0 a party of men with picks will be employed on left of Raid Zone, and endeavour to make themselves heard; otherwise there will be no noise in own front line before 0.
Stretcher Parties will use out trench only.

A hot drink will be provided for each member of Raid at 0-30.

Own front line trench will be cleared for Raid Party at 0-60. A few men only being left as temporary garrison, (the remainder will go to dugouts in rear), who will remain at their posts throughout raid. Those of the front line garrison on the immediate Right and Left of Raid Zone (with the exception of as few sentries as possible will be in their dugouts).

After the Raid Party has "come in", normal dispositions will be resumed.

(Sgd.) G.J.L. STONEY, Major,
for Lieut.Colonel,
Comdg. 2nd Worcesters Regt.

23/2/17.

SCHEME I.

All references to attached diagram.

Organisation of Raid Party.

A Column consisting of 3 groups and a party of R.E. under the Command of an Officer.

For composition of each group, etc., see diagram.

O.C., RAID to carry a revolver and two Mills Bombs.

He will be attended by 3 runners, two telephone men, one Instrument man.

A full N.C.O. to personally lead each group, and to be armed with revolver and 2 Mills bombs.

Bombers each to carry full supply of Mills Bombs, rifles slung, no bayonets, 9 rounds in Magazine, 1 in chamber, rifle ready for firing but safety catch back.

Bayonet men each to carry rifle with bayonet fixed, 9 rounds in magazine, 1 in chamber, ready for firing but safety catch back. O.C., Column to personally see this order carried out. Two Mills Bombs in jacket pocket, 25 rounds in other jacket pocket.

Blocking Parties will be employed as per diagram. Iron Cone men to be armed with revolvers and gloves will be provided for them.

Each member of the Raid Party will wear a white arm-band on each arm above elbow as a distinguishing mark.

Officer and each N.C.O. will carry a torch and torches will be fixed on to a proportion of the rifles for entering dugouts. Very Lights will also, if necessary, be used when entering dugouts.

No equipment will be worn; each member of Raid Party will wear a jerkin, gas box respirator and steel helmet.

Duration of Raid. 0 plus 3 to 0 plus 23.

Method of approaching enemy's line - see diagram.

Each group is allotted a separate and particular objective, to be reached as soon as possible and independently of the other.

Blocking/

SCHEME 2

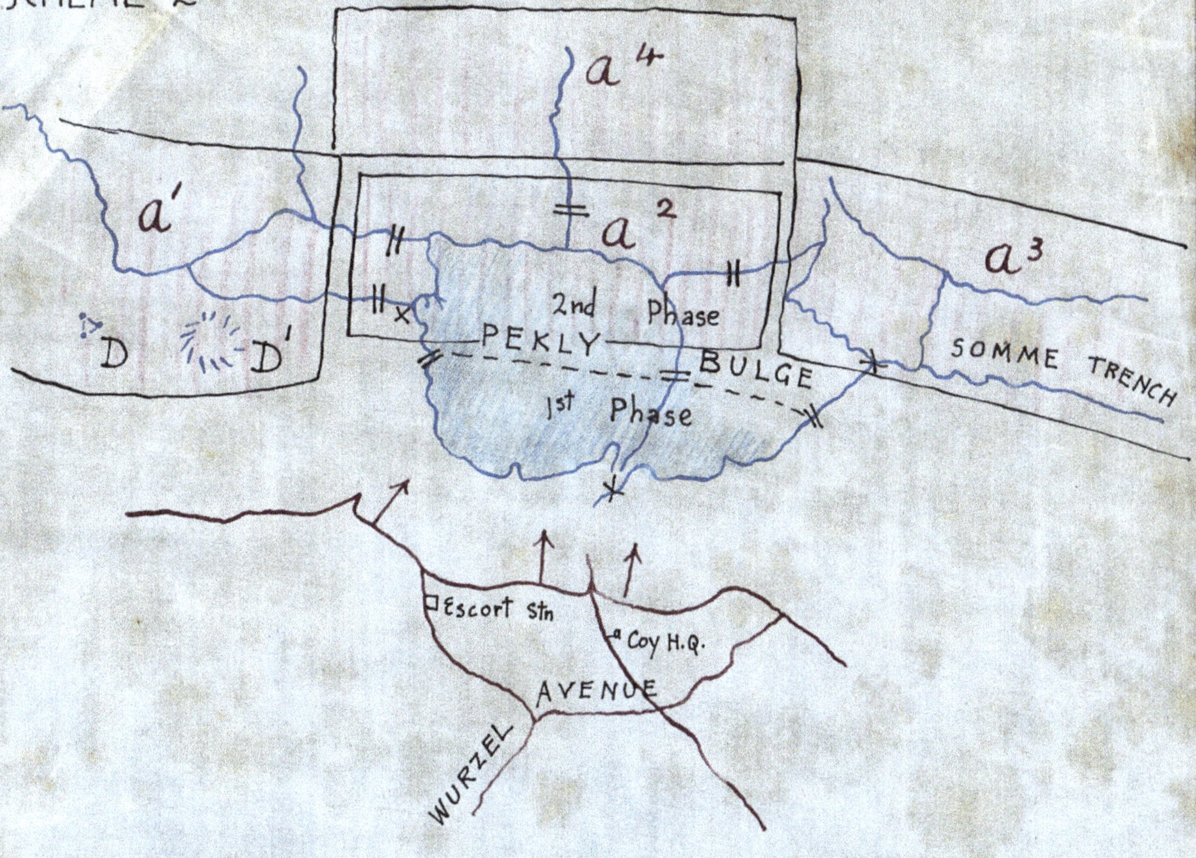

Area to be raided

Points of departure of
Raid Party from own line

In addition to foregoing the Artillery will be required to give particular attention to pts. D and D^1 (see diagram page 1).

The 100th Inf. Bde. M.G.Company will be required to co-operate with M.G. fire on enemy's parapet where previously cut by the artillery, i.e., pts. X X X also by indirect fire on likely places in rear of enemy's line where, on alarm, he may either stand to or be tempted to come out in the open by curiosity, also on strong points or suspected positions of mortars and rifle grenades.

The Bn. Lewis Guns will generally co-operate with scheme, also Rifle Grenadiers (see diagram, page 3).

For line of action and dispositions of the different Units (see diagram, page 3).

At 0, Columns will be in position as shewn on diagram, page 3.

At 0 plus 3, each group will rush straight for it's assigned objective.

Blocking parties keeping in close touch with their respective groups, they will on no account enter enemy's trench until their group has disposed of the enemy there, when they will then go straight for their objective, placing their cones in position and maintaining them there at all costs, they will be last to leave enemy's trenches on 'Come in' sounding.

The Bombers will make frontal rushes upon their objective and before entering the enemy's trench they will throw volleys of bombs, the greatest accuracy being essential in doing so, in order to get them right in, after which they will jump into enemy's trench.

With this in view it will be necessary for groups to open out immediately after passing through enemy's wire.

Bayonet men will be in readiness to deal with any rush and to take over prisoners, etc. whom they will at once escort back to point [illegible] handing over same to Police escort there. They will immediately rejoin Raid Party.

In order to guard against the danger of our bombers bombing each other and those of our adjoining columns and groups, the Countersign 'Firm' will be shouted loudly and frequently, so as to be heard/

heard.

At the conclusion of first phase a series of 'Gs' on the Bugle will sound, this to remind Officers and N.C.Os. that the barrage is lifting and that the 2nd phase begins; whereupon these blocking parties detailed to do so, will raise their cones and with the detailed groups will move forward as shewn on diagram (page 3). At conclusion of phase 2nd, the fire alarm will sound in order to draw the attention of Officers and N.C.Os. to the fact and all will 'come in'.

Each member of the raid will be dressed and equipped as in Scheme I. Men carrying cones will wear gloves. An interval of 4 hours will take place between conclusion of 1st scheme and the commencement of 2nd scheme, when there must be no noise or activity.

Similar arrangements as in Scheme I for lighting up the Raid Area by means of Very Lights will be made.

Control of Prisoners, etc. and traffic, will be similar to that in Scheme I.

A hot drink also will be arranged as in Scheme I.

(Sgd.) G.J.L. STONEY, Major,

for Lieut. Colonel,
Commanding 2nd Worcestershire Regt.

25/2/17.

"C" Form.

MESSAGES AND SIGNALS.

Army Form C. 2123.
(In books of 100.)
No. of Message 41

Prefix SM KKay Code Words 67 | Received From IGZ By Kunn | Sent, or sent out. At m. To By | Office Stamp. TELEGRAPHS 28.1.17

£ s. d.

Charges to collect

Service Instructions.

IGZ

Handed in at IGZ Office 10.50 m. Received 10.54 a m.

TO INSET

Sender's Number	Day of Month	In reply to Number	AAA
G 859	28		

Following	from	Corps	Comdr	begins
aaa	Please	convey	to	BR
Gen	BAIRD	my	congratulations	on
the	successful	raids	carried	out
last	night	by	the	2nd
Worc	aaa	The	way	in
which	the	operations	were	planned
and	carried	out	reflects	great
credit	on	all	concerned	aaa
ends	aaa	Divl	Comdr	heartily
concurs	aaa	information	gained	of
much	value	at	present	juncture

FROM ICE

PLACE & TIME 10.45 am.

* This line should be erased if not required.

(6334). Wt. W7496/M857. 500,000 Pads. 10/16. D. D. & L. (E480). Forms C/2123/3

~~Head Quarters 100th Infantry Brigade~~

Sheet I

Instructions regarding War Diaries and Intelligence Summaries are contained in F. S. Regs., Part II. and the Staff Manual respectively. Title pages will be prepared in manuscript.

WAR DIARY
or
INTELLIGENCE SUMMARY.
(Erase heading not required.)

100/33

(2 Worc R).

Army Form C. 2118.

Vol 33

Place	Date	Hour	Summary of Events and Information	Remarks and references to Appendices
In-the-Field	1st/7		A Draft of 1 Officer and 47 Other Ranks joined early in the morning. The Battalion paraded for Church Parade on the Football Field. Massed Drums and Bands played in the Square for a short time, but had to stop owing to the rain.	
In the Field	2nd/7		The Battalion paraded at 9.20 am. and marched via QUERIEU, ALLONVILLE and COISY to Billets in BERTANGLES, arriving at 2.p.m. The Billets were not good. It began to snow very heavily just after the Battalion had arrived.	
In the Field	3rd/7		The Battalion paraded at 9 am and marched from BERTANGLES to BEAUVAL, via VILLERS-BOCAGE, TALMAS and VERT-GALAND Farm. The Battalion reached Billets at about 1-30 pm., and only 2 men fell out, from weak ankles. The Brigade was rather crowded but the Battalion was fairly comfortable, especially the men in the NISSEN Huts.	
In the Field	4th/7		The Battalion paraded at 8.am and marched to NEUVILLETTE via DOULLENS and BOUQUEMAISON, reaching Billets at about 12 noon. No one fell out. The Billets were quite good although rather crowded. It rained during most of the march.	S. 33
In the Field	5th/7		The Battalion paraded at 12.30 p.m., after Dinners, and marched to Hutz	

T2131. Wt. W708–776. 500000. 4/15. Sir J. C. & S.

Sheet No. 2 Army Form C. 2118.

WAR DIARY
or
INTELLIGENCE SUMMARY.
(Erase heading not required.)

Instructions regarding War Diaries and Intelligence Summaries are contained in F. S. Regs., Part II. and the Staff Manual respectively. Title pages will be prepared in manuscript.

Place	Date	Hour	Summary of Events and Information	Remarks and references to Appendices
In the Field			outside MONDICOURT, via BOUQUEMAISON, DOULLENS and POMMERA. The Battalion reached the Huts at 6pm. Four men fell out. The huts were quite comfortable and the Battalion had plenty of room	
1 6 In the Field	6/7		A move to SOUASTRE was ordered for the 6th, but cancelled afterward, and the Battalion remained in the Huts near MONDICOURT. The day was spent in general cleaning up and inspections. The Personnel for the Depot Battalion left the Battalion in the morning	
In the Field	7/7		The Battalion paraded at about 9 am on the field just outside the Huts and marched to CHESTNUT CAMP, near BAYENCOURT, via PAS, HENU, and SOUASTRE, reaching the Huts at about midday. The Camp was very comfortable and well built but left dirty.	
In the Field	8/7		The Battalion paraded at about 9 am and marched to Billets in FONQUEVILLERS via SAILLY-LE-SEC. The roads were in a very bad condition. The accommodation in FONQUEVILLERS was not good, and a number of men slept in the open. The Dug-outs had nearly all fallen in and the village was much more knocked about than when we were holding this part of the	

T2134. Wt. W708–776. 500000. 4/15. Sir J. C. & S.

Instructions regarding War Diaries and Intelligence Summaries are contained in F. S. Regs., Part II. and the Staff Manual respectively. Title pages will be prepared in manuscript.

WAR DIARY
or
INTELLIGENCE SUMMARY.
(Erase heading not required.)

Sheet No 3 Army Form C. 2118.

Place	Date	Hour	Summary of Events and Information	Remarks and references to Appendices
			line in September. The C.O. and Company Commanders reconnoitred the new position between CROISILLES and BECQUERRELLE, and saw part of the HINDENBURGH line	
In the Field	9/4/17		The Battalion remained in FONQUEVILLERS, and Great-coats, Haversacks, and the men's dirty change of clothing were withdrawn and stored in the Brigade Store at BIENVILLERS, and all preparations made for a move. The Battalion was ready to move at 6 hours notice.	
In the Field	10/4/17		The Battalion remained in FONQUEVILLERS. All Blankets were stacked at the Q.M. Stores at 8 am. in view of a possible move, and the Battalion was ready to move at very short notice. A Plane landed behind our Head Quarters in the morning owing to engine trouble and was smashed up. The Pilot and Observer were unhurt. It snowed off and on during the day. Very good news was received from the whole front	
In the Field	11/4/17		The Battalion remained in FONQUEVILLERS ready to move at short notice.	
In the Field	12/4/17		The Battalion received orders to move at 9.20 am, and marched off at	

Instructions regarding War Diaries and Intelligence Summaries are contained in F. S. Regs., Part II. and the Staff Manual respectively. Title pages will be prepared in manuscript.

WAR DIARY
or
INTELLIGENCE SUMMARY.
(Erase heading not required.)

Army Form C. 2118.

Sheet No. 4

Place	Date	Hour	Summary of Events and Information	Remarks and references to Appendices
			about 11 am. via BIENVILLERS, MONCHY, ADINFER, to trenches near MERCATEL.	
			The Transport and 1st Reinforcements remained at FICHEUX. The Battalion was billetted in trenches, with a few dug-outs and shelters, and was "standing to at 1 hours' notice.	
In the Field	13/4/17		The Transport and Re-inforcements joined the Battalion near MERCATEL during the morning. Two working parties of 1 Officer and 50 men were supplied during the day, and a Guard of 1 Officer and 25 men was sent to ACHICOURT to guard a water-point, taking over the duties from a Guard of the 38th Division.	
In the Field	14/4/17		Two working parties of 1 Officer and 50 Other ranks were furnished in the morning. The C.O. and Company Commanders rode up to reconnoitre the line at about 4 pm., and the Battalion received orders to move to ST. LEGER as soon as possible. The Battalion moved off at about 7 pm, and marched via BOILEAUX-AU-MONT-BOYELLES to MAISON ROUGE, where Guides took their respective Companies to their position, via ST. LEGER and CROISILLES. "C" Company and 1 Platoon of 'D' Coy in CROISILLES, and 'A' and 'B' Coys on the left and right, of the right sector of the Brigade front, holding an Outpost	

T.2134. Wt. W708-776. 500000. 4/15. Sir J. C. & S.

Sheet N° 5.

Army Form C. 2118.

Instructions regarding War Diaries and Intelligence Summaries are contained in F. S. Regs., Part II. and the Staff Manual respectively. Title pages will be prepared in manuscript.

WAR DIARY
or
INTELLIGENCE SUMMARY.
(Erase heading not required.)

Place	Date	Hour	Summary of Events and Information	Remarks and references to Appendices
			line in front of CROISILLES. The relief was not completed until about 3.30 am. The 9th Bn H.L.I. were on our left, and the 62nd Division on our right	
In-the-Field	15/4/17		A very quiet day on our front. The Fifth Army were attacked on our right, but regained everything lost, and took 300 prisoners.	
In-the-Field	16/4/17		A very quiet day, fine in the morning, but turning to rain in the afternoon and evening. "A" and "B" Coys were relieved by "C" and "D" Coys respectively during the evening. The relief was quite satisfactory but 2 Sections of "B" Coy got lost for a short time.	
In-the-Field	17/4/17		A wet day. The Germans shelled CROISILLES and ST. LEGER intermittently during the day.	
In-the-Field	18/4/17		The 2nd Bn Royal Welch Fusiliers came up to reconnoitre the line during the afternoon.	
In-the-Field	19/4/17		The Battn was relieved in the evening by the 2/R.W.F. The relief was very satisfactory and was completed by about 10.45 pm. Coys moved back to Bivouacs in the Railway cutting in front of JUDAS FARM. These Bivouacs has been made by the 1st Re-inforcements from "B" Echelon	

Instructions regarding War Diaries and Intelligence Summaries are contained in F. S. Regs., Part II. and the Staff Manual respectively. Title pages will be prepared in manuscript.

WAR DIARY
or
INTELLIGENCE SUMMARY.
(Erase heading not required.)

Sheet No 6.

Army Form C. 2118.

Place	Date	Hour	Summary of Events and Information	Remarks and references to Appendices
In the Field	20/4/17		The Battalion furnished a working party of 100 men to work on the roads near MERCATEL	
In the Field	21/4/17		The Battalion furnished a working party of 200 men to work under the R.E. The Battalion relieved the 2/R.W.F. in the Right Sector, in the evening, moving off at 8 p.m. The relief was completed by 10.45 p.m. 'A' & 'B' were the left and right front Companies, 'C' in Reserve, and 'D' in Support. The Germans were active during the night, particularly on the sunken road in the Left Company area, where 5 men were buried, three of whom were killed.	
In the Field	22/4/17		Our Artillery bombarded the HINDENBURGH LINE preparatory to the attack on the 23rd and the Germans retaliated on the Companies and also on ST. LEGER. In the evening 'B' and 'C' Coys supplied 16 Guides each to take the "Queen's" and "K.R.R's" to the QUARRY. 'C' Coy carried up 20 food containers of hot tea for the attacking Battalions.	
In the Field	23/4/17		The attack commenced at 4.40 a.m. The "Queen's" attacked the HINDENBURGH LINE. The 98th Brigade attacked FONTAINE on the left, and the remainder of the 3rd Army attacked on their left. The 100th Brigade attack penetrated the	

Instructions regarding War Diaries and Intelligence Summaries are contained in F. S. Regs., Part II. and the Staff Manual respectively. Title pages will be prepared in manuscript.

WAR DIARY
or
INTELLIGENCE SUMMARY.
(Erase heading not required.)

Sheet No 7

Army Form C. 2118.

Place	Date	Hour	Summary of Events and Information	Remarks and references to Appendices
			front line, but owing to a shortage of Bombs and a counter-attack, the Queens and K.R.R.C. were driven out to the QUARRY. The 98th Brigade attacked again at 3 p.m. without success. The Germans shelled heavily during the night and it was reported that they had withdrawn behind FONTAINE	
In-the-Field	24/4/17		Reports were received in the morning to the effect that the Germans had withdrawn, and strong patrols were sent out by 'B' Coy to reconnoitre the HINDENBURGH LINE. The C.O. and Company Commanders of the 7th Leicesters came up to reconnoitre the line during the afternoon. Our patrols found out that the Germans were still holding the H. LINE opposite us.	
In-the-Field	25/4/17		A quiet day. The Battalion was relieved in the evening by the 7th Leicesters. 'B' Coy marched back to POMMIER independently on relief and got in about 3 a.m. "A", "C" and "D" Coys marched independently as far as HAMELINCOURT, where they halted for Teas, and then marched closed up to POMMIER via BOIRY St MARTIN, ADINFER, MONCHY, BIENVILLERS, getting in at 6 a.m. No one fell out	
In-the-Field	26/4/17		The Battalion rested in Billets, the first reinforcements doing the work.	

Instructions regarding War Diaries and Intelligence Summaries are contained in F. S. Regs., Part II. and the Staff Manual respectively. Title pages will be prepared in manuscript.

WAR DIARY
or
INTELLIGENCE SUMMARY.
(Erase heading not required.)

Army Form C. 2118.

SHEET. No 8.

Place	Date	Hour	Summary of Events and Information	Remarks and references to Appendices
			The Billets were quite good, and there was plenty of room. A Gas Dump blew up in ARRAS during the afternoon.	
In-the-Field	27/4/17		The whole of the day was spent in cleaning up, inspecting Iron Rations, Gas Helmets Equipment &c. The Rifles were inspected by the Armourer Sergeant.	
In-the-Field	28/4/17		The Battalion marched to old German trenches and had Battalion Drill till 10 am. & afterwards Company Drill, Platoon Training and Classes under Specialists.	
In-the-Field	29/4/17		Divine Service was held at 9.45 am, in the Football Field W. of the Village, by the Revd. E.V. Tanner.	
In-the-Field	30/4/17		Company Training under Company Commanders, N.E. of HENNESCAMP in Intensive Digging, Platoon Attacks, Patrol work &c. Two Classes (Lewis Gun, and Bombing) were started.	

In-the-Field.
1st May 1917.

M.K. Pardoe
Lieut-Colonel
Commanding 2nd Bn The Worcestershire Regiment

T2134. Wt. W708–776. 500000. 4/15. Sir J. C. & S.

2 Worc R.

Army Form C. 2118.

Instructions regarding War Diaries and Intelligence Summaries are contained in F. S. Regs., Part II. and the Staff Manual respectively. Title pages will be prepared in manuscript.

WAR DIARY
or
INTELLIGENCE SUMMARY.
(*Erase heading not required.*)

First Sheet.

Vol 34

Place	Date	Hour	Summary of Events and Information	Remarks and references to Appendices
In the Field	1/6/17		The Battalion paraded at 7.45 am, marched to FICHEUX and were billeted in Bivouacs and Tents	
-"-	2/6/17		The morning was spent in cleaning up the Camp and in Physical Training. The Battalion assembled at 12.40 pm & marched to HAMELINCOURT and bivoucked.	
-"-	3/6/17		During the morning Coys were at the disposal of Coy Commanders for Physical Training, Inspection of Feet &c.	
-"-	4/6/17		Physical Training before Breakfast, afterwards Coys were under Coy Commanders for Platoon Drill, etc, Feet Inspection and rubbing. The Divisional Commander held a conference which all Officers attended.	
-"-	5/6/17		Physical Training before Breakfast, afterwards Platoon Training, manning & blocking trenches, & Musketry.	
-"-	6/6/17		Divine Service in field W. of HAMELINCOURT at 9.45 am by Rev. E. V. Tanner. Musketry for "C" Coy.	
-"-	7/6/17		Physical Training before Breakfast, afterwards Feet Inspection, Musketry, Blocking trenches, Platoon & Coy Training.	
-"-	8/6/17		Physical Training before Breakfast, afterwards advancing in waves, Musketry and	S.34

T2134. Wt. W708—776. 500000. 4/15. Sir J. C. & S.

Instructions regarding War Diaries and Intelligence Summaries are contained in F. S. Regs., Part II. and the Staff Manual respectively. Title pages will be prepared in manuscript.

WAR DIARY
or
INTELLIGENCE SUMMARY.
(Erase heading not required.)

Second Sheet.

Army Form C. 2118.

Place	Date	Hour	Summary of Events and Information	Remarks and references to Appendices
			Company Drill.	
In the Field	9/5/17		Physical Training before Breakfast, afterwards the Battalion paraded and marched to a field about 3 miles N.W. of Camp, & practised advancing in Waves, by Coys, to Trenches. "A" & "D" Coys did the attacking, "B" & "C" Coys supplied Reserves also men for carrying parties, returning to Camp about 2.30 pm.	
-.-	10/5/17		Physical Training before Breakfast. The Battalion assembled and marched to practise ground 3 miles N.W. of Camp, & again practised advancing by Coys in Waves to trenches, returning to Camp at 1 pm.	
			The Battalion assembled at 9 pm for Night Operations and marched to parade ground. The object was to practise attacking by Coys in Waves on trenches by night, to get men accustomed to keeping in touch. After reaching objective Flares were lit. Battalion returned to Camp about 2 am.	
-.-	11/5/17		The Battalion paraded at 7.30 pm & moved by Coys via JUDAS FARM to the Railway Crossing where guides of the 6th Leicesters met them. "A" & "B" Coys were on the Left and Right respectively, "C" Coy in Support just N. of CROISILLES and "D" Coy in Reserve W. of CROISILLES. Battn H.Qrs was near the Reserve Coy. The relief was	

T2134. Wt. W708—776. 500000. 4/15. Sir J. C. & S.

Instructions regarding War Diaries and Intelligence Summaries are contained in F. S. Regs., Part II. and the Staff Manual respectively. Title pages will be prepared in manuscript.

WAR DIARY
or
INTELLIGENCE SUMMARY.
(Erase heading not required.)

Third Sheet.

Army Form C. 2118.

Place	Date	Hour	Summary of Events and Information	Remarks and references to Appendices
			completed by 12 m.n.	
In-the-Field	12.5.17		The 2/5th Warwicks (62nd Division) were on our right and the 9th H.L.I. on our left. The Corps on the right attacked in the early morning, and the Germans shelled them during the morning. A quiet day on our front. Considerable aeroplane activity in the evening.	
— " —	13.5.17		A quiet day on our front, but considerable activity on either flank, especially in the evening when the 62nd Division were heavily shelled.	
— " —	14.5.17		Reports were received that the Enemy was likely to retire to the QUEANT-DROCOURT Line shortly, & the Brigade was ordered to endeavour to take a prisoner in order to confirm this report if possible. The "Queen's" and ourselves both sent out small parties for this purpose. Our party was under Lieut. GILLESPIE, and consisted of 25 men, 15 of whom were to enter the Enemy's line. The party was observed on reaching the hostile wire, and had a stiff fight to get back as the Germans sent parties round their flanks & also advanced against them in front, so that at one time they were practically surrounded. However they succeeded in getting through and killing 14 Germans. We had 5 men severely wounded & several missing.	

Instructions regarding War Diaries and Intelligence Summaries are contained in F. S. Regs., Part II. and the Staff Manual respectively. Title pages will be prepared in manuscript.

WAR DIARY
or
INTELLIGENCE SUMMARY.
(*Erase heading not required.*)

Fourth Sheet

Army Form C. 2118.

Place	Date	Hour	Summary of Events and Information	Remarks and references to Appendices
			Lieut. GILLESPIE was wounded but not severely.	
In-the-Field	15.7		A quiet day. The Battalion was relieved in the evening by the 1st Cameronians. The relief was completed by 10 pm & was satisfactory. The Batt. marched to Bivouacs near ST. LEGER	
–"–	16.7		Practise Attack in the morning. All preparations were made for an Attack on the HINDENBURGH LINE on the morning of the 17th. This attack was cancelled in the evening. A wet night.	
–"–	17.7		The Battalion marched to a Camp near MOYENNEVILLE at 10.30 am.	
–"–	18.7		A practise attack was held in the morning. The G.O.C. VII Corps presented medals to the Brigade in the afternoon, then a Brigade practise attack was held.	
–"–	19.7		A practise Attack was held in the morning. The Battalion moved up to a position of Assembly E. of CROISILLES in the evening, halting for Teas near MAISON ROUGE FARM. The move was completed by 1. am.	
–"–	20.7		The Battalion deployed at about 3.30. am. prior to the attack on the HINDENBURGH front and support lines at 5.15 am. "D" & "A" Coys were in the front line with the HINDENBURGH first Line as their objective, "C" & "B" Coys in the 2nd Line with the	

T2134. Wt. W708–776. 500000. 4/15. Sir J. C. & S.

Instructions regarding War Diaries and Intelligence Summaries are contained in F. S. Regs., Part II. and the Staff Manual respectively. Title pages will be prepared in manuscript.

WAR DIARY
or
INTELLIGENCE SUMMARY.
(Erase heading not required.)

Army Form C. 2118.

Fifth Sheet.

Place	Date	Hour	Summary of Events and Information	Remarks and references to Appendices
			HINDENBURGH Support line as their objective. The 5th Bn Scottish Rifles attacked on the right, and the 9th H.L.I. on the left. There was a thick mist when the Attack was launched so that the first line got into their objective with very few casualties, the mist however made it very difficult for the second line to keep direction etc, and only a few men reached the support line, some of whom were taken prisoners. Eventually 'A', 'B' & 'D' Coy's consolidated the front line & 'C' Coy occupied the sunken road in front. A continuous Bombing attack went on at the right block which was held by a party of 'A' Coy.	
In the Field	21/5/17		'C' Coy was forced to retire to the front line as the Germans nearly surrounded them. Consolidation of the line and bombing on the right went on throughout the day. In the evening the Battalion was relieved by the 2nd R.W.F. and moved back to the trenches W. of CROISILLES previously occupied by the Battalion. The move was completed by 4.30 am.	
"	22/5/17		Remained in CROISILLES rest trenches during the day. Casualties about 250. Strength of Battalion about 280. In the evening Coys moved back independently to the camp at MOYENNEVILLE. The Drums met Coys at HAMELINCOURT & marched	

T2134. Wt. W708—776. 500000. 4/15. Sir J. C. & S.

Instructions regarding War Diaries and Intelligence Summaries are contained in F. S. Regs., Part II. and the Staff Manual respectively. Title pages will be prepared in manuscript.

WAR DIARY
or
INTELLIGENCE SUMMARY.
(Erase heading not required.)

Army Form C. 2118.

Sixth Sheet.

Place	Date	Hour	Summary of Events and Information	Remarks and references to Appendices
In the Field	23 5/17		them past.	
			Rested at the Camp at MOYENNEVILLE.	
—"—	24 5/17		The Brigadier addressed the Battalion. The Divisional and Corps Commanders walked round the camp during the day.	
—"—	25 5/17		Early morning parade. Platoons under Platoon Commanders, Armourer's Inspection, & general inspections. A Draft of 2 Officers & 40 men arrived in the evening. Aerial activity in the evening & during the night	
—"—	26 5/17		Early morning parade & Coy parades during the morning. In the evening the Battalion moved up to the Assembly trench E. of CROISILLES, near the HENDECOURT ROAD.	
—"—	27 5/17		Remained in assembly trench during the day and were shelled heavily at intervals. The 19th and 98th Brigades made an attack on the HINDENBURGH Support Line which was unsuccessful. In the evening we were relieved by the 5th Scottish Rifles & returned to the rest trenches W. of CROISILLES.	
—"—	28 5/17		The Battalion rested during the day & moved up to the Assembly trenches in the evening, relieving the 5th Bn Scottish Rifles. The night was spent in	

T2134. Wt. W708—776. 500000. 4/15. Sir J. C. & S.

Instructions regarding War Diaries and Intelligence Summaries are contained in F. S. Regs., Part II. and the Staff Manual respectively. Title pages will be prepared in manuscript.

WAR DIARY
or
INTELLIGENCE SUMMARY.
(Erase heading not required.)

7th Sheet.

Army Form C. 2118.

Place	Date	Hour	Summary of Events and Information	Remarks and references to Appendices
			improving the trench.	
In the Field	29/5/17		We were shelled occasionally during the day. In the evening the Battalion relieved the 9th H.L.I. in the right Sector of the Brigade front. 1 Coy of the 16th K.R.R.C. was attached to us; the Coys were disposed as follows:- 'A' Coy - Left. 'B' Coy - Left centre. 'C' Coy - Centre. 'D' Coy - Right Centre. KRRC — Right. The relief was completed at midnight; the night was fairly quiet.	
—"—	30/5/17		The Battn spent a fairly quiet day in the HINDENBURGH Trenches, although there was intermittent shelling all day. The C.O. of the 12th Northumberland Fusiliers came up to arrange the relief.	
—"—	31/5/17		The Battalion was relieved in the evening by the 12th Northumberland Fusiliers and moved back to MOYENNEVILLE.	

In the Field
31st May 1917

G. W. Pardoe
Lieut-Colonel
Commanding 2nd Bn. The Worcestershire Regiment

T2134. Wt. W708—776. 500000. 4/15. Sir J. C. & S.

Instructions regarding War Diaries and Intelligence Summaries are contained in F. S. Regs., Part II. and the Staff Manual respectively. Title Pages will be prepared in manuscript.

2 Worck

WAR DIARY
or
INTELLIGENCE SUMMARY
(Erase heading not required.)

Army Form C. 2118.

2 Worcester Rgt
Vol 35

Place	Date	Hour	Summary of Events and Information	Remarks and references to Appendices
In the Field	1/6/17		The Battalion paraded at 8.45 am & marched to Billets in POMMIER via AYETTE, ADINFER, arriving at 1 pm. The Billets were good and the Battalion marched well.	
— " —	2/6/17		The Battalion rested and cleaned up during the day.	
— " —	3/6/17		The Battalion paraded for Divine Service in the Orchard behind 'B' Coys Billets. The Divisional Band played during the afternoon.	
— " —	4/6/17		The C.O. inspected Coy Billets during the morning. The Officers beat the Sergeants at cricket in the evening.	
— " —	5/6/17		The Musketry Range was allotted to Coys during the morning. In the afternoon 'A' & 'D' Coys played a cricket match. 'D' Coy won.	
— " —	6/6/17		The Battalion was allotted the Field Firing Range during the morning 1½ hours for each Coy. The "Shrapnels" performed in the evening.	
— " —	7/6/17		Physical Training, Coy Drill & Musketry parades were held in the morning.	
— " —	8/6/17		The Battalion paraded in full marching order, on the Cricket Ground at 9.15 am for C.O.'s inspection. Colonel Butler gave a Lecture on Artillery Co-operation in the morning.	
— " —	9/6/17		The Range was allotted to Coys in the morning. A Battalion Boxing Competition was held in the evening at which Bombardier Wells gave an Exhibition. Pte Dugmore, Cpl. Davis, Ptes Horne and Denning won their respective fights. The Divisional Band played.	
— " —	10/6/17		Church parade at 11.15 am. The Battalion played the 1st Queen's at Cricket which we lost.	
— " —	11/6/17		A wet day which necessitated the Brigade Cricket match being cancelled.	

V. 35

Instructions regarding War Diaries and Intelligence Summaries are contained in F. S. Regs., Part II. and the Staff Manual respectively. Title Pages will be prepared in manuscript.

WAR DIARY
or
INTELLIGENCE SUMMARY
(Erase heading not required.)

Army Form C. 2118.

Second Sheet

Place	Date	Hour	Summary of Events and Information	Remarks and references to Appendices
In the Field	12/6/17		The Corps Rifle Range was allotted to the Battalion in the afternoon. In the morning the Battalion went a short Route March. In the evening Cricket matches.	
— " —	13/6/17		½ Coy Drill in the morning. In the afternoon we beat the 7th Corps School at cricket, & also won several Competitions in the 100th Machine Gun Coys Gymkhana which was a great success	
— " —	14/6/17		Companies on the Range. F.G.C. Martial all the morning and afternoon.	
— " —	15/6/17		All Officers under Major Stoney during the morning. F.G.C.M. continued & finished. Battalion Drill under C.O. In the afternoon K.R.R.C. Sports at which Pte Denning won the "Mile." Band lent to VII Corps School for afternoon	
— " —	16/6/17		Battalion did Field Firing on F.F. Range in the morning. In the afternoon H.L.I. sports at which Pte Denning won the "Mile". Very good Sports	
— " —	17/6/17		Brigade Rifle meeting all day. The Battalion won all the competitions.	
— " —	18/6/17		Brigade Boxing Competition which was a great success. The 1st Queen's had a Rifle meeting	
— " —	19/6/17		A quiet day preparatory to the move.	
— " —	20/6/17		The Battalion paraded at 7 am & moved to Camp B at MOYENNEVILLE arriving at 1 pm. The camp was quite good & accommodation sufficient	
— " —	21/6/17		Cleaning up in the morning. The Battalion paraded for Battn Drill during the morning	
— " —	22/6/17		The Battalion practised the attack on some ground near HAMELINCOURT.	

2449 Wt. W14957/M90 750,000 1/16 J.B.C. & A. Forms/C.2118/12.

Instructions regarding War Diaries and Intelligence Summaries are contained in F. S. Regs., Part II. and the Staff Manual respectively. Title Pages will be prepared in manuscript.

WAR DIARY
or
INTELLIGENCE SUMMARY

(Erase heading not required.)

Army Form C. 2118.

Third Sheet

Place	Date	Hour	Summary of Events and Information	Remarks and references to Appendices
In the Field	23 6/17		The C.O. and Company Commdrs reconnoitred the line in the morning. The Battalion carried out an attack practise in the morning. In the afternoon the Army Commander watched this done again.	
—"—	24 6/17		The Corps Commander presented medals after Church parade in the morning. In the evening the Battalion moved into the trenches in the CROISILLES Sector, prior to an attack on 25th.	
—"—	25 6/17		Attack cancelled at last minute. The Battalion was relieved in the evening by the 16th K.R.R. Corps, & marched back to Camp A, arriving about 4 am.	
—"—	26 6/17		A quiet day in Camp A. The attack was cancelled by the Brigadier in the afternoon.	
—"—	27 6/17		A quiet day in Camp A. In the evening the Battn moved up into Brigade Support, leaving camp by Coys at 8 pm. It rained during the evening and night.	
—"—	28 6/17		The Battalion remained in the Support Position behind CROISILLES. "B" Echelon in camp near HAMELINCOURT.	
—"—	29 6/17		The 1st Bn "Queens" made an unsuccessful raid. The Battalion remained in Support behind CROISILLES. The 1st Reinforcements and "B" Echelon Details moved to POMMIER	
—"—	30 6/17		The Battalion was relieved in the evening by the 21st Division & moved back to Camp B.	

[illegible] Lieut-Colonel
Comdg 2nd Bn The Worcestershire Regiment

2449 Wt. W14957/M90 750,000 1/16 J.B.C. & A. Forms/C.2118/12.

Headquarters
100th Infy Bde

Instructions regarding War Diaries and Intelligence Summaries are contained in F. S. Regs., Part II. and the Staff Manual respectively. Title pages will be prepared in manuscript.

WAR DIARY
or
INTELLIGENCE SUMMARY.
(Erase heading not required.)

1st SHEET.

Army Form C. 2118.

Vol 36

Place	Date	Hour	Summary of Events and Information	Remarks and references to Appendices
In the Field	1/7		The Battalion paraded at 10.15 am. and marched back to Billets in POMMIER, arriving at about 3.30 p.m. The boys occupied the same Billets as previously.	
— " —	2/7		The Battalion rested at POMMIER.	
— " —	3/7		The Battalion paraded at 7 am. and marched via ST. AMAND - SOUASTRE - BAYENCOURT - SAILLY-AU-BOIS - BERTANCOURT - ACHEUX - FORCEVILLE, arriving at HEDAUVILLE at 12.30 p.m. 38 men fell out. The Billets were quite good but very dirty.	
— " —	4/7		The Battalion paraded at 4.30 am. and marched to PIERREGOT. It rained hard during the first hours march. 3 men fell out. Route VARENNE - HARPONVILLE - TOUTENCOURT - HERISSART - RUBEMPRE.	
— " —	5/7		The Battalion paraded at 4.10 am. & marched to PICQUIGNY via RAINNEVILLE - COISY - BERTANGLES - ST SAVEUR - AILLY - BREILLY, arriving at 10.30 am. We halted for one hour during the march and the men had tea. One man fell out and the Battalion marched very well. The Billets were very dirty and not good.	
— " —	6/7		Spent in general cleaning up.	
— " —	7/7		Spent in cleaning up and inspections, also improvement of Billets etc.	

S. 36

T2134. Wt. W708—776. 500000. 4/15. Sir J. C. & S.

Instructions regarding War Diaries and Intelligence Summaries are contained in F. S. Regs., Part II. and the Staff Manual respectively. Title pages will be prepared in manuscript.

WAR DIARY
or
INTELLIGENCE SUMMARY.
(*Erase heading not required.*)

2nd SHEET.

Army Form C. 2118.

Place	Date	Hour	Summary of Events and Information	Remarks and references to Appendices
			Lieut-Colonel Gogarty arrived in the afternoon and took over Command of the Battalion.	
In-the-Field	8/7		Church parade was held in the field behind the H.Qrs Mess at 11 am. The Commanding Officer inspected Billets after parade, it rained during the morning and evening	
—"—	9/7		Coy's were at the disposal of Coy Comdrs for Coy Drill & Training and Specialists under Specialist Instructors. The Pioneers constructed a Rifle Range. A Draft of 130 men arrived.	
—"—	10/7		Bathing parade before Breakfast. The Battalion marched out to the training ground near the BOIS-DE-CAVILLON at 9.15 am, and returned from training at about 1.15 pm.	
—"—	11/7		The Battalion paraded at 8 am., marched to CAVILLON, we then attacked through the wood but closed on to central path on account of the thickness of the wood "A" Coy acted as Enemy. Pte Shelley was buried at the Cemetery, PECQUIGNY, in the afternoon.	
—"—	12/7		The Divisional General inspected the Coy's at Training in the morning	

T2134. Wt. W708—776. 500000. 4/15. Sir J. C. & S.

3rd SHEET.

Instructions regarding War Diaries and Intelligence Summaries are contained in F. S. Regs., Part II. and the Staff Manual respectively. Title pages will be prepared in manuscript.

WAR DIARY
or
INTELLIGENCE SUMMARY.
(Erase heading not required.)

Army Form C. 2118.

Place	Date	Hour	Summary of Events and Information	Remarks and references to Appendices
			One Coy was on the Ranges and all Classes paraded. The "Shrapnels" performed in the evening.	
In-the-Field	13/7		Coy's paraded for Company training. One Company on the Ranges. All Classes paraded. The Commanding Officer inspected Kits in the afternoon	
— " —	14/7		Bathing parade before Breakfast. Coy's were at the disposal of O.C. Coys during the morning, and all Specialists paraded under their own Instructors	
— " —	15/7		The Battalion paraded for Church with the 1st Bn Queen's, on the parade ground behind the H.Q. Mess. The Massed "Drums" played in the Square after the Service. A Fishing Competition was held, which was won by Pte Williams, 'D' Coy, who caught a 2¾ lb Bream.	
— " —	16/7		Coy's were at the disposal of Coy Commanders, & Classes under Specialist Officers. One Company was allotted the Ranges.	
— " —	17/7		The Battalion paraded at 5.30 am, and marched to the Training ground for Attack practise. The remainder of the day was a Holiday, and the men were able to go to the Divisional Horse Show which was held near	

4th Sheet

Army Form C. 2118.

Instructions regarding War Diaries and Intelligence Summaries are contained in F. S. Regs., Part II. and the Staff Manual respectively. Title pages will be prepared in manuscript.

WAR DIARY
or
INTELLIGENCE SUMMARY.
(Erase heading not required.)

Place	Date	Hour	Summary of Events and Information	Remarks and references to Appendices
			CAVILLON Wood. Our mules won a First Prize in the Class for pairs of L.D. Mules ride + drive. "Ginger" ridden was second in "over 15 jumping"	
In the Field	18/7		The Battalion had a whole Holiday on the second day of the Show. One of our Mules won a Third Prize. No 1 Coy Train, A S C, won the Divisional Cup.	
— " —	19/7		The Battalion marched to the Horse Show Ground where the Divisional Gas Officer gave a Demonstration.	
— " —	20/7		A Divisional Exercise lasting 24 hours commenced, which the Commanding Officer and Adjutant attended. Coy's were at the disposal of O.C. Coys	
— " —	21/7		Coys were at the disposal of O.C Coy's. 'B' Coy was allotted the Range	
— " —	22/7		The Battalion paraded for Church parade at 10 am on a Field near the Cemetery. The "Queen's" paraded with us.	
— " —	23/7		Bathing parade before Breakfast. 'C' Coy fired on the Range during the morning and 'A', 'B' + 'D' Coys constructed strong points on the Bombing Field. Instructional Classes in the afternoon	
— " —	24/7		Bathing parades before Breakfast. The Battalion paraded at 8 am. and	

Instructions regarding War Diaries and Intelligence Summaries are contained in F. S. Regs., Part II. and the Staff Manual respectively. Title pages will be prepared in manuscript.

WAR DIARY
or
INTELLIGENCE SUMMARY.
(Erase heading not required.)

5th Sheet

Army Form C. 2118.

Place	Date	Hour	Summary of Events and Information	Remarks and references to Appendices
			marched to the Training Ground where an Open-Warfare Attack was practised. All Platoons were then shown four different Strong points on the Bombing Ground.	
In the Field	25/7/17		Bathing parades before Breakfast. Coy's practised wood fighting during the morning. Classes paraded under Specialist Instructors.	
-"-	26/7/17		A Battalion Rifle Meeting was held. Competitions were as follows:- 1. Grouping. 2 Snap-shooting. 3 Rapid. 4 Team Competition. 5 Lewis Gun Competition. 6 Rifle Grenade. 7. Sniping. The Shooting was good on the whole.	
-"-	27/7/17		Bathing parade before Breakfast. Coy's practised Drill Outposts during the morning. Classes under Specialist Instructors. In the evening the Commanding Officer gave a Lecture on the Lewis Gun.	
-"-	28/7/17		"A" + "B" Coy's went for Coy Route Marches. "C" & "D" Coy's filled in the trenches on the Bombing Ground.	
-"-	29/7/17		It rained hard during the morning, and Church parade was cancelled.	
-"-	30/7/17		Coy's were at the disposal of Coy Commanders during the morning and	

Instructions regarding War Diaries and Intelligence Summaries are contained in F. S. Regs., Part II. and the Staff Manual respectively. Title pages will be prepared in manuscript.

WAR DIARY
or
INTELLIGENCE SUMMARY.
(Erase heading not required.)

6th Sheet.

Army Form C. 2118.

Place	Date	Hour	Summary of Events and Information	Remarks and references to Appendices
			attended a Sniping Demonstration. The Medical Officer lectured to Officers & N.C.O's on First Aid in the evening.	
In-the-Field	31/7		The Billetting party left by an early train for DUNKERQUE. The Battalion less "A" Coy paraded at 2.30 pm. and marched to LONGPRE, after having Teas at LONGPRE we entrained at 9 pm. & proceeded by rail via ABBEVILLE, BOULOGNE and CALAIS to DUNKERQUE	

H E Gogarty Lieut. Colonel
Comdg 2nd Bn The Worcestershire Regiment

T2134. Wt. W708—776. 500000. 4/15. Sir J. C. & S.

1st Sheet. 2 Worc R

Army Form C. 2118.

Vol 37

Instructions regarding War Diaries and Intelligence Summaries are contained in F. S. Regs., Part II. and the Staff Manual respectively. Title pages will be prepared in manuscript.

WAR DIARY
or
INTELLIGENCE SUMMARY.
(Erase heading not required.)

Place	Date	Hour	Summary of Events and Information	Remarks and references to Appendices
In the Field	1 8/17		We arrived at DUNKERQUE, & marched via TETEGHEM to UXEM, reaching Billets, which were rather crowded, at 2pm. 'A' Coy entrained at LONGPRÉ at 2.pm.	
— " —	2 8/17		'A' Coy arrived at UXEM. A wet day spent in general cleaning up and inspections	
— " —	3 8/17		The C.O and Adjutant reconnoitred the line. The Battalion paraded at about 1 pm, & moved to a camp of Huts and Tents at GHYVELDE. The accomodation was good	
— " —	4 8/17		A wet day spent in general cleaning up.	
— " —	5 8/17		The Battalion paraded for Church parade in a large tent in the morning	
— " —	6 8/17		Coy Training during the morning & early afternoon. One Coy paraded for Engineering, one for Bombing on the beach at BRAY DUNES, 'D' Coy for Bombing & Lewis Gun, & 'B' Coy for a Tactical Exercise. All Classes paraded under Specialist Instructors.	
— " —	7 8/17		Coy Training. Coy's paraded for the same parades as on Monday. A practise Gas Alarm was held in the afternoon.	

T2134. Wt. W708—776. 500000. 4/15. Sir J. C. & S.

37

Second Sheet

Instructions regarding War Diaries and Intelligence Summaries are contained in F. S. Regs., Part II. and the Staff Manual respectively. Title pages will be prepared in manuscript.

WAR DIARY
or
INTELLIGENCE SUMMARY.
(Erase heading not required.)

Army Form C. 2118.

Place	Date	Hour	Summary of Events and Information	Remarks and references to Appendices
In the Field	8/8/17		Coy Training. Two Coy's paraded on the beach, & two on the training ground. It rained hard during the evening & there was considerable artillery activity out at sea.	
— " —	9/8/17		All Coy's paraded on the training ground for Engineering & Coy attacks, as the 19th Brigade were making use of all the shore. It rained hard during the afternoon.	
			Lieut-Col. H. E. Gogarty took over Command of the Brigade & Lieut-Col. J. K Pardoe of the Battn temporarily	
— " —	10/8/17		The Battn paraded at 8.30 a.m. & marched to the beach between BRAY DUNES & LA PANNE. Coy's then paraded for Physical Training, leap frog etc & afterward the whole Battn bathed. We returned to Camp about 1.30 p.m. A Battalion Team played the R.A.M.C. in the evening.	
— " —	11/8/17		The Comdg Officer inspected the Kits of the Coy's during the morning. Coy's played inter-Platoon Cricket matches in the afternoon.	
— " —	12/8/17		Church parade was held in a large Marquee near the Depot Battn. Camp in the morning.	

3rd Sheet

Army Form C. 2118.

WAR DIARY
or
INTELLIGENCE SUMMARY.
(Erase heading not required.)

Instructions regarding War Diaries and Intelligence Summaries are contained in F. S. Regs., Part II. and the Staff Manual respectively. Title pages will be prepared in manuscript.

Place	Date	Hour	Summary of Events and Information	Remarks and references to Appendices
In the Field	13/8/17		Coy's paraded for Engineering & Tactical Exercises on the training ground, & C Coy held a Field firing practise on the beach.	
—"—	14/8/17		Two Coy's paraded for Bathing & Field firing on the beach. The other two paraded in Camp.	
—"—	15/8/17		The Battalion paraded at 8.30. am & marched to the Training ground for an Attack Practise. The Corps M.G.O. lectured to Officers of the Brigade, in the Cinema, at 12 noon, and in the afternoon a Machine Gun Demonstration was held on the beach between BRAY DUNES & LA PANNE	
—"—	16/8/17		The Battalion paraded at 9.am & marched to a position of Assembly for a Tactical Scheme. The Battalion attacked FAIR TRENCH, which was the fourth Objective, passing through the 9th H.L.I, who who were in the front line and took the first 3 Objectives. The 1st Queen's were on the right & 19th Bde on the left. A Contact Patrol was present during the attack	
—"—	17/8/17		Coy's paraded for Tactical Schemes, Coy parades & Bathing. Captain Huntingdon lectured on Bayonet fighting during the morning The minimum Reserve left for the Depot. All preparations were made	

T2134. Wt. W708—776. 500000. 4/15. Sir J. C. & S.

4th Sheet

Army Form C. 2118.

Instructions regarding War Diaries and Intelligence Summaries are contained in F. S. Regs., Part II. and the Staff Manual respectively. Title pages will be prepared in manuscript.

WAR DIARY
or
INTELLIGENCE SUMMARY.
(Erase heading not required.)

Place	Date	Hour	Summary of Events and Information	Remarks and references to Appendices
			for the move on the following day.	
In the Field	18/8/17		The Bn paraded at 5.45 am & marched to CANADA CAMP near LE PANNE, via ADINKERKE, reaching Camp at 10 am. The Camp was situated on the Dunes & was very comfortable with plenty of room.	
— " —	19/8/17		Voluntary Services were held in the morning in the Church Army Tent. The remainder of the day was spent in generally cleaning up the Camp. A few heavy shells came over during the night.	
— " —	20/8/17		Major Huntingdon A.G.S. lectured to the Battalion on Bayonet Fighting in the morning. All Coys marched down to the sea near COXYDE BAINS & bathed. A few heavy shells came over in the night & fell near COXYDE BAINS.	
— " —	21/8/17		Coys paraded for Company training & bathing. Specialists & Classes paraded under Specialist Instructors.	
— " —	22/8/17		The C.O. reconnoitred the high dune land near COXYDE preparatory to a Scheme with all Officers & N.C.O's. The Coys paraded under C.S. Majors.	
— " —	23/8/17		The Battalion paraded at 7.45 am & marched to a position of assembly	

Instructions regarding War Diaries and Intelligence Summaries are contained in F. S. Regs., Part II. and the Staff Manual respectively. Title pages will be prepared in manuscript.

WAR DIARY
or
INTELLIGENCE SUMMARY.
(Erase heading not required.)

5th Sheet

Army Form C. 2118.

Place	Date	Hour	Summary of Events and Information	Remarks and references to Appendices
			in the Training Ground. At 9 am which was Zero hour, "C" + "D" Coy's advanced on the right and left respectively + captured the 3rd Objective "A" + "B" Coy's following at Zero + 5 and captured the 1st + 2nd Objectives. After all Objectives were taken dispositions for a counter attack were taken up, and a Counter-attack launched by a Skeleton Enemy was held up on the line of Tactical Wire put up by "A" + "B" Coy's who were the 2 Coy's in readiness to counter the counter attack. Heavy rain ended the operations.	
In-the-Field	24/8/17		Coy's paraded under Coy arrangements. All specialists + Classes paraded under Specialist Instructors.	
—"—	25/8/17		The Battalion assembled at a position of Assembly on the DUNES near COXYDE BAINS + carried out a practise attack. It rained during part of the morning, but the attack + subsequent consolidation was successfully carried out.	
—"—	26/8/17		The Spray Baths at COXYDE were allotted to the Battalion during the morning + the whole Battalion was able to get a bath.	

6th Sheet.

Army Form C. 2118.

WAR DIARY
or
INTELLIGENCE SUMMARY.
(Erase heading not required.)

Instructions regarding War Diaries and Intelligence Summaries are contained in F. S. Regs., Part II. and the Staff Manual respectively. Title pages will be prepared in manuscript.

Place	Date	Hour	Summary of Events and Information	Remarks and references to Appendices
In the Field	27/8/17		Move orders were received at 8 am to the effect that the Battalion was to move back to GHYVELDE. The Battalion paraded at 11 am. & marched to GHYVELDE with 200 yds interval between Coy's, via LA PANNE & ADINKERKE, reaching Camp at 2.30 pm. It was a good day for marching & the Battalion marched well.	
— " —	28/8/17		The Battalion paraded at 8.50 am, & marched with 200 yards intervals between Coy's from GHYVELDE to Camp "C", on the Dunes near the FORT DES DUNES & ROSENDAEL. It was a very windy day. The whole Battalion was in Tents, except the Transport which was about 2 miles away near TETEGHEM.	
— " —	29/8/17		A wet day. The Coy's paraded on the beach when it was fine enough for Musketry, & practise in the Attack and Consolidation of Strong Points. A large training Area was allotted to the Battalion including a part of the beach.	
— " —	30/8/17		Coy's paraded for half an hour before Breakfast. Between 9 am & 12.30 pm "A" & "B" Coy's held Musketry parades, & "C" & "D" Coy's practise Attacks over the Dunes, which afforded a very excellent training ground. In the evening the "Drums"	

T2134. Wt. W708—776. 500000. 4/15. Sir J. C. & S.

Instructions regarding War Diaries and Intelligence Summaries are contained in F. S. Regs., Part II. and the Staff Manual respectively. Title pages will be prepared in manuscript.

WAR DIARY
or
INTELLIGENCE SUMMARY.
(Erase heading not required.)

7th Sheet

Army Form C. 2118.

Place	Date	Hour	Summary of Events and Information	Remarks and references to Appendices
			played in the Battery DE ZUIDCOOTE which was garrisoned by the 1st Regiment of French Heavy Artillery. Most of the Transport left for WORMHOUDT.	
In the Field	31/8/17		The Billeting party under Lt Green bicycled to EPERLEQUES where they met the Staff Captain & arranged Billets, leaving Camp at 3 am. The remainder of the Transport left under Lt Butler at 3.30 am, & entrained at DUNKIRK at 5 am, arriving at GANSPETTE at about 4.30 pm. The Battalion moved off from the Camp at 8 am, & entrained in No 3 Train at PREYCINET Station, DUNKIRK at 9.30 am. The Train reached WATTEN at about 1 pm, where the Battalion detrained & marched about 2 miles to Billets in GANSPETTE. The Billets were dirty & very scattered. The Transport which moved by road arrived about 2 pm, just before the Battalion.	
			In the Field 1st Sept. 1917 — C. W. Fox Capt. Lt Col for Lieut-Colonel Commanding 2nd Bn The Worcestershire Regiment	

T2134. Wt. W708–776. 500000. 4/15. Sir J. C. & S.

Army Form C. 2118.

100/33

First Sheet.

2 Worc R

Vol 38

Instructions regarding War Diaries and Intelligence Summaries are contained in F. S. Regs., Part II. and the Staff Manual respectively. Title Pages will be prepared in manuscript.

WAR DIARY
or
INTELLIGENCE SUMMARY
(Erase heading not required.)

Place	Date	Hour	Summary of Events and Information	Remarks and references to Appendices
In the Field	1/9/17	–	The day was spent in general cleaning up & inspections under Coy arrangements. The CO inspected Billets during the morning.	
– " –	2/9/17	–	The Bn. paraded for Church Parade in the morning. The CO inspected billets after Church Parade.	
– " –	3/9/17	–	"A" Coy marched over to the range near NORSLEOLINGHAM in the morning & spent the day there. "B" "C" & "D" Coys paraded on Coy parade grounds for training classes & specialists paraded under instructors. The "Shrapnels" performed in the evening.	
– " –	4/9/17	–	"C" & "D" bathed at EPERLECQUES in the morning & "A" & "B" in the afternoon. When not bathing Coys paraded for Coy training in the village.	
– " –	5/9/17	–	The Bn moved off by Coys at 7.45 am to the training ground near WESTROVE & carried out a practise attack finishing at 12.30 p.m.	
– " –	6/9/17	–	Coys paraded for Coy training from 7.30 - 8 & 9 - 12.30. The 55th Division held a Horse Show in the afternoon near NORDAUSQUES. In the evening we received orders to move "B" & "D" Coys from their billets to billets in HELLEBROUCK recently vacated by the Corps Cyclists as the personnel of the XIXth Corps moved into our billets.	S-38

2449 Wt. W14957/M90 750,000 1/16 J.B.C. & A. Forms/C.2118/12.

Instructions regarding War Diaries and Intelligence Summaries are contained in F. S. Regs., Part II. and the Staff Manual respectively. Title Pages will be prepared in manuscript.

WAR DIARY
or
INTELLIGENCE SUMMARY
(Erase heading not required.)

Army Form C. 2118.

Second Sheet.

Place	Date	Hour	Summary of Events and Information	Remarks and references to Appendices
In the Field	7/9/17	-	Coys paraded for Coy training from 7.30 - 8 + 9.30 - 12.30 and practised attacking an unexpected strong point. In the afternoon Major Pardol held a Map reading class + the C.O. saw all officers ie. training	
— " —	8/9/17	-	The battalion marched over to the GIEMY Field Firing range at 9 a.m. arriving at 12 noon + each platoon held a demonstration attack on a strong point, using live rifle grenades + bullets. Coys marched back independently the last Coy getting in at about 10. p.m.	
— " —	9/9/17	-	Range "B" was alloted to the Bn. as from 2.30 pm onwards + each Coy fired individual practise at 500 Yds. The C.O. + O.C Coys reconnoitred the ground for the Brigade Field day.	
— " —	10/9/17	-	Range "B" was again allotted to the battalion from 12.30 p.m. onwards + each Coy fired a Snap shooting + running man practise. The baths at EPERLECQUES were allotted to the battalion	
— " —	11/9/17		Coys paraded for Coy training during the morning. Range "A" was allotted to "C" + "D" Coys in the morning + "A" + "B" Coys in the afternoon for individual and tactical practises.	

2449 Wt. W14957/M90 750,000 1/16 J.B.C. & A. Forms/C.2118/12.

Instructions regarding War Diaries and Intelligence Summaries are contained in F. S. Regs., Part II. and the Staff Manual respectively. Title Pages will be prepared in manuscript.

WAR DIARY
or
INTELLIGENCE SUMMARY
(Erase heading not required.)

Army Form C. 2118.

Fourth Sheet.

Place	Date	Hour	Summary of Events and Information	Remarks and references to Appendices
In the Field	17/9/17		The battalion paraded at 9.30 a.m. & marched from STEENVOORDE to BERTHEN reaching BERTHEN at 1.30 p.m. The billets were fairly good. Some of the men were in huts.	
— " —	18/9/17		A day spent in general cleaning up & daily parades.	
— " —	19/9/17		The battalion paraded at 2 p.m. & marched to CHIPPEWA CAMP near LA CLYTTE, reaching Camp at about 5 p.m. The camp was in good repair.	
— " —	20/9/17		Spent in cleaning up & daily parades.	
— " —	21/9/17		Spent in daily parades and improving the protection of the huts against bombs by sandbagging them. The C.O. lectured on Gheluvelt in the afternoon in the Church Army Hut. Enemy aeroplanes were very active in the evening & dropped bombs fairly close to the Camp.	
— " —	22/9/17		Spent in daily parades and improvement of the Camp. The personnel detached as minimum reserve marched to the Brigade Depot Bn. near BERTHEN	
— " —	23/9/17		The Bn. paraded at 6.30 a.m. & marched to bivouacks near BEDFORD HOUSE. Two Coys were in dugouts and 2 in bivouacks.	
— " —	24/9/17		The Bn. moved into the line in the afternoon, relieving the 11th Sherwoods, 9th Yorks, & 11th West Yorks in the left centre subsector. The 4th Kings were on the left and the 9th H.L.I. on the right.	

2449 Wt. W14957/M90 750,000 1/16 J.B.C. & A. Forms/C.2118/12.

Instructions regarding War Diaries and Intelligence Summaries are contained in F. S. Regs., Part II. and the Staff Manual respectively. Title Pages will be prepared in manuscript.

WAR DIARY
or
INTELLIGENCE SUMMARY
(Erase heading not required.)

Third Sheet.

Army Form C. 2118.

Place	Date	Hour	Summary of Events and Information	Remarks and references to Appendices
In the Field	12 9/17	–	The Bn. paraded at 6 am. + marched via WESTROVE to a position of assembly near NORT LEULINGHAM. A practice brigade attack took place at 9 o.c. am. The battalion was on the left with "A" + "B" Coys in the front line and "B" + "D" in the second. The operation ended at about 12 noon + the battalion marched back. The Corps Commander watched the attack.	
– " –	13 9/17	–	The Bn. paraded at 8 am. and marched to a position of assembly near NORT LEULINGHAM. A practice brigade attack took place at 11.15. am with the same scheme as on the 12th. General Plumer was present at the attack + held a conference of officers afterwards. The battalion got back by about 3 p.m.	
– " –	14 9/17	–	Range "A" was allotted to the battalion. "A" + "B" Coys used it in the morning + "C" + "D" Coys in the afternoon. All Coys fired one individual + one rapid practise.	
– " –	15 9/17		The Bn. paraded at 9 am and marched from GANSPETTE to OOST HOUCK via WATTEN and BROERE, reaching billets at 12.30 p.m. The billets were very good but scattered.	
– " –	16 9/17		The Bn. paraded at 6.30 am. + marched to STEENVOORDE via CASSEL. The billets were rather scarce + also scattered. The battalion arrived at 12 noon.	

Instructions regarding War Diaries and Intelligence Summaries are contained in F. S. Regs., Part II. and the Staff Manual respectively. Title Pages will be prepared in manuscript.

WAR DIARY
or
INTELLIGENCE SUMMARY
(Erase heading not required.)

Army Form C. 2118.

Fifth Sheet.

Place	Date	Hour	Summary of Events and Information	Remarks and references to Appendices
In the Field	25/9/17		Relief completed about 1.0 A.M. 24/25. German Counter Attack commenced about 5.40 am which was finally repulsed about 11 am. Remainder of the day was quiet till about 2 pm when another Counter Attack developed from the direction of Polderhoek Chateau. The attack was repulsed & Artillery Fire continued throughout the night. Capt & Adjt C.A.R. Fox was killed about 10 a.m. & at the same time Colonel Gogarty was slightly wounded in 4 places but remained in the line. R.S. Major Davis was badly wounded by the same shell.	
— " —	26/9/17		Early in the morning Operation Orders were received and despatched to Coys about 5.30 am. Enemy Artillery Barrage became intense, missing first line, but very severe on Bn. H.Q. & west of it. Our attack commenced at 5.50 am & a constant Fire Fight with the enemy was kept up. About 4.45 pm the enemy attacked "Queens" (R.W. Surrey's) near MENIN Road, & KING'S (Liverpool Rd) but no attack developed against the Battalion. During the night Artillery Fire was constant but nothing of interest occurred.	
— " —	27/9/17		About 7 am Enemy's Artillery Fire ceased altogether; remainder of the day was quiet. Orders for relief came in about 7 pm. Relief commenced about 9 pm by 11th Sherwood Foresters. About 7 pm very heavy Enemy fire, heaviest ever experienced came down on the area, & again from 3.30 am to about 6.45 am. The relief was completed at 7 am Sept 28th.	

2449 Wt. W14957/M90 750,000 1/16 J.B.C. & A. Forms/C.2118/12.

Instructions regarding War Diaries and Intelligence Summaries are contained in F. S. Regs., Part II. and the Staff Manual respectively. Title Pages will be prepared in manuscript.

WAR DIARY
or
INTELLIGENCE SUMMARY
(Erase heading not required.)

Army Form C. 2118.

Sixth Sheet

Place	Date	Hour	Summary of Events and Information	Remarks and references to Appendices
In the Field	28/9/17		The Battalion assembled in BREWERY CAMP N.E. of DICKEBUSH. Capt. Fox was buried at DICKEBUSH Cemetery with Military honours. Casualties during the action 9 offrs. + 208 O. Ranks. At 1 pm the Battn paraded + marched to RENINGHELST Station + from there moved by rail to EBLINGHEM. + by road to GERCUS. Moves completed by 10.30 pm.	
— " —	29/9/17		Battalion rested. Billets were separated but fairly good	
— " —	30/9/17		Church parade at 3.30 pm.	

H E Gogarty
Lieut. Colonel
Comdg 7Bn The Worcestershire Regt

100/33

THE SECOND WORCESTERSHIRE REGIMENT.

IN THE ACTION ON THE MENIN ROAD, SEPTEMBER 25th-27th, 1917.

by

Lieutenant-Colonel H.E. Gogarty. Commanding.

Handed to Section by Capt. Stacke. 8-1-26.

THE SECOND WORCESTERSHIRE REGIMENT.

IN THE ACTION ON THE MENIN ROAD, SEPTEMBER 25th-27th, 1917.

by

Lieutenant-Colonel H.E. Gogarty. Commanding.

On the 23rd of September, the 2nd Worcestershire Regiment left Chippewa Camp. near Dickebusch, and marched to Bedford House. The C.O's of the Brigade went on by car to reconnoitre the line to be taken up by their Battalions and to arrange the relief. The relief by the 2nd Worcestershire Regiment was complicated by the fact that it had to take over from no less than three Battalions - the 9th Yorks, 11th West Yorks and 11th Sherwood Foresters. The country, too, was difficult. It was a mass of shell-holes interspersed with marshes. The only landmarks were the various German concrete dug-outs, Inverness Copse, or what remained of it, and the numerous derelict Tanks. Of the dug-outs, one was more conspicuous than any of the others. There was a two-storied, loopholed, round Tower East of Inverness Copse, which was within fifty yards of the Headquarters dug-out of the 2nd Worcesters, and which was used as an Observation Post and Signal Station. There was a buried Cable to it, a 'phone to the Headquarters dug-out, and, from it, visual signalling was possible to Brigade Headquarters at Tor Top, about two miles to the south-west; a power buzzer was also installed there and baskets of carrier-pigeons.

The Battalion started from Bedford House at 1.30 on the 24th, to march by Platoons at 100 yards interval to the 69th Brigade (afterwards 98th Brigade) Headquarters at Stirling Castle. The route was by Maple Copse, Doring House and Zillebeke. On arrival at Stirling Castle the Companies were to have tea and move off at intervals to their place in the line.

There was a story after the action that a German officer prisoner had declared that the enemy was fully acquainted with this relief, having picked it up on his listening sets during the previous twenty-four hours. Whether this was so or not, the Germans must have had ample notice from their aeroplane which hovered over the track and, apparently without interference from our air-service, signalled by means of colossal lights to their guns.

The 98th Brigade were relieving the same day and seem to have used the same track as the 100th Brigade, though a more westerly one was available. Partly owing to this and to unpunctuality on the part of some units and to failure to keep the prescribed distances between Platoons, there was a constant stream of Infantry moving along the Zillebeke track throughout the 24th, and appreciable casualties were caused by the enemy's artillery. The effect, too, on the troops, of the dead bodies along a track which should have been a fairly safe one, cannot have been good.

There was also a dangerous concentration of troops in the vicinity of Sterling Castle, where there was no adequate cover. It was due to good fortune alone that the enemy's shells did not fall on this area, and that only a few casualties were incurred there. Guides met the Companies at Stirling Castle, and at 4 p.m., "A" Company, under Captain Booth, marched off and relieved a company of the 11th West Yorks in and around the concrete dug-outs about 150 yards north-west of Brigade headquarters.

It was followed at 6 p.m., by "C" Company, under Captain Ripley, which marched via Herentage Chateau and took over the dug-outs south of Brigade headquarters from the 9th Yorks. Both these reliefs must have been observed by the enemy, and they were carried out under considerable artillery fire, as were all the subsequent reliefs.

At 6.30, the Headquarters company, under Second-Lieutenant

Turley, marched off, and, passing through Inverness Copse, relieved the 9th Yorks at the Tower and Headquarters dug-out.

"B" Company followed by the same route at 7 p.m., and reached the front line at 9.30 p.m., where it took over from "A" Company, 11th Sherwood Foresters. One-and-a-half Platoons were put into the front line, half a Platoon, under Second-Lieutenant Pointon, whose guide was killed, was temporarily lost, and the third Platoon arrived in the Support line at about 2 a.m.

"D" Company, under Captain Smith, was taken by its guide at 7.30 p.m. to a trench dug the previous night by the 11th Sherwood Foresters south of Northampton Farm. This trench was so full of water that the Company got into shell-holes behind it.

The C.O. - Lieutenant-Colonel Gogarty - and the Adjutant - Captain Fox - arrived at B Headquarters at 7 p.m. The O.C. 9th Yorks left on the completion of the relief, at about twelve, midnight.

The Battalion strength on coming into the line was:-

"A" Company		123;
"B" "		117;
"C" "		127;
"D" "		134;
H.Q. "		66;
	Total	567 with 21 officers.

The attack of the 100th Brigade on the Polderhoek Chateau line was timed to take place on the 26th. Final orders were therefore now written and issued at 2.30 a.m., on the 25th September.

This done, the C.O. and Adjutant started to go round the line, taking the orders for "B" and "D" Companies with them. Both on this and subsequent occasions, the difficulty of finding the way amid the mass of shell-holes, especially by night, was very noticeable. It interfered not only with the communication by runner but also with the supply of stores and ammunition.

Notification was received during the night of the 24th/25th that an army practice barrage would take place on the morning of the 25th, and a Corps barrage during the afternoon. The former started at about 5 a.m. and a German barrage commenced at approximately the same time. The German barrage was in three portions. The first was evidently intended for our front-line, and, on this occasion, it actually fell on "B" Company. It did not remain there long, however, but shifted about thirty yards west, where it remained during the rest of the fighting. The second portion was placed on the line of the three concrete dug-outs, only some 250 yards further West, and was evidently intended for our support line. The next, and apparently the main barrage, extended from in front of the Tower well to the West of Inverness Copse. This barrage was very severe. The Tower received direct hits certainly every fifteen minutes, probably much oftener. The fire came mainly from the East, but a good deal was from guns somewhere south of Gheluvelt, and this latter fire increased considerably and became especially severe on the 26th. The shells were mostly of medium calibre, up to 5.9 guns and howitzers.

As it grew light, the ground East of the Tower was so covered with smoke from the shells of both sides that little or nothing could be seen. At about 8 a.m., a runner arrived from the front line with a message to the effect that reinforcements and S.A.A. were required there, that a number of the Battalion on the immediate right had surrendered, men of the Battalion on the Menin Road had also been seen to surrender as had some of the adjoining Brigade beyond the Reutel Beek.

The C.O. and Adjutant at once came down from the Tower and orders were issued to deal with the situation.

From subsequent information the story of what had happened in the front line would appear to be approximately as follows:-

Although the 100th Brigade had taken over the line more or less correctly, during the previous night, owing to the darkness, the difficulty of the country and the ignorance of it on the part of the relieved troops, there was a good deal of confusion. Especially was this the case with the Highlanders on our right. Many of their men were mixed up with other battalions and the general line occupied, instead of facing East, faced North.

The Germans had planned an attack on our line below the Menin Road and Polygon Wood for the morning of the 26th September. The artillery fire was to start at 5.15 a.m., and it was to be followed by an Infantry attack at 5.45 a.m. The enemy's front line was to stand fast while three battalions passed through it, one North of the Reutel beek, one South of it, and a Battalion of Storm troops along the Menin Road, which was held by two Companies of the 1st Queen's with two companies in support.

When it began to get light, "B" Company, which was not in touch with the Highlanders on the right, found considerable numbers of the enemy in its front and in a low wood (the Osier beds) on its right flank. The enemy evidently did not quite know the situation and was nervous. A few men on the right of "B" Company opened fire with such good effect that the remainder of the Company, rapidly gaining confidence, joined in and brought the German advance in this part of the field to a standstill. "B" Company, however, was able from its position to see the surrenders already reinforced and sent up the message which reached the C.O. in the Tower.

Evidently the first thing was to get reinforcements of men and S.A.A. to "B" Company. "A" Company was therefore turned out and ordered up to the front line. Some S.A.A. boxes were opened, and each man as he filed past the Headquarters was handed two or three bandoliers to carry with him.

The Company advanced very steadily under a heavy artillery fire, and under rifle fire probably from the small wood already mentioned, and from the Menin Road. It reached the Front Line where it took up a position in Echelon on "B" Company's right rear. It lost two officers and eight or ten men during its advance. Captain Brooks had his leg broken by a shell, either on the way up or shortly after getting into position. This left 2/Lieutenant Loder in command, 2/Lieuts. High and Ashcroft being wounded.

There was now time to look round and try and grasp the situation, which was very obscure. On the ridge near the "Pimple" lines of men, apparently Germans, could be seen advancing. Close to the "Pimple" itself, which was a concrete tower south-west of Polderhoek Chateau, were a number of British soldiers, some of them carrying a wounded man. To the right, near the Menin Road, Highlanders could be seen walking along with their hands up.

The situation was rendered no clearer by a machine gun opening fire on Battalion Headquarters, apparently from a position South of it, and between it and the Menin Road. This fire was fortunately high.

At this moment a Platoon of Highlanders arrived at Battalion headquarters on its say up to reinforce the front line. Bandoliers of ammunition were served out to the men as they passed and the Platoon went off in the direction of the Menin Road. Whether the machine gunner was under the impression that he was in danger of being cut off by this party, or for some other reason, he ceased fire and apparently retired.

The C.O., Adjutant, R.S.M., and others, were now standing outside the Battalion headquarters dug-out, endeavouring to make out what was happening, when a shell struck the concrete wall of the dug-out behind them, killed Captain Fox, badly wounded R.S.M. Davis and scratched and bruised the C.O.

The latter, however, was able to remain at duty. By this time the front line had been further reinforced by "D" Company on the personal initiative of Captain Smith (vide Sketch), and, in spite of the presence of the enemy in the Copse on the right of "B" Company, the situation was well in hand. That this was the case was principally due to the admirable arrangements made by Captain Barker and to the good shooting of the men, which not only confined the Germans on the front and right flank to their shell-holes, but also stopped these being reinforced by section rushes from the "Pimple" slope.

The expenditure of S.A.A. was heavy, and supplications for more continued to be received. One Platoon of "C" Company, under 2/Lieut. Johnson, was therefore sent up soon after midday with a fresh supply. The Platoon was especially well handled. Lieut. Johnson himself, with his runner, reported to Captain Barker, found out exactly where his men were required, and then skilfully brought them up to a position on the right flank of the Worcestershire's line as shown in the sketch. This occurred shortly after 1 p.m.

At about 2 p.m. a message came from the Brigade by runner, to say that one company, 16th K.R.R.C., was being sent up to the Battalion as a reinforcement. Other messages were received shortly afterwards to say that the enemy was massing on the south-east and that counter-attacks were to be expected. During the afternoon the K.R.R. company, under Captain Chadwick, arrived, and was ordered to take up a position about half-way between the Tower and the front line in rear of the gap between the 2nd Worcesters and the Highlanders, and to counter-attack should the enemy penetrate the gap. The company did not reach this position but occupied either the trench shown south of Northampton Farm or the ground near it. Late in the evening it was withdrawn to the concrete dug-outs originally occupied by "A" Company, from where it rendered valuable assistance in carrying up supplies of S.A.A. and water through the barrage.

At about 3.30 p.m., an S.O.S. signal was sent up from the front line. This was repeated from the Tower, and (as no reply came) from Battalion headquarters. It was twenty minutes before our barrage came down, and then it was weak. No information was received as to the reason for this S.O.S. which apparently came from somewhere on the right.

Another S.O.S. signal was given about 4.30, with very different results. The machine-gun barrage fire followed immediately, and a minute or so later came a perfect artillery barrage.

Second-Lieut. Turley, who was the Worcestershire O.O. in the Tower at this time, was able to see a body of the enemy, estimated at a Battalion, advance past the South of Polderhoek Chateau towards our line. About five minutes later another body, estimated at two Battalions, appeared in mass on the north of the Chateau. Both these formations were caught by our barrage and suffered such heavy losses that their advance was completely stopped.

The chief difficulties experienced during the 25th and, indeed, throughout the operations, were (a) Communication and (b) Provision of Supplies.

The provision for Communication was :-

<u>Pigeons</u>. These worked well and were very useful.

<u>Buried Cable</u>. Useless, on account of the heavy shelling.

<u>Power Buzzer</u>. Did not work; reason unknown.

<u>Visual</u>. Lamps were placed in the Front Line and signalled back O.K. at intervals, to the Tower. A flag on the Tower and lamps at its foot outside, sent messages to the Brigade. This worked fairly well, but both lamps and signallers suffered from the shells.

Runner. On the whole this was good, if slow, but it failed once or twice on account of the enemy fire.

It will be noticed that, with the exception of runners, there was no communication from rear to front. Probably it would have been better had visual messages been sent. The fire could not have been heavier than it was, as the enemy knew our positions, and the danger of his reading our code would not have been great. It was unfortunate that the Battalion signalling officer was sick and unable to come into the line. There is no doubt that the arrangements for communication might have been improved upon.

As regards supplies, the difficulty was due to two causes, viz., the violence of the enemy's fire and inadequate preparation. Had the latter been more complete, and numerous dumps of S.A.A., Very Lights, S.O.S. Signals, Water and Rations been established, the fire would not have been so great an obstacle. The few dumps that did exist were quite insufficient.

THE 26th.

During the night of the 25th - 26th, Brigade orders were received for the attack of the next day. The scheme had been modified. The 4th King's was to advance about 500 yards, pivotting on its right; the remainder of the 100th Brigade was to stand fast or retake any portions of the line lost, while the troops on the left carried out the original scheme. Battalion orders to this effect were issued about 2 a.m.

The operations of the 26th were to commence with the Artillery preparation at 5.30 a.m., and the Infantry advance was to follow at 5.50 a.m. The German artillery fire which had been kept up throughout the night, started with redoubled intensity at about 5.30. New guns, or rather

Howitzers, were employed, and the direct hits on the roof of the Headquarters became so frequent that it seemed doubtful whether the building would hold out. Had it failed to do so, the only possible place for Headquarters was one of "A" or "C" Company's shelters. To carry on in the open under such a fire was impossible. The whole ground was churned up, even the bodies of the killed soon disappeared. It would have been well worth the enemy's while to have detailed one or two heavy guns expressly for the dug-outs. Had they gone control would have become difficult, if not impossible. Fortunately, the building stood, and the Infantry attack presently caused the fire of the new howitzers to be diverted elsewhere.

The front companies were engaged in a fire-fight throughout the day and never lost the ascendancy they had gained. They were able to inflict losses on the enemy near the "Pimple" and the Chateau and also on the enemy opposite the 98th Brigade beyond the Reutel beek at ranges up to 50 yards. At about 2 p.m., the O.C. "B" Company received a message from the Highlanders that they were going to attack in twenty minutes time in order to join up with his right and the Queen's left. Just then the Germans started shelling the neighbourhood of the Highlanders with great violence, and the attack did not develop until 4.30. In its initial stage it was a right wheel, and it was followed by an advance through the Copse. It was carried out with great dash and determination. About seventy Germans were driven out from the Copse, and, as they passed "B" Company's flank, were caught in enfilade by two Lewis guns. Only four escaped. They were closely followed by a machine gunner, who was killed, but a second man took the gun and almost reached the German line before he too fell. The gun was not captured, but the spare parts box was taken off the body of the first man.

While the attack of the Highlanders was in progress,

a party of Germans appeared, about J.16. central, and advanced towards Jut Farm - strength about one company. This company was engaged by the left Company of the 2nd Worcesters, who knocked over a considerable number and brought the advance to a standstill, Shortly after this our guns shelled the hollow in rear of the "Pimple", and drove the Germans in it towards us on the crest of the ridge. Many of them tried to get into the Pimple Tower and were caught by our shrapnel and the fire of the Worcestershire front Line Companies. Their situation was so unpleasant that they could be seen fighting and knocking each other down in order to get into the shelter of the Tower.

During the whole of the action the Infantry were worried by low flying enemy aeroplanes firing their machine guns. Our own planes were probably engaged elsewhere, in any case they were conspicuous by their absence on the 25th and 26th. Two of these enemy planes were brought down by rifle and machine-gun fire.

At the side of the Headquarters dug-out was a small German first-aid post, in which were installed the aid posts both of the 4th King's and the 2nd Worcesters. Some 340 wounded men passed through this post during the fighting. The congestion was very great. Every available place was filled with wounded and an overflow post was established in one of the "C" Company's dug-outs. Things were made worse by the fact that, for 24 hours, no stretcher bearers arrived to evacuate these wounded, on account of the severity of the artillery fire between Battalion Headquarters and the first relay post at Clapham Junction. Eventually the Chaplain, the Rev. E.V. Tanner, went back himself through the barrage and brought back stretcher-bearers with him. Both the Chaplain and the Medical Officer, Captain Morris-Jones were recommended for the D.S.O., on account of their gallant and self-sacrificing conduct during the operations.

Though no further Infantry actions developed in the B attalion front during the remainder of the 26th, the artillery fire was continuous and severe.

At midnight, Br.-General Baird, Commanding 100th Brigade, visited Headquarters and brought the news that the Battalion would be relieved by the 23rd Division on the following night. Orders for this arrived a few hours later.

THE 27th.

At dawn on the 27th, the fire on both sides ceased, and, with the exception of odd shells and casual rifle or machine-gun fire, did not recommence until about 4 p.m. Advantage was taken of this to supply the front Companies with water and S.A.A. Rations had not arrived, and men had to subsist on their iron ration during the 26th and 27th. Many iron rations, together with the packs, had been destroyed by shells while the men were digging, so that some men were without food.

At about 3 p.m., the representative of the Sherwood Foresters arrived to arrange the relief and was followed by the O.C. at about 6 p.m. At about 7 p.m., the heaviest barrage yet experienced was directed on the line of the Tower and lasted for two hours. A further barrage was put down by the enemy from about 3.30 a.m. to 6.45 a.m. on the 28th. The Battalion was relieved between the hours of 1 a.m. and 7 a.m. on the 28th, the process being much facilitated by tapes which had been put down as guides.

-x-x-x-x-x-x-x-x-

Instructions regarding War Diaries and Intelligence Summaries are contained in F. S. Regs., Part II. and the Staff Manual respectively. Title pages will be prepared in manuscript.

WAR DIARY
or
INTELLIGENCE SUMMARY.
(Erase heading not required.)

2 Worc R

Army Form C. 2118.

100/33

Vol 39

Place	Date	Hour	Summary of Events and Information	Remarks and references to Appendices
In the Field	1.10.17		Battn paraded under Major Pardoe for rehearsal by C in Chief	
" "	2.10.17		Battn paraded under Colonel Gogarty for inspection by the C in Chief. The following N.C.O's were awarded Medals:- C.S.M. Bragg, Sergt. Haggit, L/Cpl Williams, L/Cpl Compton. C in Chief extremely pleased at general turnout, special mention being made about handling of arms.	
" "	3.10.17		Battn paraded for baths at BLARINGHEM	
" "	4.10.17		Major Pardoe took over command of the Battn during Lt. Col. Gogarty's absence on a fortnight's leave.	
" "	5.10.17		Battn paraded 9.30 AM for march to SALPERWICK. Route taken was via RENESCURE - FORT ROUGE - ARQUES - outskirts of St Omer to SALPERWICK. ~~[illegible] ARQUES~~. The Battn arrived in Billets at 3.30 P.M. Billets were good but scattered.	
" "	6.10.17		Battn marched to WIZERNES Station at 8.40AM and entrained at 10.30AM for BAILLEUL arriving there at 1P.M. On arrival Battn marched ~~by march route~~ to Camp at WHEAL Camp about 400 yards S of NEUVE EGLISE on the NEUVE EGLISE - STEENWERCKE road. H.Qrs Coy & Officers were in huts, but rest of Battn were in tents.	

T2134. Wt. W708—776. 500000. 4/15. Sir J. C. & S.

Instructions regarding War Diaries and Intelligence Summaries are contained in F. S. Regs., Part II. and the Staff Manual respectively. Title pages will be prepared in manuscript.

WAR DIARY
or
INTELLIGENCE SUMMARY.
(Erase heading not required.)

Army Form C. 2118.

Place	Date	Hour	Summary of Events and Information	Remarks and references to Appendices
Surth-Field	7.10.17		Battn under O.C. Coys for general cleaning up of Camp. Divine Service at 10 A.M.	
— " —	8.10.17 9.10.17		Battn paraded under Coy arrangements.	
— " —	10.10.17		Coys fired on the range during the day. Major Pidel proceeded to England on light duty, and Captain H.I.E. RIPLEY took over command of the Battn until Lt/Col. Gogarty's return.	
— " —	11.10.17		Coys paraded under O.C. Coys for the day. Battn commanders conference at 3 p.m. at Bde. H.Q.	
— " —	12.10.17		Coys paraded for work on the range. Coy commanders and Battn commander visited trenches.	
— " —	13.10.17		Coys paraded for work on the range. Adjutants parade in early morning.	
— " —	14.10.17		Church parade at 10. A.M. Battn moved up into the trenches at 5 P.M. in front of WULVERGHEM. A Coy L. Front Coy. C Coy R. Front Coy. D Coy Support. B Coy Reserve. Relief completed about mid-night.	
— " —	15.10.17		Battn in the line. During night Support Coy & Battn H.Q. shelled without effect by 4.2 & 5.9 Hows. Several casualties amongst reserve coy whilst employed in carrying to the front line.	

T2134. Wt. W708—776. 500000. 4/15. Sir J. C. & S.

Army Form C. 2118.

Instructions regarding War Diaries and Intelligence Summaries are contained in F. S. Regs., Part II. and the Staff Manual respectively. Title pages will be prepared in manuscript.

WAR DIARY
or
INTELLIGENCE SUMMARY.
(Erase heading not required.)

Place	Date	Hour	Summary of Events and Information	Remarks and references to Appendices
In the Field	25.10.17		Battn moved by lorry route to the MENIN GATE YPRES for working parties to 1st ANZAC CORPS. Relief was completed by 5 p.m.	
— —	26/31st (inc)		Working parties of every available man were supplied daily for work under 253 Coy R.E. The ~~rest of the men~~ stragglers were employed in making the camp which ~~was in a disgraceful condition~~ consisted of rough shelters in wet ground. It rained hard on the 26th & the camp got into such a condition that accommodation was arranged for two Companies in the Old Cavalry Barracks YPRES & a drying room & other accommodation constructed from material supplied by C.R.E. Corps troops. Full moon was on the 29th & the camp & its neighbourhood was bombed nightly by enemy planes.	

H. E. Gogarty Lt Col
Comdg 2nd Bn The Worcestershire Regt.

T2134. Wt. W708—776. 500000. 4/15. Sir J. C. & S.

WAR DIARY
or
INTELLIGENCE SUMMARY.
(Erase heading not required.)

Army Form C. 2118.

Instructions regarding War Diaries and Intelligence Summaries are contained in F. S. Regs., Part II. and the Staff Manual respectively. Title pages will be prepared in manuscript.

Place	Date	Hour	Summary of Events and Information	Remarks and references to Appendices
In the Field	16.10.17 / 17.10.17		Battn in the line. H.Q. & Support line shelled during night but no damage done except to trench.	
— " —	18.10.17		Battn were relieved by 1st Queens. Relief started at 6 pm and finished at 12 midnight. 'B' Coy remained in reserve to the Queens owing to their weak ~~strength~~ numbers & 'D' Coy went into Battn Support Coy. at BETHLEEM FARM. A & C Coys went into dug-outs at BRISTOLL CASTLE close to N. MIDLAND FARM (Brigade HQ)	
— " —	19.10.17 / 20.10.17 / 21.10.17		A & C Coys remained at BRISTOLL CASTLE and were employed as carrying fatigues for the first line and support trenches.	
— " —	22.10.17		Battn relieved by 4th Kings & went into hutments at BULFORD CAMP on the NEUVE EGLISE – NIEPPE road. Relief commenced 6 pm & finished 11 pm. Total casualties for the tour about 25.	
— " —	23.10.17		Battn spent day in cleaning up camp. A & C Coys used for Bde. fatigues	
— " —	24.10.17		Battn had use of range during morning and baths in the afternoon.	

T2134. Wt. W708–776. 500000. 4/15. Sir J. C. & S.

16

2 Worcester R.

Vol 40

Army Form C. 2118.

Instructions regarding War Diaries and Intelligence Summaries are contained in F. S. Regs., Part II. and the Staff Manual respectively. Title pages will be prepared in manuscript.

WAR DIARY
or
INTELLIGENCE SUMMARY.
(Erase heading not required.)

Place	Date	Hour	Summary of Events and Information	Remarks and references to Appendices
In the Field	Nov. 1st		Working parties were supplied for the 203rd Coy Art. R.E. Orders were received for the Battn to be relieved on the evening of the 2nd by the 4th Suffolks	
	Nov. 2nd		The Battn was relieved by the 4th Suffolks in the afternoon. Battn marched by Coys to the Asylum YPRES where they embussed and proceeded to CANTEEN CORNER CAMP near NEUVE EGLISE.	
	Nov. 3rd		The Battn spent the day in cleaning up and inspections under Coy arrangements. Six officers of the 1st Queens were attached to the Battn owing to the Battn being very short of Officers. One was posted to B Coy. One to D Coy. and two each to A & C Coys.	
	Nov. 4th		A wiring demonstration was held at WULVERGHEM. Orders were received that Divl Commander would present Medal Ribbons on the 5th Nov. Coys paraded under Coy arrangements for Physical Training, Gas Drill etc.	
	Nov. 5th		The Battn paraded at 12.30 pm on field behind camp for the Medal Ribbon distribution. Div. Commander arrived at 12-45 pm, presented ribbons and spoke to the Battn about the 1st battle of YPRES congratulating all ranks. He also praised the Battn considerably for the defence of the captured positions in the	5.40

See Sheet 2

T2134. Wt. W708–776. 506000. 4/15. Sir J. C. & S.

Sheet 2

Instructions regarding War Diaries and Intelligence Summaries are contained in F. S. Regs., Part II. and the Staff Manual respectively. Title pages will be prepared in manuscript.

WAR DIARY
or
INTELLIGENCE SUMMARY.
(Erase heading not required.)

Army Form C. 2118.

Place	Date	Hour	Summary of Events and Information	Remarks and references to Appendices
In the Field			neighbourhood of POLDERHOEK on the 25th of September	
	Nov. 6th		Coys paraded under Coy arrangements in the morning. A conference of all officers was held in HdQr Mess after dinner.	
	Nov. 7th		Battn moved up to support in the evening relieving 1st Cameronians at BRISTOL CASTLE. Relief was reported complete by midnight.	
	Nov. 8th		The whole Battn were on working parties all day and the work on the new support line was taken over from the 19th Bde.	
	Nov. 9th		Working parties were found by the Battn all day and support line and New Cross C.T. were worked on all night.	
	Nov. 10th		Working parties as before. 1st Queens carried out a raid on the enemies trenches during the night. One prisoner was taken.	
	Nov. 11th		The 1st Queens were relieved by the Battn in the evening on the right subsector. B Coy went up to the left front sector. D Coy went to the right front sector. C Coy went from BETHLEHEM FARM where they had been while the Battn was at BRISTOL CASTLE to POLLARD SUPPORT. A Coy remained at Bn HdQrs in reserve where they had also been during the Battns tour at BRISTOL CASTLE	

See Sheet 3

Sheet 3.

Instructions regarding War Diaries and Intelligence Summaries are contained in F. S. Regs., Part II. and the Staff Manual respectively. Title pages will be prepared in manuscript.

WAR DIARY
or
INTELLIGENCE SUMMARY.
(Erase heading not required.)

Army Form C. 2118.

Place	Date	Hour	Summary of Events and Information	Remarks and references to Appendices
In the Field			The relief was reported complete about 10 P.M.	
	Nov. 12th		A very quiet day followed by a quiet night.	
	Nov. 13th		A quiet day. A little T.Ms of the left front coy otherwise all quiet.	
	Nov. 14th		Australians came up during the day to take over dispositions etc. Battn was relieved during the evening by the 30th Aust. Battn in the right subsector. On completion of relief Battn marched back by platoons to BULFORD CAMP near NEUVE. ÉGLISE.	
	Nov. 15th		Battn spent the day in cleaning up clothing etc.	
	Nov. 16th		Battn marched to a camp in the LOCRE area. Battn paraded at 8-30 AM and passed starting point forked roads at NEUVE. ÉGLISE at 9-13 AM. Arrived in new camp about midday.	
	Nov. 17th		Battn spent the day in cleaning up of clothing and inspections.	
	Nov. 18th		Battn embussed on the LOCRE-DRANOUTRE ROAD for ST. LAWRENCE CAMP BRANDHOEK. Arrived in camp at 11-45 AM.	
	Nov. 19th		Battn spent the day in cleaning up the camp which had been taken over from the Canadians. This occupied the whole day.	

Sheet 4

Sheet 4

Instructions regarding War Diaries and Intelligence Summaries are contained in F. S. Regs., Part II. and the Staff Manual respectively. Title pages will be prepared in manuscript.

WAR DIARY
or
INTELLIGENCE SUMMARY.
(*Erase heading not required.*)

Army Form C. 2118.

Place	Date	Hour	Summary of Events and Information	Remarks and references to Appendices
In the Field	Nov. 20th		Battn continued cleaning up the camp during the morning, and at 11-30AM, range was commenced. C.O's kit inspection in the afternoon.	
	Nov. 21st		Lt Col: H. E. Gogarty D.S.O. relinquished Command of the Battn and proceeded to ITALY as A.A.G. L.O.C. Major S. G. Roman D.S.O took over Command. The Battn paraded under Coy arrangements.	
	Nov. 22nd		Company Parades. 2/Lt Bryant appointed Bde Gas Officer.	
	Nov. 23rd		Refit of box respirators. Baths. Orders to move into Rivl. Support.	
	Nov. 24th		Battn to Camp in LANCER FARM took over from 1st Middlesex Rivl. Support. PASSCHENDAELE SECTOR.	
	Nov. 25th		All Battn on Working parties.	
	Nov. 26th		Battn ready to move at ½ hours notice.	
	Nov. 27th		Battn ready to move at ½ hours notice.	
	Nov. 28th		All Battn on working parties.	
	Nov. 29th		Battn moved into Right Support in SEINE FARM. Started 5-30pm. Relief complete 8-20pm.	

See Sheet 5

Sheet 5

Instructions regarding War Diaries and Intelligence Summaries are contained in F. S. Regs., Part II. and the Staff Manual respectively. Title pages will be prepared in manuscript.

WAR DIARY
or
INTELLIGENCE SUMMARY.
(Erase heading not required.)

Army Form C. 2118.

Place	Date	Hour	Summary of Events and Information	Remarks and references to Appendices
Infantry Field	Nov. 3rd		Relieved 20th Fusiliers in Right Subsector of PASSCHENDAELE. A, C Coys front line. D Coy in Support. B in reserve. Bn Hd Qrs at HAMBURG	

L. C. Dorman. Major
Comdg 2nd Bn The Worcestershire Regt.

T2134. Wt. W708—776. 500000. 4/15. Sir J. C. & S.

2 Worc Regt

Army Form C. 2118.

Instructions regarding War Diaries and Intelligence Summaries are contained in F. S. Regs., Part II. and the Staff Manual respectively. Title pages will be prepared in manuscript.

WAR DIARY
or
INTELLIGENCE SUMMARY.
(Erase heading not required.)

Vol 41 Dec 17

Place	Date	Hour	Summary of Events and Information	Remarks and references to Appendices
In the Field	Dec 1st		Battalion in the line	
	Dec 2nd		Battalion in the line	
	Dec 3rd		Battalion was relieved in the line by the 9th H L I. Battalion moved back to Right Support relieving the 2/9 Manchesters at DARLING CROSSING	
	Dec 4th		Battalion in Support	
	Dec 5th		Battalion was relieved in support by the 4th Suffolks. On completion of relief Battalion moved back down Mule Track and ZONNEBEKE ROAD to ST-JEAN camp at ST-JEAN.	
	Dec 6th		Battalion entrained at ST-JEAN Station for BRANDHOEK from there marched to ST-LAWRENCE Camp.	
	Dec 7th		Day spent in general cleaning up of clothing, equipment and the camp.	
	Dec 8th		Capt Peake joined the Battalion and took over command of "C" Company 2nd Lieut Wickham joined and was posted to "A" Company Baths were allotted to the Battalion.	
	Dec 9th		Devine Service by Rev: E V Tanner. Billeting party proceeded to WINNEZEELE	
	Dec 10th		Battalion moved to Billets in WINNEZEELE area, route VIA POPERINGHE-ST-JANSTER-WATOU-BIEZEN	
	Dec 11th		Battalion spent the day in general cleaning up. Billets in new area very scattered. 2nd Lieut Bond joined the Battalion and was posted to "D" Coy.	
	Dec 12th		Companies were at disposal of Coy Comdrs for general Training	

Contd

T2134. Wt. W708—776. 500000. 4/15. Sir J. C. & S.

Instructions regarding War Diaries and Intelligence Summaries are contained in F. S. Regs., Part II. and the Staff Manual respectively. Title pages will be prepared in manuscript.

Sheet 2

WAR DIARY
or
INTELLIGENCE SUMMARY.
(Erase heading not required.)

Army Form C. 2118.

Place	Date	Hour	Summary of Events and Information	Remarks and references to Appendices
	Dec 13th		Battalion moved to ST-JEAN area for work on Roads and Mule Tracks. Battalion entrained at GODEWAERSVELDE detraining at ST-JEAN Station. On detraining Battn marched to Canvas camp at ST-JEAN.	
	Dec 14th		Spent in improving camp.	
	Dec 15th		Battalion on Fatigue, 2nd Lieuts Burton and Bryant joined from 7th reserves	
	Dec 16th		Battalion on Fatigue.	
	Dec 17th		Battalion on Fatigue.	
	Dec 18th		Battalion on Fatigue.	
	Dec 19th		Battalion on Fatigue	
	Dec 20th		Battalion on Fatigue.	
	Dec 21st		Battalion was relieved by the 5th Scottish Rifles. Battn entrained at ST-JEAN Station for GODEWAERSVELDE, from there marched to original billets in WINNEZEELE area.	
	Dec 22nd		General smartening up.	
	Dec 23rd		General smartening up.	
	Dec 24th		Companies at the disposal of Coy Comdrs for Training etc:	

Contd

T2134. Wt. W708—776. 500000. 4/15. Sir J. C. & S.

Instructions regarding War Diaries and Intelligence Summaries are contained in F. S. Regs., Part II. and the Staff Manual respectively. Title pages will be prepared in manuscript.

Sheet 3

WAR DIARY
or
INTELLIGENCE SUMMARY.
(Erase heading not required.)

Army Form C. 2118.

Place	Date	Hour	Summary of Events and Information	Remarks and references to Appendices
In the field	Dec. 25th		Xmas Day	
	Dec. 26th		Companies continued programmes of work.	
	Dec. 27th		" " " " "	
	Dec. 28th		" " " " ". Lt Col H. W. Weldon (Leinster Regt.) on joining the Battn, took over Command vice Major L. C. Dorman R.S.O. to second-in-command.	
	Dec. 29th		Voluntary R.C. parade. All Officers & NCOs down to the rank of Cpl paraded for a demonstration by Commanding Officer. The remainder of Battn cleaned up their equipment.	
	Dec. 30th		Companies continued their programmes of work.	
	Dec. 31st		Spent as a Holiday.	

H. W. Weldon a/Lt Col
Comdg 2nd Bn the Worcestershire Regt.

Instructions regarding War Diaries and Intelligence Summaries are contained in F. S. Regs., Part II. and the Staff Manual respectively. Title pages will be prepared in manuscript.

100/33

WAR DIARY
or
INTELLIGENCE SUMMARY.
(Erase heading not required.)

Army Form C. 2118.

2/8th Worcester Regt.

Vol 42

Place	Date	Hour	Summary of Events and Information	Remarks and references to Appendices
In the Field	1/1/18		Football match against 9th H.L.I. Capt G. J. L. Stoney on rejoining Battn takes over 2nd in command vice Major L. C. Rorman R.S.O. to a Reinforcement Camp. Major Bt Lt Col J. O. Nelson joined Battn.	
	2/1/18		Battn's box respirators were tested at WINNEZEELE.	
	3/1/18		Moved to ST LAWRENCE CAMP BRANDHOEK.	
	4/1/18		Battn ready to move to POTIJZE area.	
	5/1/18		Battn moved to ALNWICK CAMP POTIJZE.	
	6/1/18		Spent in organizing and cleaning camp. The Battn provided 260 men for working parties.	
	7/1/18		Battn provided the same working parties.	
	8/1/18		Battn on working parties. F.G.C.M. held on 13071 Pte J. Edwards.	
	9/1/18		Battn provided same working parties. Major G. J. L. Stoney M.C. takes over command vice Lt Col H. H. Weldon to command 2nd Leinsters. Half the Battn had baths.	
	10/1/18		Battn provided same working parties.	
	11/1/18		— Do —	
	12/1/18		— Do —	

S.42

T2134. Wt. W708—776. 500000. 4/15. Sir J. C. & S.

Instructions regarding War Diaries and Intelligence Summaries are contained in F. S. Regs., Part II. and the Staff Manual respectively. Title pages will be prepared in manuscript.

Sheet 2

WAR DIARY
or
INTELLIGENCE SUMMARY.
(Erase heading not required.)

Army Form C. 2118.

Place	Date	Hour	Summary of Events and Information	Remarks and references to Appendices
Intheried	13/1/18		Battn provided same working parties	
	14/1/18		— Do —	
	15/1/18		— Do —	
	16/1/18		— Do —	
	17/1/18		Battn relieved 5th Scottish Rifles in support at HAMBURG	
	18/1/18		Battn in support	
	19/1/18		Battn relieved 4th Suffolks in the front line	
	20/1/18		Battn in front line	
	21/1/18		Battn moved to BRANDHOEK	
	22/1/18		Baths and MO's inspection. Armourer Sgt inspected rifles. 2/Lt's A Rudd & A Hurley joined Battn and were posted to B & C Coys respectively.	
	23/1/18		Coys at the disposal of Coy Commanders. Armourer Sergt inspected the remainder of the Battn's rifles.	
	24/1/18		Baths allotted to the Battn for Anti-Trench foot treatment	
	25/1/18		Battn relieved the 5th Scottish Rifles in the front line	
	26/1/18		Battn in front line	

Contd

T2134. Wt. W708—776. 500000. 4/15. Sir J. C. & S.

Instructions regarding War Diaries and Intelligence Summaries are contained in F. S. Regs., Part II. and the Staff Manual respectively. Title pages will be prepared in manuscript.

Sheet 3

WAR DIARY
or
INTELLIGENCE SUMMARY.
(Erase heading not required.)

Army Form C. 2118.

Place	Date	Hour	Summary of Events and Information	Remarks and references to Appendices
In the Field	27/1/18		Battn were relieved in the front line by the 4th Kings. On completion of relief the Battn moved to BRANDHOEK	
	28/1/18		Battn entrained at BRANDHOEK and detrained at WIZERNES. Marched to billets in LEULINES area	
	29/1/18		General cleaning up and company inspections.	
	30/1/18		— Do —	
	31/1/18		Coys at the disposal of Coy Commanders for training etc	

G. J. Money Major
Comdg 2nd Bn The Worcestershire Regt.

Instructions regarding War Diaries and Intelligence Summaries are contained in F. S. Regs., Part II. and the Staff Manual respectively. Title pages will be prepared in manuscript.

WAR DIARY
or
INTELLIGENCE SUMMARY.
(Erase heading not required.)

2 Worc Rgt

Army Form C. 2118.

Vol 43

Place	Date	Hour	Summary of Events and Information	Remarks and references to Appendices
In Field	Feb 1st		Battn fired on the range at QUELMES Inspection of Coys by C.O	
	Feb 2nd		Parade service at ETRETHEM	
	Feb 3rd		Coys continue training programme	
	Feb 4th		C Range at Q 35 C 18 allotted to Battn Musketry was fair 1st Queens left Bde to go to 98th	
	Feb 5th		Battn moved to SETQUES from LEULINE AREA F G C M assembled to try Sgt Day for drunkenness	
	Feb 6th		Coys continue training programme 8983 Sgt Adkins awarded Belgian Croix de guerre	
	Feb 7th		Coys continue training programme C.O inspected new draft of 61 physique good and generally a good draft Lecture for all the officers in the evening	
	8th Feb		Coys continued programme	
	Feb 9th		A R A Competition two platoons per Coy B Coy won	
	Feb 10th		Box Resp of Battn tested at ESQUERDES	
	Feb 11th		Coys continue programme of training "B" Coys platoon practice the assault	

Contd

5.43

Stat 2

Instructions regarding War Diaries and Intelligence Summaries are contained in F. S. Regs., Part II. and the Staff Manual respectively. Title pages will be prepared in manuscript.

WAR DIARY
or
INTELLIGENCE SUMMARY.
(Erase heading not required.)

Army Form C. 2118.

Place	Date	Hour	Summary of Events and Information	Remarks and references to Appendices
In the Field	F.11th		According to A R A rules	
	F.12th		Coys Continue training programme Bde final of A R A Competition B Coy won easily.	
	F.13th		Coys continue training programme All officers attended lecture on [illegible]	
	F.14th		Coys continue programme of work Baths at SETQUES allotted to Battn	
	F.15th		Low flying aeroplane demonstration at HALLINES	
	F.16		Parade Service at SETQUES	
	F.17		Coys Continue programme of work Divisional final of A R A competition "B" Coy second	
	F.18th		Battn parade for Counter attack Scheme at ESQUERDES	
	F.19th		Coys at disposal of Coy Commanders	
	F.20th		Battn move to St LAWRENCE CAMP at BRANDHOEK entrained at WIZERNES at 8 45 am	
	F.21st		Battn moved to YPRES entraining at BRANDHOEK at 12 noon	
	F.22nd		Battn parade for work on Corps defence lines	
	F.23rd		Coys at disposal of Coy Commanders	

T2134. Wt. W708—776. 500000. 4/15. Sir J. C. & S.

Contd

Sheet 3

Instructions regarding War Diaries and Intelligence Summaries are contained in F. S. Regs., Part II. and the Staff Manual respectively. Title pages will be prepared in manuscript.

WAR DIARY
or
INTELLIGENCE SUMMARY.
(Erase heading not required.)

Army Form C. 2118.

Place	Date	Hour	Summary of Events and Information	Remarks and references to Appendices
In the Field	Feb 24th		Battn paraded for work on Corps defence line	
	Feb 25th		Battn moved to Brigade Support at SEINE leaving YPRES at 5.30 pm relief completed at 11.30 pm	
	Feb 26		Battn in Support.	
	Feb 27		Battn in Support.	
	Feb 28		Battn in Support.	

[illegible] Lieut for Lt/Col
Commanding 2/Bn The Worcestershire Regt

T2134. Wt. W708—776. 500000. 4/15. Sir J. C. & S.

Instructions regarding War Diaries and Intelligence Summaries are contained in F. S. Regs., Part II. and the Staff Manual respectively. Title pages will be prepared in manuscript.

WAR DIARY
or
INTELLIGENCE SUMMARY.
(Erase heading not required.)

100/33

Army Form C. 2118.

2 Worc Rgt

Vol 44

Place	Date	Hour	Summary of Events and Information	Remarks and references to Appendices
[illegible]	1916 March			
	1st		Battalion in Support at SEINE.	
	2nd		Battalion relieved 16th K.R.R.C. in front line	
	3rd		Battalion in Line; Lieut. H. H. S. Laughton evacuated (Sick)	
	4th		Battalion in Line — Visited by Welsh M.P.'s and Major General Pinney and Brigadier — — Rev. T. V. Tanner C.F. rejoined.	
	5th		Battalion in Line	
	6th		Battalion relieved by 9th H.L.I. — moved back to Billets in YPRES	
	7th		General cleaning up and baths	
	8th		Musketry under O.C. Companies.	
	9th		Battalion on Working Party in Corps Defence Line — Summer time comes into force at 11.0 p.m.	
	10th		Battalion Parade for Divine Service.	
			Relieved 16th K.R.R.C. in support at SEINE — Capt. E. S. [illegible] wounded	
	11th		Battalion in Support	
	12th		Battalion in support, — Capt. E. S. [illegible] died of wounds	
	13th		Battalion in Support	

S 44

Instructions regarding War Diaries and Intelligence Summaries are contained in F. S. Regs., Part II. and the Staff Manual respectively. Title Pages will be prepared in manuscript.

WAR DIARY
or
INTELLIGENCE SUMMARY
(Erase heading not required.)

Army Form C. 2118.

Place	Date	Hour	Summary of Events and Information	Remarks and references to Appendices
In the Field	1918 March			
	14th		Relieved by 9th H.L.I. and go forward and relieve 16th K.R.R.C. in Front Line	
	15th		Battalion in Line	
	16th		Battalion in Line.	
	17th		Battalion in Line – One prisoner gives himself up to Left Front Company Patrol of 'B' Company captures 4 prisoners.	
	18th		Relieved by 9th H.L.I. and return to YPRES Capt. Morris-Jones M.C. (R.A.M.C.) evacuated (Sick)	
	19th		General cleaning up. Lieut. Jones (U.S.A.) A.M.C. joins Battalion.	
	20th		Battalion work on Corps Defence Line.	
	21st		Companies at disposal of O's. C. Companies for Musketry and Inspections F.G.C.M. – Trial of No. 13603 Pte. Bent	
	22nd		Companies entrain at ST. PIERRE SIDING preparatory to Battalion relieving 16th K.R.R.C. in Support at CORDIAL FACTORY. Capt. Adj. W.L. Smith rejoins from leave	
	23rd		Battalion in Support.	

Instructions regarding War Diaries and Intelligence Summaries are contained in F. S. Regs., Part II. and the Staff Manual respectively. Title Pages will be prepared in manuscript.

WAR DIARY
or
INTELLIGENCE SUMMARY
(Erase heading not required.)

Army Form C. 2118.

Place	Date	Hour	Summary of Events and Information	Remarks and references to Appendices
In the Field	1918 March			
	24th		Battalion in Front Line, relieving Right Front Company of 16th K.R.R.C., and Left Front Company of 1/6th West Yorks.	
	25th		Battalion in Front Line.	
	26th		Battalion in Front Line.	
	27th		Battalion in Front Line. Lieut Jones (U.S.A.) leaves for 101st F.A. Capt Boag R.A.M.C. joins Battalion.	
	28th		Battalion in Front Line. – Side-step southwards 1 Coy. Frontage. Bn. H.Q. move to RETALIATION FM.	
	29th		Battalion in Front Line. Lieut. L.R. Tilling wounded on patrol.	
	30th		Battalion relieved by 16th K.R.R.C. and move to YPRES.	
	31st		Battalion on Working Party building the Div. Reserve Line. Lieut. W.H. Smyth and 2Lt. E.W. Edmonds return from leave.	

G.F.L. Stones[?] Lieut.-Col.
Comdg. 2nd. Bn. The Worcestershire Regt.

2449 Wt. W14957/M90 750,000 1/16 J.B.C. & A. Forms/C.2118/12.

100th Brigade.

33rd Division.

2nd BATTALION

WORCESTERSHIRE REGIMENT

APRIL 1918.

Report on Operations attached.

Instructions regarding War Diaries and Intelligence Summaries are contained in F. S. Regs., Part II. and the Staff Manual respectively. Title pages will be prepared in manuscript.

33/120

Army Form C. 2118.

WAR DIARY
or
~~INTELLIGENCE~~ SUMMARY.
(*Erase heading not required.*)

APRIL 1918

2 Worc Regt

Vol 43

Place	Date	Hour	Summary of Events and Information	Remarks and references to Appendices
YPRES	1.4.18		Battalion in cellars in YPRES, in Bde support. Coys at disposal of Coy Officers for general cleaning up, kit inspections etc. Working party of 1 off and 80 OR provided to work under 222 Coy RE. Some promiscuous shelling of the city	
YPRES	2.4.18		One working party of 1 off 150 OR provided for 222 Coy RE. Remainder of Bn firing on the moat ranges. C.O. reconnoitred Div. Res. Line	
YPRES	3.4.18		Companies again firing all morning on moat ranges. Marching order & kit inspection at 2 pm. Rumours of the Division moving to ARRAS sector	
YPRES	4/4/18		Companies doing musketry, physical training etc. Lewis Guns sent to DADOS for overhauling	
BRANDHOEK ~~YPRES~~	5/4/18		Battalion left YPRES, and marched to BRANDHOEK on a wet drizzly morning, – accommodated in B Camp there, pending a further move.	
BRANDHOEK	6/4/18		Companies doing musketry & general training in the morning. A concert given to the Battalion in afternoon by 29th Div. Troup. Visit from Colonel Clarke of 4th Bn. At 12.00 pm Battalion moved off on march to PESELHOEK, where the Bde entrained. 2 Guns mounted on trucks for AA defence.	

S.45

2

Instructions regarding War Diaries and Intelligence Summaries are contained in F. S. Regs., Part II. and the Staff Manual respectively. Title pages will be prepared in manuscript.

WAR DIARY
or
~~INTELLIGENCE SUMMARY~~.
(Erase heading not required.)

Army Form C. 2118.

Place	Date	Hour	Summary of Events and Information	Remarks and references to Appendices
IZEL-LES-HAMEAU	7.4.18		Battalion detrained at about 6am at TINCQUES Station, marching from there to billets in village of IZEL-LES-HAMEAU. Batt in 3rd Army Reserve. Billets all good. H.L.I. in same village, also Bde H.Q.	
IZEL-LES-HAMEAU	8.4.18		Lewis Gun classes commenced, all coys fired on the ranges near the village. Lecture to Officers & NCOs in the school room at 6pm by the Commanding Officer - Illustration of dispositions etc	
IZEL-LES-HAMEAU	9.4.18		All companies doing range practise from 9.30 am to 1.0 pm. Classes as usual - 80 men under L. Gun training. Lecture by Div. Commander to Officers & NCOs of the Bde at 3pm, on recent fighting etc.	
IZEL-LES-HAMEAU	10.4.18		Bn passed starting point at 9am on march to SUS-ST-LEGER, to be in reserve to VI Corps. Recalled on line of march, and sent back to old billets - rumours of a strong enemy offensive near ARMENTIERES and BETHUNE. Ready to move at very short notice till orders in the evening sent the Bn marching to AUBIGNY, where the Bde entrained	
CAESTRE- NEUVE EGLISE	11.4.18		Bn detrained at CAESTRE. After taking up extra S.A.A., embussed to METEREN. Stream of refugees coming down the roads, laden with goods. No definite news - but great noise of artillery. Attached to IX Corps. Marched through BAILLEUL - all desolate & ruined, to RAVELSBERG, and there got into fighting order. Div Commander arrived before the Bn finally marched away, & gave orders, C.O. and Brigadier General went in advance to take	

T2134. Wt. W708—776. 500000. 4/15. Sir J. C. & S.

3

Instructions regarding War Diaries and Intelligence Summaries are contained in F. S. Regs., Part II. and the Staff Manual respectively. Title pages will be prepared in manuscript.

WAR DIARY
or
~~INTELLIGENCE SUMMARY.~~
(Erase heading not required.)

Army Form C. 2118.

Place	Date	Hour	Summary of Events and Information	Remarks and references to Appendices
(continued)				
NEUVE EGLISE	11-4-18		over our front. Attacked a position in Army Line, due N. of NEUVE EGLISE, relieving K.O.Y.L.I.	
NEUVE EGLISE	12-4-18		Quiet day, until attacked in evening. Attacks repulsed. Two patrols sent out in morning, both of which claimed many killed. Many enemy seen in & around PLOEGSTRAET WOOD, and in the fields towards ARMENTIERES. Heavy barrage on C Company - 12 casualties. A & B Coys in front line; D support & C Coy reserve. 'B' Echelon sent into front line - unknown to B.H.Q. & but attacked twice.	
NEUVE EGLISE ~~ARRAS~~	13-4-18		Enemy attacked & held NEUVE EGLISE until ejected by a counter attack from C Coy - in which 2LT GREEN killed, & 2LT VERNON wounded. Situation thoroughly restored. In evening 2 platoons of B Coy moved back into Bn reserve, and companies wheeled round to face their original right flank. Bn H.Q. established in MAIRIE, NEUVE EGLISE. Enemy put very strong barrage over, and attacked. Nothing more seen of CAPT PEAKE, or CAPT. MATTHEWS after 5pm. Siege of Bn H.Q. all night long. Enemy apparently all around our right flank.	
NEUVE EGLISE	14/4/18		Enemy seen on all sides. Sortie made from Bn H.Q. - was successful in driving the enemy completely away, & opening a way for communication. Many casualties	

T2134. Wt. W708—776. 500000. 4/15. Sir J. C. & S.

4

Instructions regarding War Diaries and Intelligence Summaries are contained in F. S. Regs., Part II. and the Staff Manual respectively. Title pages will be prepared in manuscript.

WAR DIARY
or
~~INTELLIGENCE~~ SUMMARY.
(Erase heading not required.)

Army Form C. 2118.

Place	Date	Hour	Summary of Events and Information	Remarks and references to Appendices
NEUVE EGLISE	14.4.18		from M.G. & Trench Mortar fire. Enemy attacked again in force at about 1.30 pm. MAIRIE evacuated at 1.45 pm – no word from companies obtainable, or from unit on our right. No casualties in evacuation though heavy M.G. fire brought to bear on path. Bn placed in Bde reserve	
HILL 70 N.E.	15.4.18		Remains of Bn trickling back all morning. At 3pm as result of a 'Stand to' Bn took up a reserve position on the ridge S of RAVESBERG, now held by the enemy.	
HILL 70 N.W. NEUVE EGLISE	16.4.18		Hard fighting. Bn now in front line – people in front having withdrawn. Attacks – heavy barrages & trench mortar fire. 9/N FUSILIERS counter-attacked & took over some of our front – only 5 officers being left	
HILL 70 N.W. NEUVE EGLISE	17.4.18		More attacks & heavy barrages throughout the day. French Artillery lending support. Finally relieved by KOYLI & YORKS & LANCS REGT.	
MONT DES CATS	18.4.18		Bn marched back to a camp near WESTOUTRE; after a rest marched on to the Monastery at MONT DES CATS. Visited by Bde & Div Commanders.	
MONT DES CATS	19.4.18		Muster parade of Men – approximate strength 300. Cleaning up & resting.	
NOORDPEENE	20.4.18		Bn marched from 6.30 am till 2.0 pm into billets near NOORDPEENE.	

T2134. Wt. W708–776. 500000. 4/15. Sir J. C. & S.

5

Instructions regarding War Diaries and Intelligence Summaries are contained in F. S. Regs., Part II. and the Staff Manual respectively. Title pages will be prepared in manuscript.

WAR DIARY
or
~~INTELLIGENCE~~ SUMMARY.
(Erase heading not required.)

Army Form C. 2118.

Place	Date	Hour	Summary of Events and Information	Remarks and references to Appendices
NOORDPEENE	21.4.18		Battalion paraded at 6.45 am for march to Div HQ at TROIS ROIS – turned back on line of march, & returned to billets. No work – Sunday. Back in XV Corps. Draft of 2 officers & 325 OR.	
NOORDPEENE	22.4.18		Battalion inspected, and addressed on its recent performance in the fighting at NEUVE EGLISE by Div Commander. Major TK PARDOE DSO arrived & took over command of the Battalion vice Lt Col S.S.L. STONEY MC	
NOORDPEENE	23/4/18		Companies being refitted with clothing etc, and carrying on with their programme of work. A draft of 11 officers joined the Battalion	
NOORDPEENE	24/4/18		In the morning Companies doing musketry, physical drill and arm drill etc, when not bathing in NOORDPEENE. C.O. interviewed newly joined officers at HQ at 6 pm	
NOORDPEENE	25/4/18		Companies continuing general training. All recommendations for services etc awards despatched to Bde. Readiness to move at ½ hours notice removed.	
ST MARIE CAPELL	26/4/18		Battalion & transport paraded at 7.30 am, & marched via BAVINCHOVE to aerodrome near ST. MARIE CAPELL, arriving about 12 noon. 19th Bde also here. Standing to ready to move at short notice. In 2nd Army Reserve. Lt H.S.L. WARD rejoined	

6.

Instructions regarding War Diaries and Intelligence Summaries are contained in F. S. Regs., Part II. and the Staff Manual respectively. Title pages will be prepared in manuscript.

WAR DIARY
or
~~INTELLIGENCE SUMMARY.~~

(Erase heading not required.)

Army Form C. 2118.

Place	Date	Hour	Summary of Events and Information	Remarks and references to Appendices
ST. MARIE CAPELL	27/4/18		Companies continuing their programme of work, L. Gun, bombing, PT. & N.C.O. classes commenced under Bde & Bn arrangements. Bn played 33rd R.G. Battalion at football	
			Div Concert party played in evening. Draft of 181 men from 14th Bn HANTS. REGT.	
ST. MARIE CAPELL	28/4/18		Div. Commander inspected yesterday's newly joined draft at 10.am. Draft very deficient of kit. Church parade under REV. E.V. TANNER. C.F. at 10.45am. One company firing on range. C.O. & 1 off per coy reconnoitred XV Corps Reserve line. Batt. warned of move to WARDRECQUES area tomorrow	
ST MARIE CAPELL	29/4/18		Bn paraded – & passed starting point at 9.0 am. – & began march via STAPLE and EBBLINGHEM to WARDRECQUES. Billeting party sent in advance. Beyond STAPLE, S.S.O.S. Division came with orders for Bde to turn about & return to the previous billets. Remainder of day spent in pitching tents etc.	
ST MARIE CAPELL	30/4/18		Bn. at 2 hrs notice to move. Companies doing musketry etc. and a practise attack under supervision of Major SIDNEY. R.C. Draft of 1 offr & 37 OR. 2Lt CROYDON TURNER appointed L.G.O. Conference at Bde HQ. attended by C.O. & 2nd in Command.	
			[illegible] Lt for Regt Cmmdg 2 [illegible] Regt	

11 July 1918.

IX Corps Special Order No 3.

The following record is to be made of the action described below:—

2nd Bn The Worcestershire Rgt

Neuve Eglise, 11 - 14 April 1918.

On the evening of the 11th April the 2nd Bn The Worcestershire Rgt took over a section of the Line to the East of Neuve Eglise. The night was spent in strengthening & concealing the defences of the position. The following morning, two strong patrols in charge of Lieuts NICKLIN and PARRY were pushed far out & quickly came into touch with superior enemy forces, which they fought to a standstill, inflicting heavy losses. They were withdrawn later, but not until the enemy had been obliged considerably to strengthen his patrols, & to postpone his impending attack.

During the day, enemy activity greatly increased, & the Battalion patrols were constantly engaged in stopping small parties who were endeavouring to work their way into the lines. At 7.30 in the evening, after heavy artillery & machine gun preparation, the enemy developed an attack to both right & left of the line held, breaking through to the right. He was ejected, & the position restored. Early on the morning of the 13th, he again attacked to the right, reached NEUVE EGLISE village & thus took the Battn line in the rear. An immediate counter attack not only turned the enemy out of the village, but led to the annihilation of the force which had gained a footing there & to the destruction of it's machine guns.

At 6 pm the enemy attacked in great strength on the left, & the whole Battn withdrew fighting to a new position. The Mairie was organised as a strong point; the garrison effectively dealt with Enemy parties which had crept up to the main cross roads on the right.

During the night, attack after attack was launched against the Battn, & eventually touch was lost with the Companies holding the left. They were last heard of holding on against overwhelming odds, fighting it out to the last.

Meanwhile the enemy had crept nearer & nearer to the Mairie, which was held by Battn HQrs. At dawn on the 14th he was seen to be occupying NEUVE EGLISE in strength, & soon after, the Mairie was completely surrounded. 2/Lt JOHNSON at once volunteered to try & work his way through to the Brigade & report the situation. His gallant attempt was unsuccessful, & he did not return.

Clever manoeuvering & well directed fire forced the enemy to relinquish his hold & to retire to the high ground on the right, & to the Church on the left. 2/Lt CROWE with a small party worked round the flank of the former position, & surprising the enemy, forced him further up the rise. The success of this feint was completed by a very daring sortie led by the same officer & 2/Lt POINTON, & supported by accurate fire from the Mairie, which compelled the Germans to withdraw to the centre of the village.

Early in the afternoon the enemy was observed to be preparing for a violent attack upon the Mairie. A withdrawal was decided upon, & in spite of heavy fire carried out without loss, to the Railway, where British troops had already taken up their positions.

By their well planned & spirited defence under very difficult conditions, the Battn kept the enemy at bay for three days, without rest, & in the face of greatly superior numbers. This patrol work delayed & harassed the preparation of attacks; rapidity of counter-attacks, coupled with skilful disposition of forces in response to every enemy move, obliged him time after time to relinquish his gains; tenacity when all seemed hopeless, opened a way to safety; while the daring & gallantry of individual officers & men did much to prevent the effective use of the larger forces at the Enemy's disposal, & exacted a heavy price for every yard of ground gained.

(Signed) R.L. Montgomery
for
Brig. Gen
General Staff, IX Corps.

Report on the part taken by the 2nd Worcestershire Regiment in the defence of NEUVE EGLISE April 11th to April 14th, 1918.

On the evening of April 11th the Battalion took over the Army Line E. of NEUVE EGLISE, then held by the 1/4th K.O.Y.L.I., this latter unit on relief prolonged the line from my left flank.

The dispositions for defence were as follows :-

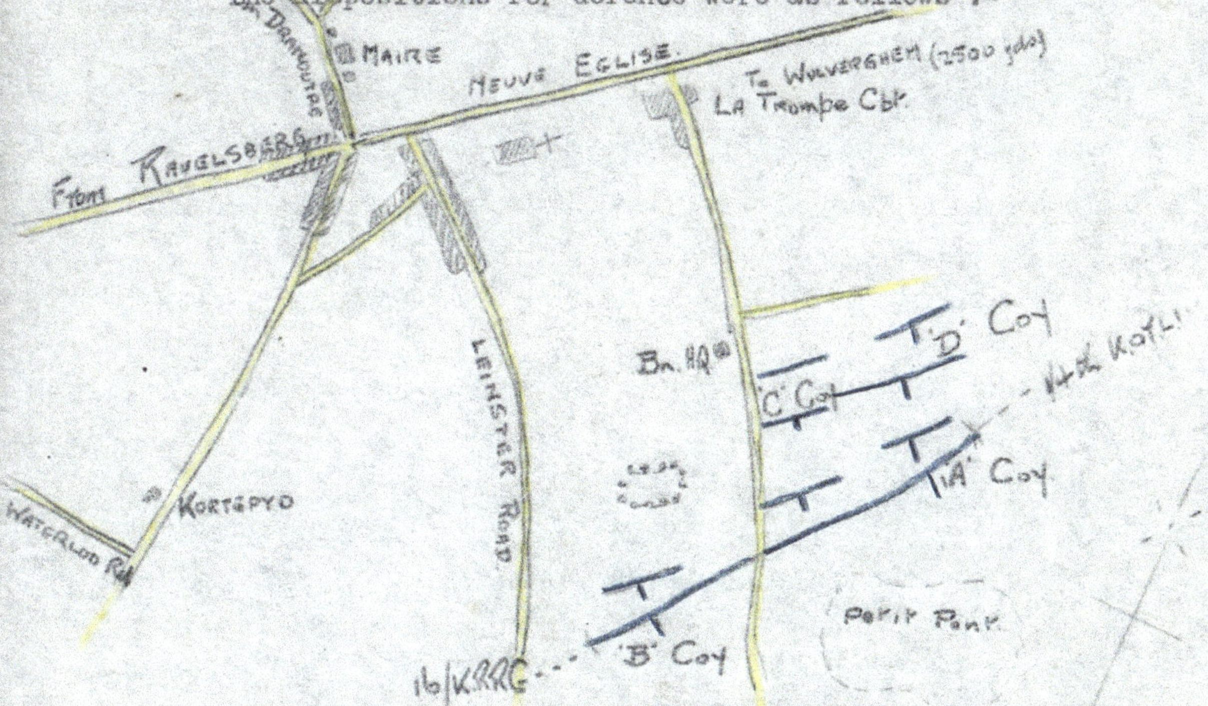

A and B Companies in the front line with D and C Companies in close support to them respectively.

As it appeared clear that my left flank was the most threatened I withdrew C Company to a position of Reserve and ordered it to dig in along the lane which crossed the LA TROMPE CBT. - PETIT PONT RD., close to Battalion H.Qs. (which was in a cement dugout there).

By daylight on the 12th this Company was well dug in and screened from view by the hedge which ran along the lane.

At dawn on April 12th, acting on instructions from Brigade I pushed out two strong patrols (25 and a Lewis Gun), each under an Officer (2nd Lts. NICKLIN and PARRY), their orders were to go out beyond the Army Line and locate and engage the enemy, the object being to deceive the latter as to our real line of defence. These patrols almost immediately got into touch with superior forces of Germans whom they engaged and held at bay inflicting heavy losses upon them, and it was not till later in the day when, owing to heavy hostile shelling and enveloping pressure by increased enemy numbers and Machine Guns, were these patrols forced to withdraw to our lines. They rendered a most splendid service by thus considerably delaying the pending enemy attack.

Throughout the 12th a continuous stream of small parties of Germans could be seen, with the naked eye, moving in a S. direction from MESSINES RIDGE towards PLOEGSTEERT WOOD. German artillery also came into action in full view of our positions and opened fire at almost point blank range.

Whilst this irregular movement was taking place across our front small parties of enemy trickled across the country towards our line sometimes coming clearly into view, and then disappearing again in the folds of the ground and behind hedges. They kept no formation. Some wore equipment and packs, others did not. Some mounted men also were seen moving amongst these parties of Germans.

Fire was not opened from the Army Line at this period, as the enemy were not close enough and the intention then was to conceal our real line of defence, our advanced patrols however, engaged these parties of the enemy.

A7

A hostile 'plane came over during the morning and locating our advanced patrols, dropped lights, whereupon the latter were almost immediately shelled by German artillery.

Considerable movement developed along the whole Brigade Sector about mid-day. Enemy M.G's seemed to increase in number and their fire was very active being directed all over our position.

I was not quite satisfied as regards my right flank and foreseeing the posibility of an attack from this point upon the village, sent a platoon from C Company (Reserve) to occupy the further hedge of the enclosure immediately in support of B Company (front right).

Towards evening enemy activity showed a marked increase along the whole Brigade Sector, the village was heavily shelled throughout, also very heavy M.G. fire.

At about 7.30 p.m. the 1/4th K.O.Y.L.I. were attacked and a part of the enemy approached my left, but were easily driven off.

The dispositions of the Battalion were as follows :-
(7.30 p.m. 12th April).-

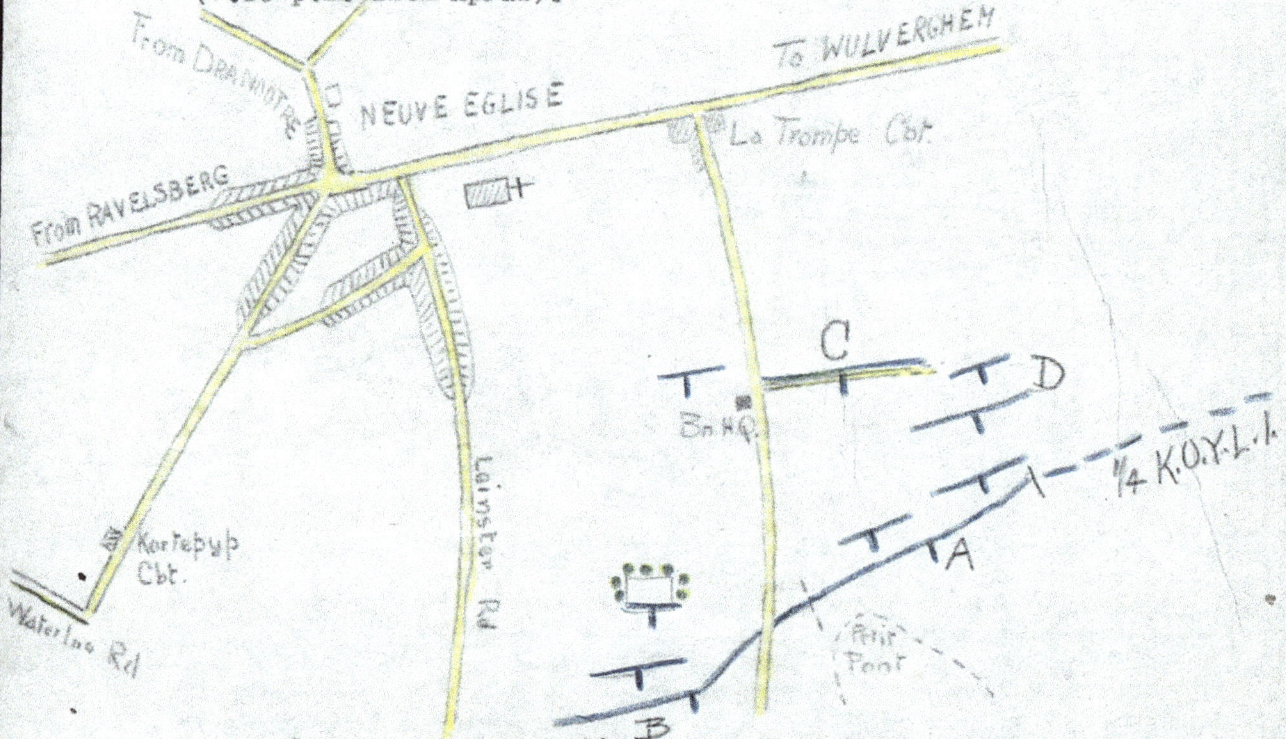

Almost at the same time I received the report that the 16th K.R.R.C., on my immediate right had been attacked and their line broken, so I immediately ordered C Company (Reserve) to form a defensive flank across this portion of NEUVE EGLISE which appeared to be in danger.

The positions to which C Company was directed were as follows:-

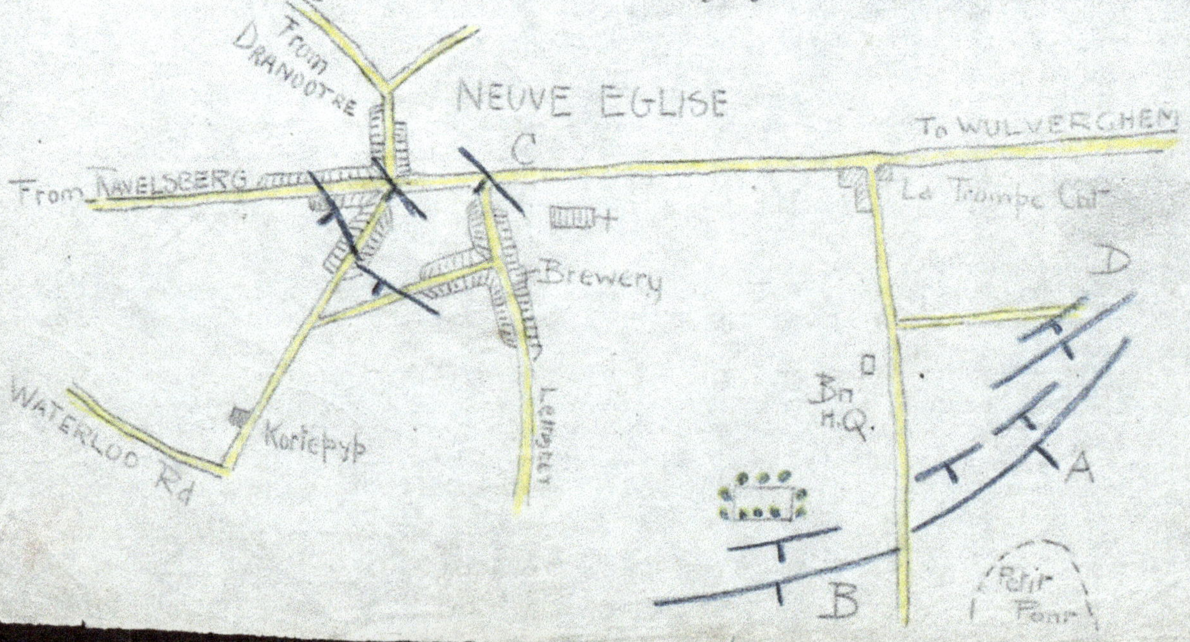

Information being received that the line held by the K.R.R.C. Had been re-established the above dispositions were not made until the following morning, (13th).

During the night Battalion H.Qs. moved to the Brewery, here I was more centrally placed and in close touch with the units on my flanks, moreover, LA TROMPE CBT. - PETIT PONT RD. was under direct observation by the enemy, where all movement had to be done under direct M.G.fire.

Early on the morning of the 12th the enemy broke through the K.R.R.C., reached the village and got past the Brewery and my H.Qs. 2nd Lieut. Pointon collected all available men at H.Qs., rushed to the cross roads W. of the Church, at the same time I ordered C Company to immediately counter-attack the enemy and occupy those positions I had indicated on the previous evening. This counter-attack was carried out promptly and thoroughly, with the reseult that the enemy's stay in the village was short, for withdrawing down the LEINSTER RD. he was caught between our counter-attack and a party of the Hallamshire Rgt., who were then coming up. All these Germans were accounted for, some 60 being killed and about 20 taken prisoner, besides about 6 machine guns, these latter were destroyed as it was not possible then to get them away.

The dispositions of the Battalion were now as follows :- (mid-day April 13th).-

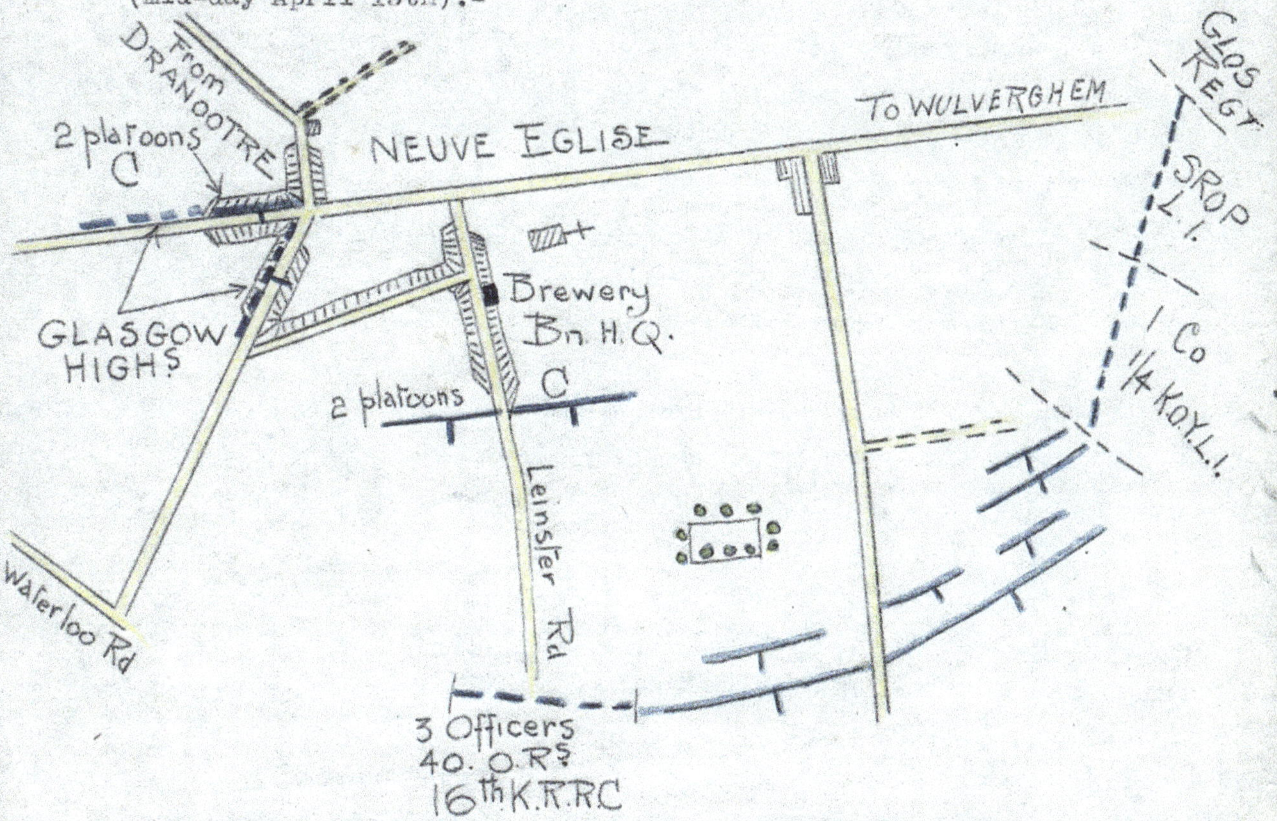

Early in the afternoon an Officer of the Glasgow Highlanders and two platoons reported to me at the Brewery and asked for instructions. I therefore ordered him to prolong the right of my Reserve Coy. (C) then thrown across LEINSTER RD., and to endeavour to obtain touch with a party of his own Battalion, believed to be on the NEUVE EGLISE-KORTEPYP CABT. RD. A portion of my Reserve Coy. were then in touch with some Glasgow Highlanders on the NEUVE EGLISE - RAVELSBERG RD.

Until about mid-day I had been in telephonic communication with the O.C., Glasgow Highlanders, but this had now ceased.

During the afternoon I ordered the following dispositions :-

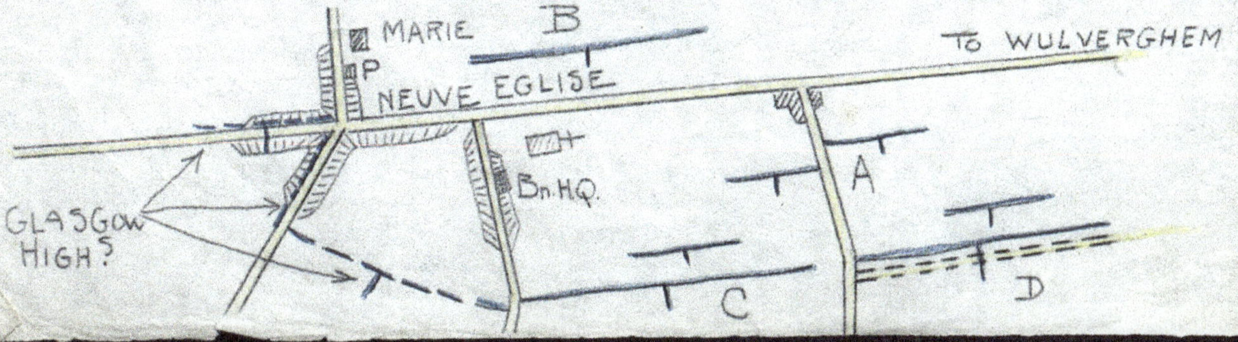

That portion of C Company then holding the cross roads of the village and were in touch with the Glasgow Highlanders on the RAVELSBERG - NEUVE EGLISE RD., was to rejoin its Company at LEINSTER RD. at dusk, when the above dispositions would be made.

I considered this alteration of my line necessary in view of the fact that my right flank was now almost completely in the air and the unit on my left, had, with the exception of one Company, withdrawn from the Army Line, and that one still remaining had thrown back across the NEUVE EGLISE - WULVERGHEM RD.

B Company was to move to the N. side of the village by the Church and be in Battalion Reserve.

These above moves by Companies were to be carried out with the greatest caution, one party covering the other's withdrawal with fire.

At about 6 p.m. I received a message from O.C., A Company, saying that the enemy were attacking in strength and that if his line was not to be broken it was necessary to carry out the new arrangement immediately. I therefore ordered my front Companies to immediately withdraw fighting, to their new positions.

At 6.30 p.m. I moved Battalion H.Qs. to the MAIRIE and at once decided to hold it as a strong point, and issued instructions for its defence as follows :-

2 platoons were to be held as final reserve in the cellars,

1 platoon in addition to H.Qs. personnel were to defend the building.

1 platoon to occupy the house marked P.

Lewis Guns were to be placed in position on the ground floor behind windows and to cover the ground E. of the MAIRIE and also the main roads of the village and Church area.

3 riflemen were to man each window.

A M.G. which had just reported to me, was ordered to assist the Lewis Guns.

The platoon allotted to the house marked P. was to hold the road and generally act as a buffer to the MAIRIE.

At about 8 p.m. the O.C., B Company arrived at the MAIRIE with only two platoons, he reported to me that on the request from Os.C., A and D Companies, he had sent a platoon to each of them as they were being very hard pressed by the enemy whilst carrying out the re-arrangement of their line. There was now very heavy M.G. and rifle fire all along the village and a good deal of shelling over the village.

It was impossible now for two platoons to be held as a final reserve, so half a platoon was placed in the house marked P. and a large supply of bombs were issued (this house was about 40 yards in front of the MAIRIE). The remaining one and a half platoons and Battalion H.Qs. manned the MAIRIE.

Reliefs were arranged so that a certain number of fresh men were ready to relieve those on duty. A large supply of bombs was found and they were issued out.

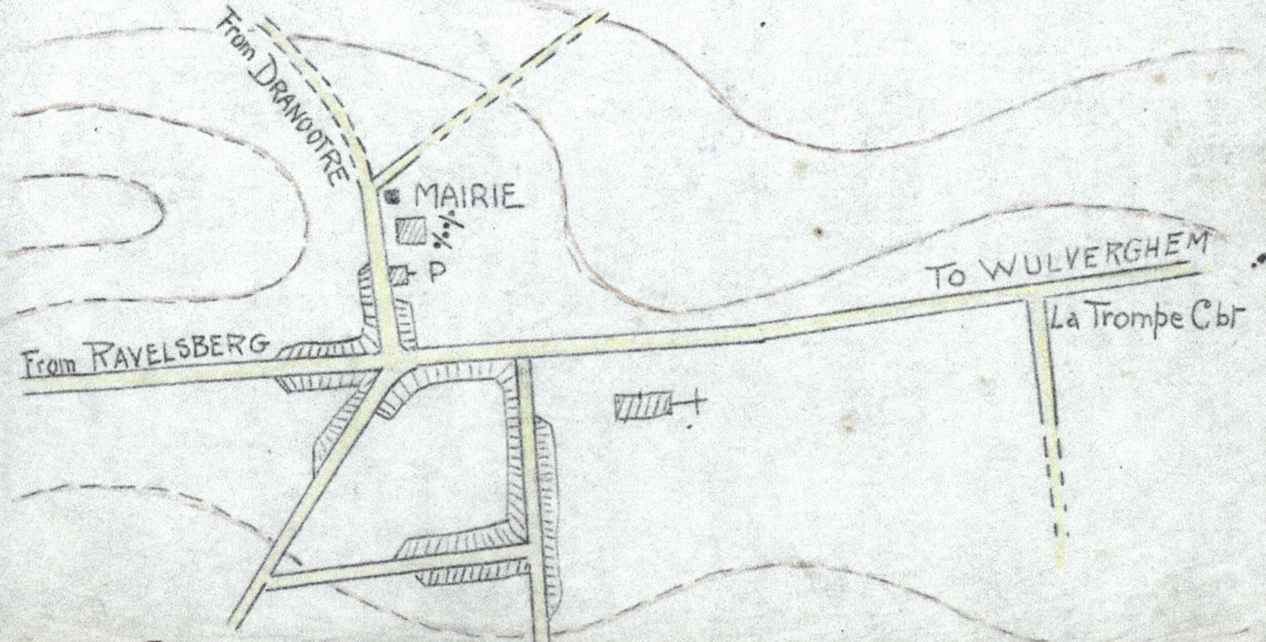

Runners who were sent forward to the front line Companies to ascertain the situation there and to report the position of the new Battalion H.Qs., did not return.

Almost as soon as it was dark a very light was fired about 80 yards distant from the MAIRIE and in line with the Church, this was followed a few minutes later by more very lights, by the light of which a party of about 12 Germans were detected moving round the left of the building. Our M.G. immediately opened fire, whereupon the Germans withdrew leaving one dead on the ground. Shortly after this a very sharp M.G. fire was directed on to our M.G. putting it out of action.

Much activity was noticed at the cross roads of the village from which point very heavy M.G. fire was directed down the DRANOUTRE RD. in the direction of the MAIRIE, numerous very lights were fired from the high ground on the right.

A motor machine gunner also had reported at Battalion H.Qs. earlier in the evening, engaged the enemy M.G. at the cross roads, when a lively duel kept up for a considerable time until the motor Machine gunner was wounded.

Attempts were then made to silence the M.G. at the cross roads by means of rifle grenades fired from the garden in front of the MAIRIE. This met with success,for the M.G. fire down the road now ceased, but heavy fire from the direction of the Church still continued.

At about 1 a.m. movement was heard on the road which ran past the MAIRIE and a party of Germans were seen to be approaching from the rear of the building, the sentries at once opened fire and the Germans cleared off leaving one, a Company Sgt. Major, lying on the road, this man very severely wounded was taken into the Aid Post and interrogated.

The situation had become somewhat quieter, but towards morning the garrison of house P was forced to withdraw to the MAIRIE owing to heavy M.G. fire and bombs, which made communication between them and H.Qs. most difficulty.

A bomb was thrown from the rear of the MAIRIE and actually fell into one of the cellars, through the window which faced our rear, causing two casualties.

It was a very dark night making it extremely difficult to see exactly what was happening, and to obtain reports from the Companies was now impossible, for those runners sent out did not return, the enemy appeared to have managed to get almost completely round our position.

The greatest vigilance had to be maintained from all quarters of the MAIRIE. As soon as it became sufficiently light, the enemy was seen to be occupying the village in strength, movement could be observed in almost every house and also in the open ground by the Church. Lewis gun and rifle fire was at once opened on all hostile parties.

Trench Mortar shells began to fall about the MAIRIE, several direct hits being obtained two burst inside the rooms causing many casualties. M.G. fire increased from the direction of the Church, the cross roads and also the high ground on our right, whilst small groups of Germans were seen to rush forward. Sniping was directed upon our back windows and doors from the outhouses.

At about 8 a.m. we were absolutely surrounded and it was clear that a determined assaultwas imminent.

2nd Lt. Johnson begged permission to try and get through to the Brigade, giving him the situation, verbally, I very reluctantly consented to his request. This very gallant Officer has not since been heard of.

A further attempt was made to communicate with our troops on the left, though it was not known where they were, one of two runners who attempted to cross from the outhouses to the lane in rear, was shot the instant he emerged from the building, the other had to come back.

Every/

Every effort was now directed towards checking the enemy's further approach, so a lewis gun was mounted in one of the top windows of the MAIRIE and every available sniper was posted in position of observation. 2nd Lt. Turley directed rifle grenade fire into the outhouses and also on to the road and adjacent houses. This combined action soon took effect, for the sniping from the rear ceased and the enemy were noticed clearing out of the houses near P. But he still maintained his hold on the high ground on our right and also the Church area; certain it was, however, that a way to our rear must be kept open, otherwise our position would very soon become untenable.

2nd Lt. Crowe therefore volunteered to take a small party with a view to clearing the enemy from our rear, this very gallant Officer met with considerable success for on reaching the road a hostile party with M.G. was encountered and driven off on to the high ground. Leaving 2 N.C.O's and 5 men here to guard the road, 2nd Lt. Crowe went forward with only 2 men in order to work round the outer flank of their party, which he succeeded in doing, and by opening rapid fire in co-operation with those he had left on the road under 2nd Lt. Pointon, forced the Germans to withdraw still further up the hill.

By a determined and quick forward movement now by both 2nd Lts. Crowe and Pointon, the latter having being reinforced from the MAIRIE the enemy was pushed back to the line of the houses leaving many dead on the ground and 3 machine guns captured.

A line of defence was now established close to the crest of the high ground and a strong post on the road maintaining communication with Battalion H.Qs.

During the above described very daring and energetic sortie on the part of 2nd Lts. Crowe and Pointon, hot fire was kept up from the defenders of the MAIRIE, fire being directed onto the houses and the cross roads, where the Germans offered a fine target.

The Germans now were seen to be withdrawing by small groups to the centre of the village, this opportunity I at once seized of once again trying to get in touch with units on either flank, runners were therefore sent with messages requesting the O.C's. the units concerned to co-operate in a combined and converging attack upon the centre of NEUVE EGLISE.

I received a reply from the O.C., unit on my left, who had moved back to the N. of NEUVE EGLISE, saying that he would do all he could, but no reply came from my right.

An Officer from the VIII Corps School Bn. came to my H.Qs. during this lull (about 11 a.m.) and stated that he had been ordered forward with a party to reconnoitre the situation. I gave him a letter to "O.C., troops DRANOUTRE" stating the situation, and requesting that a Battalion if possible be sent up without delay, and that if the O.C., would report to me I would direct him: this I considered most urgent if the village of NEUVE EGLISE was to be saved.

At about 1 p.m. what appeared to be a party of Highlanders was seen moving through the village from the rear of the Church and towards LEINSTER RD. I therefore concluded that the assistance I had asked for from my flanks was actually being effected. But this almost as quickly proved to be a delusion, for a few minutes later Germans were seen forming up in the street by the brewery.

Coinciding with this the bombardment of the MAIRIE by trench mortars re-opened, also M.G. and rifle fire was again directed from the high ground on the right and also the Church - several casualties occurred in the MAIRIE.

By the numbers of the enemy in the village and the activity of his M.G's on our flanks, it was clear that another and more violent attack on the MAIRIE was determined. From the top windows the German troops were to be seen moving up in fours. (1.30 p.m.).

The covering party was still in position on the hill, but these men could not maintain their ground if attacked in any force.

It was impossible to reinforce them as all forward movement came under close M.G. fire.

The troops from DRANOUTRE which I had hoped to see had not turned up and I knew that if the enemy again succedded in surrounding the MAIRIE all our communications would be finally closed.

I therefore came to the decision that our position had to be given up in order to save Battalion H.Qs. and to regain touch with those of our troops on either flank.

At 1.45 p.m. I ordered all in the MAIRIE to evacuate. 2nd Lt. Crowe made his way to our men in position on the hill and the post on the road, instructing them to cover the withdrawal of the remainder.

The withdrawal of the entire garrison and also the covering party was effected without loss, in spite of a very heavy and continuous enemy M.G. fire which continued to sweep the slopes of the ground until the railway line was reached. 3 of our wounded who could not be moved, were left behind in the cellars of the MAIRIE, their wounds previously being dressed.

Withdrawing across the railway we passed through positions in rear held by our troops. 2nd Lt. Pointon who had moved towards the DRANOUTRE RD. was fired upon by British sentries who thought we were hostile troops.

Early on the morning of 14th runners who had been sent out from Battalion H.Qs. to find out the position of those units on our flanks, reached their positions near the railway, when they were told that there were no British troops to their front, that these positions were then the British front line..

Passing through these troops I reported to the G.O.C., 175th Inf. Bde., who directed me to LOCRE when I ascertained the position of 100th Inf. Bde., to whom I reported at about 6.30 p.m. (14th April).

The last occasion on which communication with the Companies of the Battalion was effected was at about 6 p.m. on 13th, when O.C., A Company sent a message saying that he was being heavily attacked and required ammunition, at the same time requesting permission to carry out <u>then</u> the new dispositions which were to take effect at dusk.

After that every attempt to gain touch failed.

A runner who was sent from Battalion H.Qs. at about 7 p.m. to the Brewery, the Battalion H.Qs. we had just handed over to O.C., C Company, in order to take a message to O.C., C Company, returned to say that Germans were in occupation of the Brewery.

Other runners sent forward and to the flanks, from that hour on, failed to return. Similarly no further information of any kind came from the Companies to Battalion H.Qs.

A Sergt. of the 16th K.R.R.C. reported to me on the evening of 13th at the MAIRIE at about 7 p.m. and said that he and 3 Officers and 40 O.R. had been on the right of my B Company throughout that day, but had to withdraw. He asked for orders. I instructed him to report to my O.C., C Company at the Brewery, under whose command he would then come.

This party was later seen moving along the NEUVE EGLISE - WULVERGHEM RD. in the neighbourhood of LA TROMPE CBT. From this it would seem probable that on approaching the Brewery they found this latter place in the hands of the Germans.

Whilst in the MAIRIE there were some 20 - 30 casualties amongst the defenders, all with the exceptionof 3 as already stated, were evacuated.

During the operations in NEUVE EGLISE and those subsequently at Hill 70 (N.E. BAILLEUL) the following points were prominent.

(1)/

(1) The enemy preceded his attacks by sending forward small parties under specially selected senior N.C.O's who showed the greatest leadership and bravery. Accompanied by M.G's these parties siezed the earlies opportunity of penetrating into our position and then establishing their M.G's - thus to some extent securing their ground - these advanced parties paved the way for further numbers who followed up close behind with more M.G's and Trench Mortars, these latter weapons engaged our points which offered a special resistance to their advance.

(2) The rapidity and precision with which the enemy located all prominent features in our positions, and on to these prominent features, vigorous M.G. fire was instantly directed.

(3) Enemy artillery appeared to work in closest liaison with the infantry, even firing at point blank range.

(4) The use made of enemy aeroplanes to locate our advanced patrols, by dropping coloured lights, whereupon enemy artillery opened fire.

(5) During daylight the time was employed by the enemy in dribbling forward men in very small and irregular numbers, to a position of assembly, from which, when dusk came on, attacks in strength and regular formations were launched.

(6) Very lights were extensively employed at night by the enemy, either to.-
(i) Direct his columns in rear, or
(ii) to give the line for his artillery, or
(iii) to signal his progress.

(7) Where our posts were placed in the open or in front of hedges these positions were very quickly discovered by the enemy and consequently soon became the targets for his guns.

Had they been placed close behind hedges, they would have been screened both from view of the enemy observers and scouts and also from his aeroplanes, whilst at the same time would have been afforded the protection against being rushed and fire being directed through the hedges. Moreover, concealed communication to and from these posts would have been maintained, whereas communication in most cases, sooner or later became almost impossible when exposed to view of the enemy.

(8) The urgent need for infantry being supported with trench mortars and Stokes gunners was demonstrated both in the MAIRIE and at Hill 70. At the latter place when the enemy gained a footing in the wood about 300 yards in front of our posts, L.G's and M.G's failed to dislodge him, our artillery failed to get the range to this wood and direct infantry assaults, though attempted met with little success, besides being too costly. T.M's or Stokes guns could have, it is certain, made the enemy's position in this wood untenable.

(9) In the absence of aeroplane observation by our artillery, F.O.O's are imperative, and in their connections either communication by means of 'phone or visual must be maintained. Should this be impossible some kind of signal to show artillery whether they are shelling short or over could be used.

(10)/

(10) We suffered agreat number of casualties from our own shells falling short, this was particularly regrettable for our own barrage came down with such intensity on our posts that it appeared that these posts were included in the S.O.S. line.

(11) From the point of view of a Battalion Commander in the line I would like to suggest that all M.G's and Stokes guns, Trench Mortars,etc., be placed under his command in so far as their position is concerned, for in the light of recent events, when the subordinate Officer Commanding these smaller units became a casualty, the N.C.O. remaining in charge invariably came to me for instructions, which I forthwith issued, and it seems reasonable to say that the Battalion Commander has a clearer picture of the situation than these above referred to units.

(12) As regards posts. Instead of the system of having a few large posts, it might be suggested that smaller and more numerous posts could be employed with advantage. Knowing the rapidity with which the enemy locates our posts and then turns the attention of his trench mortars and artillery on to these posts it would perhaps be advisable to dig these smaller posts and employ a few men (6 - 8) to garrison them, with alternative small posts in front, so that in the event of any one post becoming untenable there would be another one to go forward to, and at the same time should any posts be hit by a direct shell then the loss would be essentially small.

That very dangerous and disastrous tendency to fall back, by the survivors of posts which have become untenable by reason of direct hits by shell fire, would then be provided against if there were alternative short lengths of trench close at hand.

The most terribly shaken soldier will readily jump into the nearest trench that gives even small cover, but in the absence of any such cover, he goes back.

(13) On these occasions when the enemy obtained a footing in our positions, by means of an immediate counter-attack he was invariably ejected, having obtained a footing he must not be given time to secure that footing, but be attacked whilst he is still 'getting his breath' and before he can get his M.G's into position.

(14) In spite of the generous provision of Lewis Guns per Company, application had to be made during the above described operations for more to replace those lost.

The supply of S.A.A. was abundant, although heavy demands were made by M.G.Corps units at Hill 70.

(15) Throughout the operations in NEUVE EGLISE, on no occasion did those units on either flank inform me of their intention to withdraw, the result being my total ignorance of their movements though I made frequent efforts to keep in touch with them.

(Sgd) G.J.L.STONEY, Major,
2nd Worcestershire Regiment.

1.

Instructions regarding War Diaries and Intelligence Summaries are contained in F. S. Regs., Part II. and the Staff Manual respectively. Title pages will be prepared in manuscript.

WAR DIARY
or
~~INTELLIGENCE SUMMARY.~~
(Erase heading not required.)

Army Form C. 2118.

2 Docs.
Vol 46

Place	Date	Hour	Summary of Events and Information	Remarks and references to Appendices
HEURINGHEM	1.5.18		The Battalion paraded at 8.30 a.m. in the aerodrome, near ST. MARIE CAPELL, and marched via STAPLE and RENESCURE, to HEURINGHEM, not far from ST. OMER. Dinners served on the road, during an hour's halt at midday. 3 men fell out on the march, and were all admitted to Field Ambulance. Billets all quite good. Visit from Divisional Commander in the evening	
	2.5.18		The Commanding Officer inspected the latest draft, from Worc. Regt. and from Hants Regt., at 9.30 am. Companies doing field work, and physical training on a large common near to billets. Bde L.G. and Bombing classes still continuing. Warning of a move tomorrow to STEENVOORDE area by bus. Conference of officers at BHQ. 6pm	
	3.5.18		Battalion doing field operations - a practise attack & defence scheme - in the morning, in the woods and on the common allotted as training area. After 2 pm Bn. standing by, ready to embus - which it did at 6.20 pm. Route - ARQUES, CASSEL, STEENVOORDE, where Bn debussed in the dark, and after marching for about an hour arrived at a field in which the whole Bde is bivouacked.	
NE of STEENVOORDE.	4.5.18.		Tents and shelters drawn, and erected by the companies. Classes continued under their instructors. Visitors from 3rd Bn, which is billeted not far away, and expecting to entrain shortly for the South.	

S.46

2

Instructions regarding War Diaries and Intelligence Summaries are contained in F. S. Regs., Part II. and the Staff Manual respectively. Title pages will be prepared in manuscript.

WAR DIARY
~~or~~
INTELLIGENCE SUMMARY.
(*Erase heading not required.*)

Army Form C. 2118.

Place	Date	Hour	Summary of Events and Information	Remarks and references to Appendices
NE of STEENVOORDE	5.5.18		Divine service under Rev E. V. TANNER R.C. – very wet and showery for the parade. Battalion to move in the morning	
SHEET 27 L.15.c.8.8.	6.5.18		Battalion paraded early in the field, passing starting point at 5.30am, and marched to a new bivouac, near POPERINGHE, at 27/L.15.c.8.8. Bivouacs shelters were erected in a little coppice – camouflage being greatly resorted to, as this area is within direct observation from KEMMEL HILL. The Bde is here in Divisional Support: Coy continued training – classes as usual. Brigadier visited Bn. in the evening	
do	7.5.18		Bn prepared to move at short notice – the front being unsettled, and an attack expected on Div. front. Rum issue to the men at night; this place is very damp, and an epidemic of ... & influenza is running through the Bn.	
do.	8/5/18		CO of 10th Bn paid a visit, re the transfer of SGT-MAJOR FARLEY to this Bn. At 1.30 pm, on receipt of orders, Bn paraded and marched into position of Div support. The move is due to an enemy attack on Div. front S.E of DICKEBUSH LAKE. Companies in fighting order – Minimum clothes left behind. Billets much better than those just left. New position N.W. of BUSSEBOOM. 28/G.16.b.4.4.	

T2134. Wt. W708–776. 500000. 4/15. Sir J. C. & S.

3.

Instructions regarding War Diaries and Intelligence Summaries are contained in F. S. Regs., Part II. and the Staff Manual respectively. Title pages will be prepared in manuscript.

WAR DIARY
~~or~~
INTELLIGENCE ~~SUMMARY.~~
(Erase heading not required.)

Army Form C. 2118.

Place	Date	Hour	Summary of Events and Information	Remarks and references to Appendices
NE of BUSSEBOOM. 28/G.11.b.4.4	9.5.18		Bn 'stood to' at 4.15 am, and was ready to move at very shortest notice. O.C. Coys reconnoitred portions of the defensive system ~~to the~~ front, in the morning with the C.O. Coys practising advancing in artillery formation. A counter attack by French troops and 19th Bde completely restored the situation in front.	
do.	10/5/18		Bn "stood to" at 4.0 am. More defensive lines and routes of approach reconnoitred by the C.O with company officers. Companies training, and Lewis Gun classes commenced. Visit from Brigadier General.	
do	11/5/18		Situation much quieter and apparently completely restored. An enemy counter attack no longer expected. HAMERTINGHE and BRANDHOEK lines reconnoitred by C.O. & 1 officer per company. No further 'stand to' required in the morning.	
do	12/5/18		Minimum reserves rejoined in the evening. H.Q. moved to an empty house at 28/G.10.a.5.1. - though companies remained in their same farm-house billets. Bde from today in II Corps Reserve; the old Divisional front having been taken over by the French troops.	

4.

Instructions regarding War Diaries and Intelligence Summaries are contained in F. S. Regs., Part II. and the Staff Manual respectively. Title pages will be prepared in manuscript.

WAR DIARY

~~or~~

~~INTELLIGENCE SUMMARY.~~

(*Erase heading not required.*)

Army Form C. 2118.

Place	Date	Hour	Summary of Events and Information	Remarks and references to Appendices
W. of BRANDHOEK 28/G.10.a.5.1.	13/5/18		Programme of work made out & issued to the companies; more classes started.	
do	14/5/18		Companies specialising in "open warfare" training – practising attacks on strong points, pillboxes etc. A Company moved to new billets in ST. LAWRENCE CAMP, where Bn. was often billeted in the winter. Some little gas shelling after dark.	
do	15/5/18		Owing to the continued hot weather, training henceforth carried out in shirt sleeves and parades commence at 6 a.m. in order that work may be done in the cool hours of the day. CAPT HOPKINS M.C. rejoined Bn. on completing six months tour of duty at home.	
do	16/5/18		Coys continuing programme of work – & practise of open warfare operations. Some gas shelling at night, causing B Company to move out of its billets at about 11 pm for about an hour.	
do.	17/5/18		Companies training. POPERINGHE shelled in afternoon. Heavy barrage fire on the front at about 9.30 pm.	
do.	18/5/18		Test of load for a L.G. limber. Practise parade of composite company for the Army Commander's inspection.	

51

Instructions regarding War Diaries and Intelligence Summaries are contained in F. S. Regs., Part II. and the Staff Manual respectively. Title Pages will be prepared in manuscript.

WAR DIARY
or
~~INTELLIGENCE SUMMARY~~

(Erase heading not required.)

Army Form C. 2118.

Place	Date	Hour	Summary of Events and Information	Remarks and references to Appendices
Nr BRANDHOEK 28/G.10.a.5.1	19/5/18		Church parade under Rev E V TANNER MC	
do.	20/5/18		Heavy fire along the front in early morning – a successful attack by the French. Parade of composite company, north of the YPRES–POPERINGHE road, under the Adjutant in the morning, and in the afternoon, under Major STONEY MC.	
do	21/5/18		Coy did a short route march 6am – 8.30am – & later in the morning practised an immediate counter attack. At 5pm composite company paraded ~~at~~ under Major STONEY MC practising for the parade tomorrow for Army Commander.	
do	22/5/18		Representative company from the Battalion marched, under the command of Major STONEY MC to the Bde assembly ground (28/A27.c.5.0) to take part in an inspection of 100th Bde by 2nd Army Commander, General Sir H.C.O. PLUMER. The inspection & march past, was followed by a congratulatory address on the fighting at NEUVE EGLISE. At 3pm F.G.C.M. held at Bn H.Q.	
do	23/5/18		Classes training as usual. Orders to relieve a Bn 98th Bde tomorrow near HOUTKERQUE.	

2449 Wt. W14957/M90 750,000 1/16 J.B.C. & A. Forms/C.2118/12.

6

Instructions regarding War Diaries and Intelligence Summaries are contained in F. S. Regs., Part II. and the Staff Manual respectively. Title Pages will be prepared in manuscript.

WAR DIARY
or
~~INTELLIGENCE~~ SUMMARY
(Erase heading not required.)

Army Form C. 2118.

Place	Date	Hour	Summary of Events and Information	Remarks and references to Appendices
N.W. of HOUTKERQUE. SHEET 27 D.30.d.9.9	24/5/18		Bn paraded early, passing starting point at 5.0 am. & marching via POPERINGHE, ST. JAN TER - BIEZEN, WATOU to a camp at 27/D.30.d.9.9. Very good camp: accomodation good. All the men very wet from the march, during which heavy rain fell. M.O. Capt BOAG RATH relieved by a new M.O. Lt MACGREGOR	
do	25/5/18		A & B Coys paraded at full strength for a muster roll call, kit inspection, and firing on the range, whilst C Coy provided all duties for the Bn. C & D Coys continuing training - musketry & coy drill.	
do	26/5/18		Battalion paraded as strong as possible at 11.30 am for Divine Service under Deputy Chaplain - General (Bishop GWYNNE) in the wood adjoining the camp.	
do	27/5/18		C & D Coys paraded at full strength for muster roll call, kit inspection, firing, whilst A & B Coys furnished reliefs for all Bn duties & harvesters work from 6 am till 6 pm. In the evening, Major STONEYDALE lectured all officers & N.C.O.s on the operations at NEUVE EGLISE 11 - 14 April; showing the different dispositions of the companies in & around the village.	

2449 Wt. W14957/M90 750,000 1/16 J.B.C. & A. Forms/C.2118/12.

1.

Instructions regarding War Diaries and Intelligence Summaries are contained in F. S. Regs., Part II. and the Staff Manual respectively. Title Pages will be prepared in manuscript.

WAR DIARY
or
~~INTELLIGENCE SUMMARY~~

(Erase heading not required.)

Army Form C. 2118.

Place	Date	Hour	Summary of Events and Information	Remarks and references to Appendices
E of HOUTKERQUE 27/D30d99	28/5/18		The morning, from 7 am, devoted to an operation identical to that carried out by the Battalion at NEUVE EGLISE, with special reference to the counter attack carried out by C Company. MAJOR STONEY in command of operations	
	29/5/18		A Bde. scheme took place in the Bn area. The 1/KRRC on the left, & the Battalion on the right, with A & B Coys taking first objective, C Company passing through them, taking the second objective, while D Coy were in reserve. The Bn had to pass through the BOIS DE ST. ACAIRE, wearing Box Respirators, as the wood was, for the purpose of the scheme, supposed to be filled with gas.	
			At conclusion, the Corps Commander, Sir CLAUD JACOB K.C.B., inspected the Battalion, wishing it every success in all future operations it has to take part in, & reminding it, that 36 yrs ago he himself joined the WORC. REGT.	
DIRTY BUCKET CORNER.	30/5/18		Bn paraded at 4.10 am, marched via WATOU, ST JAN TER BIEZEN to DIRTY BUCKET CAMP passing 19th INF. BDE. en route, whom 100th Inf Bde relieved.	
do	31/5/18.		Bn provided a working party of 100 per coy, for work on EAST. POP Line – from 5 am – 9 am. Remainder of day spent in Coys passing through gas hut for testing S.B.R.s	

G. I. L. Stoney Major
Comdg 2/Worc Regt.

2449 Wt. W14957/M90 750,000 1/16 J.B.C. & A. Forms/C.2118/12.

2 Worc R[?]

1.

Army Form C. 2118.

Vol 47

Instructions regarding War Diaries and Intelligence Summaries are contained in F. S. Regs., Part II. and the Staff Manual respectively. Title pages will be prepared in manuscript.

WAR DIARY
or
INTELLIGENCE SUMMARY.
(Erase heading not required.)

Place	Date	Hour	Summary of Events and Information	Remarks and references to Appendices
[illegible] A-30 b 4.4 (Sheet 28)	1-6-18		Companies practised withdrawals from positions by platoons & sections. Battn. on ready to man Yellow or Blue line at short notice.	
	2-6-18		Battalion paraded for Divine Service. Conference at Bn. H.Q. attended by all officers & C.S.M's. The Commanding Officer explained the system of an [illegible] [illegible] & the method by which companies should withdraw when attacked by overwhelming numbers.	
	3-6-18		Two Companies working on Green & Blue Lines. A Coy returned from RUBROUCK where they fired a musketry course. C.O. & Adjutant attended a conference at Brigade H.Q. at which the G.O.C. Brigade explained the forthcoming tour in the line & scheme of defence.	
	4-6-18		Message of congratulation sent to G.O.C. 33rd Division on his being made K.C.B. Companies & Specialists training. C.O. held a conference at Battn. H.Q. attended by Company Commanders, Lewis Gun Officer, & Signalling Officer at which he explained the points laid down at Brigade Conference of 3rd inst. Commanding Officer & Adjutant visited H.Q. 9th Norfolks to arrange details of relief for night 6/7th.	

T2134. Wt. W708—776. 500000. 4/15. Sir J. C. & S.

2.

Army Form C. 2118.

Instructions regarding War Diaries and Intelligence Summaries are contained in F. S. Regs., Part II. and the Staff Manual respectively. Title pages will be prepared in manuscript.

WAR DIARY
or
INTELLIGENCE SUMMARY.
(Erase heading not required.)

Place	Date	Hour	Summary of Events and Information	Remarks and references to Appendices
	5.6.18		O's. C. Coys. 2 I.O. + S.O. reconnoitred positions to be taken over from 9th Norfolks. Companies fired on local range.	
	6-6-18		Companies training in morning. Battalion relieved 9th Norfolks at night in Ravine (H 23 d). Relief carried out without any difficulty.	
Ravine H23d 6.8 (Sheet 28)	7.6.18		2nd Lt R. BENNETT joined Bn H.Q. as Intelligence Officer. B + C Coys ready to move + occupy flank defences should enemy break through on our right. D Co. + 2 platoons A Co. at work under R.E. during the night. Very fine weather.	
	8-6-18		Enemy shelled area occupied by Battn. during the morning. Routes to defensive positions reconnoitred by all officers. A + D Coys working at night under R.E's. C. Co. wiring flank defences. All Coys. were gas shelled. Fine weather. 1 O.R. wounded.	
	9-6-18		Considerable gas shelling around Battn. lines during morning + evening. Representatives of 2nd Bn Argyll + Sutherland Highlanders visited the Battalion to reconnoitre before taking over on the 10th inst. D. Co. + 2 platoons A Co. at work under R.E. C Co. wiring flank defences. Casualties 2 O.R. wounded.	

WAR DIARY
or
INTELLIGENCE SUMMARY.
(Erase heading not required.)

3.

Army Form C. 2118.

Instructions regarding War Diaries and Intelligence Summaries are contained in F. S. Regs., Part II. and the Staff Manual respectively. Title pages will be prepared in manuscript.

Place	Date	Hour	Summary of Events and Information	Remarks and references to Appendices
	10-6-18		Quiet morning, rain fell during the morning. 2nd Lt. C.E. LIVELY. D.C.M. joined the Battalion. R.S.M. Foster joined Battalion from 10th Battalion. Lt. Col. T.K. PARDOE D.S.O. proceeded to join [illegible] Garrison Battalion at ETAPLES. Capt. T.J. CROWE proceeded on leave to United Kingdom. Major G.T.L. STONEY. M.C. assumed command of the Battalion. Battalion relieved by 2 Coys. 2nd Argyll & Sutherland Highlanders & moved back to Green Line, bivouacking in rear of the front & support lines. Casualties: Capt. A.R. SOMERS-COX wounded slightly at duty. O.R's killed 1, wounded 8, 2 to hospital with gas.	
House H.7.a.75.05 (Sheet 28)	11-6-18		Very fine weather. Companies making shelters around the line. A. B. and half C Coys. working under R.E. during night in intermediate line. Brigade Commander visited Bn. H.Q. 2½ Coys at work in forward line.	
	12-6-18		Companies continued digging shelters around GREEN LINE. 2½ Coys. at work as 11th. Company Commanders reconnoitred sector south of YPRES held by 1st Queens.	

T2134. Wt. W708—776. 500000. 4/15. Sir J. C. & S.

Instructions regarding War Diaries and Intelligence Summaries are contained in F. S. Regs., Part II. and the Staff Manual respectively. Title pages will be prepared in manuscript.

WAR DIARY
or
INTELLIGENCE SUMMARY.
(Erase heading not required.)

Army Form C. 2118.

Place	Date	Hour	Summary of Events and Information	Remarks and references to Appendices
	13.6.18		Conference held at Bn H.Q. attended by O's C Cos. C.O. explained points for special care when Battalion goes into line. 2½ Cos at work as before. Casualties 1 O.R. wounded. 2 O.R. Gas.	
	14.6.18		News received that a big enemy attack was expected on 15th or 16th. Mobile Reserve was brought up & dumps formed along Green Line. Battalion stood to at dawn but no attack developed. Conference at Bn. H.Q. attended by Co. Commanders at which C.O. explained roles Battn might be called upon to play should an enemy attack develop. Casualties 1 O.R. killed. Advance parties from Cos. went to line held by 1st Queens to remain until Battn. relieved.	
	15.6.18		A/Major O.V.L. SYMONS, Gloucestershire Regt. joined Bn. as Major on Headquarters. Battn. relieved 1st Queens in sector south of YPRES around ZILLEBEKE LAKE. B & C Coys in front line, A in reserve, D in support. Quiet relief. Casualties 2 O.R. wounded.	
In the Line H18 d 4.2.	16.6.18		2/Lt. J. WATKIN-JONES sick to hospital. Quiet day, some gas shelling at night. Brigade Commander visited Bn H.Q. Casualties O.R. 1 wounded.	

Instructions regarding War Diaries and Intelligence Summaries are contained in F. S. Regs., Part II. and the Staff Manual respectively. Title pages will be prepared in manuscript.

WAR DIARY
or
INTELLIGENCE SUMMARY.
(Erase heading not required.)

5.

Army Form C. 2118.

Place	Date	Hour	Summary of Events and Information	Remarks and references to Appendices
	17-6-18.		Trench Strength 22 Officers 517 O.R. 3 Officers 17 O.R. of American Army attached to Bn for instruction. Brigade Commander visited Battn H.Q. & support line. Casualties O.R. 4 Gas. 2nd Lt L. G. A. BRYANT sick to Hospital.	
	18-6-18.		MAJOR STONEY M.C. awarded D.S.O. CAPT. POINTON awarded M.C. REV. E. V. TANNER awarded bar to M.C. Conference at Bn H.Q held by Brigade Commander attended by C.O. O.C.T.M.B. M.G. Officer & Artillery Liason officer to arrange for raid. Heavy gas shelling during the morning Casualties 4 O.R. wounded.	
	19-6-18		Rain fell during the day. Quiet day. final arrangements made for raid. A Co relieved B Co in the line, B remaining near Co H.Q ready for raid. 2nd Lt J. WATKIN-JONES rejoined from hospital. Casualties 3 O.R. wounded.	
	20-6-18		At 12.15 a.m. party of 5 Officers (2nd Lt. BOSWELL in command, 2nd Lt. Greene R.G.A. Lt. Hill, 2nd Lt. Barnard, 2nd Lt. Lively) ~~raided~~ & 150 O.R. raided enemy lines W. of ZILLEBEKE killing many Germans & bringing back 5 prisoners.	

Instructions regarding War Diaries and Intelligence Summaries are contained in F. S. Regs., Part II. and the Staff Manual respectively. Title pages will be prepared in manuscript.

WAR DIARY
or
INTELLIGENCE SUMMARY.
(Erase heading not required.)

6. Army Form C. 2118.

Place	Date	Hour	Summary of Events and Information	Remarks and references to Appendices
(Contd)	20-6-18		We had two men slightly wounded. B Co. returned to billets in Brigade reserve. 1 Co 9th H.L.I. relieving them. Casualties 2 O.R. killed. 4 O.R. wounded. 2nd Lt. STARKEY sick to hospital. Battn relieved by 9th H.L.I. Relief carried out without interference. Bn returned to Brigade Reserve S. of VLAMERTINGHE	
	21-6-18		Following message received from Corps Commander:- "Please convey to Brigadiers & all ranks concerned my congratulations on successful raid carried out last night. Identifications were obtained which were of special importance to the Intelligence Service" Working parties found - 4 platoons. Casualties OR wounded. 1.	
	22-6-18		Fine day. Cos. cleaning up billets. A Co. badly gas shelled. Divisional Commander inspected B. Echelon. Casualties - O.R. wounded 2. Gas 5.	
	23-6-18		Fine day. Working parties of 5 platoons found. Casualties Nil	
	24-6-18		Rain during morning. Working parties found as before. Casualties	
	25-6-18		Quiet day. Bn relieved by 1st Middlesex Regt & proceeded into Divisional	
KNOLLYS FARM			Reserve at BRANDHOEK.	
H.4.c.75.00 (Sht 28)	26-6-18		Cos. cleaning up & inspecting Kits.	

Instructions regarding War Diaries and Intelligence Summaries are contained in F. S. Regs., Part II. and the Staff Manual respectively. Title pages will be prepared in manuscript.

WAR DIARY
or
INTELLIGENCE SUMMARY.
(Erase heading not required.)

7

Army Form C. 2118.

Place	Date	Hour	Summary of Events and Information	Remarks and references to Appendices
	27-6-18		C.O. & Adjutant visited B Echelon. Battalion reorganised in accordance with G.H.Q. letter for battalion strength of 900. Each platoon now 1 Lewis Gun section + 2 rifle sections. Minimum reserve reduced to 100. Working party of 200 O.R. on Green line.	
	28-6-18		Divisional Commander visited Bn H.Q. Working party of 200 O.R. on Green line. Lecture on German M.G. at Bn H.Q. C Co shelled heavily, moved nearer to Bn H.Q.	
	29-6-18		C.O. Adjutant & Os. C. Cos. visited 5th Sco. Rifles in Right Bde Sector. Advance Parties from each Co. proceeded to trenches. Casualties wounded 1 O.R. Capt. J. J. CROWE awarded V.C. for gallantry at NEUVE EGLISE	
	30-6-18		Bn area shelled heavily during the morning.	

S. A. Stones [illegible] Major
Comdg 2 Bn The Worcestershire Regt

T2134. Wt. W708—776. 500000. 4/15. Sir J. C. & S.

2 Worc Rgt

Army Form C. 2118.

Instructions regarding War Diaries and Intelligence Summaries are contained in F. S. Regs., Part II. and the Staff Manual respectively. Title pages will be prepared in manuscript.

WAR DIARY
or
~~INTELLIGENCE SUMMARY.~~
(*Erase heading not required.*)

48

Place	Date	Hour	Summary of Events and Information	Remarks and references to Appendices
	July 1	.	Violent shelling of Battn area CHATEAU SEGARD WOOD from 2.45 - 3.10am, otherwise quiet. Coys working to improve G.H.Q 1 & G.H.Q 2 Lines. Visit from Brigade Commander. Casualties 1 O.R. Wounded.	
	" 2		Quiet day, little artillery & aerial activity, till midnight when a "Chinese Barrage" on our left provoked some artillery retaliation. Casualties 1 O.R. Wounded (Self-inflicted)	
	" 3		Another quiet fine day. Nothing seen of enemy in daytime - fair amount of M.G. activity by night. Coys still working on their lines, & wiring.	
	" 4		Capt & Adjt W.B. Edwards M.C. to Hospital-Sick. Epidemic of "Flanders Grippe" in Brigade, not very pronounced in the Battn	
			Raid by 49th Divn on our left at 11 pm. Casualties 1 O.R. Killed.	
	" 5		In consequence of Divn taking over more frontage, & side-stepping & extending to the right, our front line coys & left support coy were relieved by The Glasgow Highlanders who had been relieved by a Battn of Right Brigade. Our coys temporarily accomodated in communication trenches & in the RAVINE with Brigade Support Battn (16th KRRC) Casualties 1 O.R. Wounded.	
	" 6		Very hot, coys resting & preparing for the front line again. 4 Officers & 6 N.C.Os of U.S. Army attached to Battn for instruction. At 9.30pm B & D coys relieved front line coys 11th Essex Rgt. Right of Battn rests on broad gauge railway running past SCOTTISH WOOD.	

S. 4.8

T2134. Wt. W708—776. 500000. 4/15. Sir J. C. & S.

Instructions regarding War Diaries and Intelligence Summaries are contained in F. S. Regs., Part II. and the Staff Manual respectively. Title pages will be prepared in manuscript.

WAR DIARY
or
~~INTELLIGENCE SUMMARY.~~
(Erase heading not required.)

Army Form C. 2118.

Place	Date	Hour	Summary of Events and Information	Remarks and references to Appendices
	July 6	(Contd)	At 11.45 pm The GLASGOW HIGHLANDERS carried out a raid on the enemy with 4 Offs 100 O.R. No prisoners were taken. Enemy retaliation fell on our Support Coy ("C") Casualties 1 O.R. Killed 4 O.R. Wounded.	
	" 7		Our new sector not good. Much work done by B & D Coys to improve their positions.	
	" 8		Major Symons visited the Battn, quiet day & night. Several new cases of influenza. U.S.A Officers & men relieved by another party	
	" 9		About 2.30am a German Light Machine Gun was captured by 2/Lt MORTON-HICKS, together with 2 overcoats belonging to men of 118 R.I.R. 56th Divn. R.Es covered the Brigade front with a double apron wire. Little activity.	
	" 10		Officers & N.C.Os of American Forces (119th Rgt 30th Divn) left the Battn, returning to their unit at night Battn relieved by 1st Bn MIDDLESEX RGT. Battn withdrawn into Divnl Support at KNOLLYS FARM Sheet 28 N/4. C. 75. 00. Coys in same positions. A late & long relief.	
	" 11		General cleaning up & Baths.	
	" 12		2 Coys provided working parties in Green Line. Box respirator inspection, & change of clothing	
	" 13		2 Coys provided working parties in Green Line. Lewis Gunners firing on range all day.	
	" 14		Voluntary Church Service. 2 Coys working on Green Line.	
	" 15		Battn shooting competition all day. Battn moved up into Left Sub Sector relieving SCOTTISH RIFLES. A & C Coys in front Line. 'B' in Support. 'D' in Reserve	

T2134. Wt. W708—776. 500000. 4/15. Sir J. C. & S.

Instructions regarding War Diaries and Intelligence Summaries are contained in F. S. Regs., Part II, and the Staff Manual respectively. Title pages will be prepared in manuscript.

WAR DIARY
or
~~INTELLIGENCE SUMMARY.~~
(Erase heading not required.)

Army Form C. 2118.

Place	Date	Hour	Summary of Events and Information	Remarks and references to Appendices
	July 16		B Coy provided working party on G.H.Q. 1 Line. G & H Coys 2nd Bn 120 American Infy Rgt attached to Battn & distributed to all Coys. Heavy counter preparation on Corps Front. Lt Col G.H. Stoney D.S.O. A.C. went on Leave.	
	" 17		B Coy found working parties on G.H.Q. 1 Line. 2 German prisoners captured during night 17/18th of 70th Rgt.	
	" 18		Quiet day. Lt Scott wounded. H.L.I sent strong patrol to our front, no prisoners. Americans organise into Platoons.	
	" 19		H.L.I. sent out strong patrols on our front consisting of 3 Officers & 40 O.R. One prisoner captured. Capt & Adjt W.B. Edwards A.C. rejoined in the afternoon.	
	" 20		Americans took over & relieved our Front Line Coys, who went into the BROWN LINE. B Coy provided working party on G.H.Q. 1 Line. D Coy relieved by F Coy Americans, D Coy going into G.H.Q. 1 Line.	
	" 21		Heavy counter preparation during the night, remainder of day fairly quiet.	
	" 22		B & D Coys relieved by E Coy American Battn, the latter now took over command of line, & B & D Coys & H.Q. moved to BROWN LINE.	
	" 23		Battn in Brigade reserve. Working parties of 3 Officers & 150 O.R.	
	" 24		2/Lts A.E. BARRS & M. GLYNN joined Battn for duty. Working parties as on 23rd.	

T2134. Wt. W708—776. 500000. 4/15. Sir J. C. & S.

Instructions regarding War Diaries and Intelligence Summaries are contained in F. S. Regs., Part II. and the Staff Manual respectively. Title pages will be prepared in manuscript.

WAR DIARY
or
~~INTELLIGENCE SUMMARY.~~
(Erase heading not required.)

Army Form C. 2118.

Place	Date	Hour	Summary of Events and Information	Remarks and references to Appendices
	July 25		Working parties as on 23rd. Battn relieved by 2nd Bn A & S.H. & Brigade moved into Divnl Reserve in Green & Yellow Lines.	
Knolly's Farm H.7.c.75.00 Sheet 28NW	" 26		Coys bathed, inspected & general cleaning up.	
	" 27		Working parties of 150 O.R. on Green Line. Divnl Comdr visited B.H.Q. Lt Col. G.J.L. STONEY D.S.O., M.C. rejoined from leave in France.	
	" 28		Working parties as on 27th. Major O.V.L. SYMONS went on Course at WISQUES for Commanding Officers. Party of 2 officers & 50 O.R. went for a days trip to seaside. Lt R.K. WRIGHT. M.C. joined Battn for duty from 6th BEDFORDS. 2 Coys training in advancing in small parties making use of natural cover.	
	" 29		Working parties as on 24th. 2 Coys training in use of ground.	
	" 30		Working parties as on 27th. 2/Lt H. GARRATT slightly wounded. Battn relieved the CAMERONIANS. Heavy shelling during the night.	
H30.a.7.8. Sheet 28NW.	31		Brigade Commander visited B.H.Q. Coys trying to capture prisoners as relief on this front expected. 2 strong patrols went out during night but failed to get any identification. 2/Lts H. WALFORD & C. NEALE joined the Battn for duty.	

In the Field
July 31. 1918.

G J L Stoney Lt. Col.
Comdg 2nd Bn, The Worcestershire Rgt.

T2134. Wt. W708—776. 500000. 4/15. Sir J. C. & S.

2 Worcester Regt

Army Form C. 2118.

ORDERLY ROOM No. 1414 Date 1/9/18 2nd BATTN. THE WORCESTERSHIRE REGT.

Vol 49

Instructions regarding War Diaries and Intelligence Summaries are contained in F. S. Regs., Part II. and the Staff Manual respectively. Title pages will be prepared in manuscript.

WAR DIARY
or
INTELLIGENCE SUMMARY.
(Erase heading not required.)

Place	Date	Hour	Summary of Events and Information	Remarks and references to Appendices
H.30.a.7.7.1. Sheet 28 N.W.	1-8-18.		Capt. E.O. UNDERHILL. M.C. joined the battalion for duty. Very quiet day. L. Co. 3rd Bn. 119th American Infantry Regiment attached to the Battalion for instructional purposes. 1 platoon divided amongst each of our Coys. Casualties 1. O.R. wounded.	
	2-8-18.		Daylight patrols out all along our front, remaining out in huts all day. Raid carried out by battalion on our right, captured 5 prisoners. Our fighting patrols out all night seeking for identifications. Major O.V.L. SYMONS returned from course. Order received from Brigade to carry out raid if identification not secured by night 6/7th. Casualties 9. O.R. wounded.	
	3-8-18.		Very wet day. Very little enemy activity. Brigade on left carried out raid, but found no enemy. B + D. Coys pushed out advanced posts 200-300 yds in front of our line. No enemy opposition. L. American Co. organised into platoons, one with each Co., one platoon of M.G. Co. also attached to each Company. 2 platoons of A + C. Cos. went back to green line, + 1 platoon of B + D. Cos. to make room for Americans. Disposition in line changed and defence organised in greater depth.	

S.49

T2134. Wt. W708-776. 500000. 4/15. Sir J. C. & S.

Army Form C. 2118.

Instructions regarding War Diaries and Intelligence Summaries are contained in F. S. Regs., Part II. and the Staff Manual respectively. Title pages will be prepared in manuscript.

WAR DIARY
or
INTELLIGENCE SUMMARY.
(Erase heading not required.)

Place	Date	Hour	Summary of Events and Information	Remarks and references to Appendices
4-8	4-8-18.		Service to commemorate the 4th anniversary of the war held at HOUTERKERQUE. Brigade represented by Minimum Reserves Commanded by Capt. A.C. POINTON M.C. Fighting patrols again out at night for identifications, no enemy encountered. Front line shelled & trench mortared during the morning. Dull morning changing to fine day.	
	5-8-18		Strong party of enemy encountered one of our advanced posts, caught completely by surprise, several enemy killed by bombs & Lewis Gun fire. One dead body of man belonging to 364th Pioneer Coy. was brought in. Dull day. Conference at Bn. H.Q. to arrange raid for night 6/7th. The Americans were organised into Companies, one relieving D Co. in the front line & one relieving A. Co. in reserve. Bn ordered to hold advanced posts & not to hand over to Americans; consequently C. Co. took over posts which were withdrawn at dawn to enable artillery preparation to be carried out. Raid cancelled during night. A. Co. proceeded to Green Line. Casualties nil.	

Instructions regarding War Diaries and Intelligence Summaries are contained in F. S. Regs., Part II. and the Staff Manual respectively. Title pages will be prepared in manuscript.

WAR DIARY
or
INTELLIGENCE SUMMARY.
(Erase heading not required.)

Army Form C. 2118.

Place	Date	Hour	Summary of Events and Information	Remarks and references to Appendices
	6.8.18		Divisional & Brigade Commander visited Bn. H.Q. Arrangements made for further advance of forward posts at night. Capt. J. J. CROWE. V.C. presented with the Victoria Cross by His Majesty the King at 2nd Army H.Q. A representative party from the Brigade Minimum Reserve under Capt. E.O. UNDERHILL M.C. marched to Div. H.Q. where H.M. the King drove past the assembled troops. The Brigade & Battalion Commanders attended this parade. Patrol of 2 officers + 26 O.R. of C. Co. + L. American Co. searched the battalion front covered by T.M. barrage to enable posts to be pushed forward. Patrol completed its route but failed to dislodge the enemy from some of his posts. The American Officer was killed. Our posts were not advanced. Capt. E. L. HOPKINS M.C. slightly wounded in hand remained at duty. Fine night. Casualties O.R. 1 K. 1 W.	
	7-8-18		Enemy shelled our advanced posts heavily in the morning. A. Co. relieved B. Co. in the right front line. B. Co. proceeded to Green Line. Command of Left Front Co. passed to O.C. 2/119th A.I.R. at 9 p.m. Quiet night. Casualties K. 1. W. 3. O.R.	

Instructions regarding War Diaries and Intelligence Summaries are contained in F. S. Regs., Part II. and the Staff Manual respectively. Title pages will be prepared in manuscript.

WAR DIARY
or
INTELLIGENCE SUMMARY.
(*Erase heading not required.*)

Army Form C. 2118.

4.

Place	Date	Hour	Summary of Events and Information	Remarks and references to Appendices
	8-8-18		Quiet morning. Front line Co. with exception of 1 Officer + 4 L. G. teams withdrawn to enable Heavy Artillery to fire on enemy strong points. A. Co. went back to Green Line. Brigade Commander + O.C. 119th A.I.R. visited Bn. H.Q. + took notes on organisation of hot food for men in trenches. Casualties O.R. K. 1 W. 5.	
	9-8-18		Artillery bombardment on VOORMEZEELE, no enemy retaliation. C Co. moved forward + occupied advanced posts after dark to cover relief. Battalion relieved by 2nd Bn. A + S. H. + moved back to Green Line.	
KNOLLYS FARM. H.7c.75.00 (Sheet 28 N.W.)	10-8-18		Commanding Officer inspected B Echelon & Minimum Reserve. Companies held kit inspection + devoted day to cleaning up.	
	11-8-18		Lt. Col. G. J. L. STONEY. D.S.O. M.C. proceeded on leave to United Kingdom. Major O. V. L. SYMONS assumed command. A + C. Coys at work in morning on Green Line. Capt. C. C. TOUGH M.C. commanded Brigade platoon at a service attended by H.M. the KING at TERDEGHEM. Marched past after the service. Capt. E. V. TANNER. M.C. presented to H.M. the King.	

T2134. Wt. W708—776. 500000. 4/15. Sir J. C. & S.

Instructions regarding War Diaries and Intelligence Summaries are contained in F. S. Regs., Part II. and the Staff Manual respectively. Title pages will be prepared in manuscript.

WAR DIARY
or
INTELLIGENCE SUMMARY.
(Erase heading not required.)

Army Form C. 2118.

Place	Date	Hour	Summary of Events and Information	Remarks and references to Appendices
	12-8-18		Fine weather. B & D Cos at work on Green Line. Party of 2 officers + 22 O.R's went for a day's holiday at DUNKIRQUE. Divisional Commander visited Bn. H.Q. Musketry competitions held throughout the day on small range.	
	13-8-18		A & C Cos. at work on Green Line. B & D Cos. training - strong patrols advancing + surrounding enemy posts, taking same + consolidating with Lewis Guns. Platoon training now in force in each Co for 1 hour per day. Party of 2 Officers + 22 O.R. to DUNKIRQUE for day's rest. Minimum Reserve changed over to give as many men as possible a rest from line.	
	14-8-18.		A. Co. training. B & D. Cos. working on Green Line. Commanding Officer attended conference at Brigade H.Q. Battalion relieved 1/5th Scottish Rifles in support to Left Sector between VLAMERTINGHE & DICKEBUSCH. Relief passed without event.	
Hqd I.5. Sheet 28 N.W.	15-8-18.		Fine warm day. Cos. worked on existing trenches. D. Co. at work on G.H.Q. 1. Line. Warning order received that Brigade is to be relieved by 120th American Regt. on night of 17/18th inst. Capt. INNES. D.S.O. of K.O.S.B. arrived to take over from Capt. J I MUIRHEAD. M.C. as Brigade Major.	

6.

Army Form C. 2118.

WAR DIARY
or
INTELLIGENCE SUMMARY.
(Erase heading not required.)

Instructions regarding War Diaries and Intelligence Summaries are contained in F. S. Regs., Part II. and the Staff Manual respectively. Title pages will be prepared in manuscript.

Place	Date	Hour	Summary of Events and Information	Remarks and references to Appendices
	16-8-18.		Very warm day. C. Co. at work on G.H.Q.1. line. A Co. out carrying + working all night.	
	17-8-18.		The Battalion was relieved by parts of 1st & 2nd Bn. 120th A.I.R. + trained to TUNNELLING CAMP near St. JAN TER BIEZEN.	
TUNNELLING CAMP.	18-8-18.		Very fine weather, extremely hot.	
	19-8-18.		Cos. held kit inspections. Cricket match between officers of battalion + 16th K.R.R.C. resulting in a win for the battalion by 10 wickets.	
	20-8-18.		Transport moved by road to WORMHOUDT en route for WATTEN area. Cos. paraded for medical inspection.	
	21-8-18.		Brigade entrained at PROVEN for WATTEN. Battalion marched from WATTEN + was billeted in SERQUES.	
LE MARAIS SERQUES.	22-8-18.		Cos. bathed in the canals around the area. Boating + fishing in full swing. Very hot day.	
	23-8-18.		Brigade Commander held a practise ceremonial parade outside SERQUES to get ready for presentation of medal ribands by Divisional Commander. Parade very satisfactory considering the short time the Brigade had.	

7.

Army Form C. 2118.

Instructions regarding War Diaries and Intelligence Summaries are contained in F. S. Regs., Part II. and the Staff Manual respectively. Title pages will be prepared in manuscript.

WAR DIARY
or
INTELLIGENCE SUMMARY.
(Erase heading not required.)

Place	Date	Hour	Summary of Events and Information	Remarks and references to Appendices
	23-8-18 (Contd)		been out of the line. The Brigadier General addressed the Brigade Group and complimented them on their past work. A. Co. the best coy. on parade.	
	24-8-18		Divisional Commander presented medal ribands to officers + men of Brigade Group, mostly for action at Neuve Eglise in April. Capt. A. C. POINTON. M.C. + 2nd Lt. H.E. BOSWELL. M.C. + several N.C.O's + men were amongst the recipients. Battalion mentioned for its excellent work at Neuve Eglise	
	25-8-18		Platoon training carried on during the morning. Very hot weather.	
	26-8-18		Wet morning. Platoons carried on training in billets. Warning order received that Battalion would be moving to New Army area on 27th inst.	
	27-8-18		Orders received that Bn. would entrain on 28th inst. B. Co. proceeded to entraining station ARQUES for loading purposes.	
	28-8-18		Battalion entrained at ARQUES for BOUQUE MAISON at 9 p.m. Very heavy rain all day. Lt. Col. G. J. L. STONEY DSO MC. returned from leave.	
SUS-ST-LEGER.	29-8-18		Battalion detrained at BOQUE MAISON during morning + marched to billets at SUS-ST-LEGER. Brigade H.Q. + 16th K.R.R.C. in same village.	

8.

Instructions regarding War Diaries and Intelligence Summaries are contained in F. S. Regs., Part II. and the Staff Manual respectively. Title pages will be prepared in manuscript.

WAR DIARY
or
INTELLIGENCE SUMMARY.
(Erase heading not required.)

Army Form C. 2118.

Place	Date	Hour	Summary of Events and Information	Remarks and references to Appendices
	30-8-18.		Battalion practised platoon attacks on wide frontages as carried out in new fighting. Hockey match between officers & N. C. O's. result - draw.	
	31-8-18		Training - Cos. attacking on 2 platoon frontage of 400. Yards. Fine weather. Inter-platoon football matches commenced. Lecture on co-operation between infantry & tanks attended by all officers & sergeants of Brigade.	

G. I. L. Moriey
LIEUT-COLONEL,
COMDG. 2nd Bn. THE WORCESTERSHIRE REGT.

Instructions regarding War Diaries and Intelligence Summaries are contained in F. S. Regs., Part II. and the Staff Manual respectively. Title Pages will be prepared in manuscript.

17

WAR DIARY
or
INTELLIGENCE SUMMARY
(Erase heading not required.)

Army Form C. 2118.

2/4 Worcester Rgt

100/33

WO 95/50

Place	Date	Hour	Summary of Events and Information	Remarks and references to Appendices
	1918			
SUS-ST-LEGER	Sept 1		Battn at Divine Service held by Capt the Rev E.V.TANNER M.C. Fine weather	
	" 2		Brigade exercise held, involving the capture of SUS-ST-LEGER & BEAUDRICOURT, advance covered by tanks & artillery barrage. Fine day	
	" 3		The Battn marched to HUMBERCOURT & repeated exercise of previous day. Major E.O. UNDERHILL M.C. left the Battn to join 2/4th Bn R.W.S Rgt. Conference at B.H.Q attended by all officers.	
	" 4		'A' Coy at Musketry, remaining Coys carried out tactical exercises. Lecture to all Officers & Sergeants on general principles of present warfare	
	" 5		26 Representatives from Battn attended a demonstration of tanks near ST POL & were all given a ride in same. Coys training. Fine day	
	" 6		Coys training. Lewis Gunners on range. Cricket match against Glasgow Hlanders won by latter by 23 runs. Fine day.	
	" 7		Coys training. Showery weather.	
	" 8		Divine Service held in Chapel. Very wet day. Rugby match between Battn & 16th K.R.R.C won by the latter.	
	" 9		Very wet day. Coys training in billets	
	" 10		B & C Coys on range A & D Coys training. Very wet weather interfered with outdoor work	

g.D.

S.50

2449 Wt. W14957/M90 750,000 1/16 J.B.C. & A. Forms/C.2118/12.

Instructions regarding War Diaries and Intelligence Summaries are contained in F. S. Regs., Part II. and the Staff Manual respectively. Title Pages will be prepared in manuscript.

WAR DIARY
or
INTELLIGENCE SUMMARY
(Erase heading not required.)

Army Form C. 2118.

Place	Date	Hour	Summary of Events and Information	Remarks and references to Appendices
	1918			
SUS-ST LEGER	Sept 10 contd		IX Corps Special Order received. Copy attached.	
	11		A & D Coys on range at distances of 200 & 300 yards. Competitions held in which Brigadier General took part. B & C Coys training. 2nd Lt B W Dudley joined for duty & posted to B Coy.	
	" 12		Very wet day Coys training in billets. Conference of all officers & paper examination given to all subalterns. Football match between officers & sergeants won by latter 1-0	
	" 13		Conference for all Officers & Sergeants on scheme for night practice. Battn scheme held at night including advance of 3 miles & capture of 2 villages. Fine day	
	" 14		Warning order received for Battn to be prepared to move same night by road or bus. Final of Platoon football matches held, won by No 7 Platoon B Coy. Prizes given on ground by Commanding Officer. Orders received that Battn would move night 15/16th by bus.	
	" 15		Fine day. Divl Commander gave lecture to all officers & sergeants on present situation & likely events. Battn preparing for move. Transport proceeded by road to LUCHEUX VILLE area. Battn embussed for BAZENTIN area. Lt G SCOTT M C assumed duties of Battn S.O.	
	" 16		Battn debussed at 5 am & occupied dugouts in DELVILLE WOOD identical ground which Battn captured on Aug 25, 1916. Battn rested throughout day. Officers	

Instructions regarding War Diaries and Intelligence Summaries are contained in F. S. Regs., Part II. and the Staff Manual respectively. Title Pages will be prepared in manuscript.

WAR DIARY
or
INTELLIGENCE SUMMARY

(Erase heading not required.)

Army Form C. 2118.

Place	Date 1918	Hour	Summary of Events and Information	Remarks and references to Appendices
	Sept 16 contd		reconnoitred routes eastwards. Very heavy thunderstorms at night.	
	17		Battn scheme & capture of GINCHY by flanking movements. Warning order received that Battn would move early 18th inst. Minimum Reserve under Capt F de Zulueta proceeded to LESBOEUFS	
LECHELLE SHEET 57c	" 18		Battn marched to LECHELLE accommodated in huts & tents, & was held in V Corps Reserve, for attack on VILLERS-GUISLAINS. Very wet morning. Ready to move at 20 minutes notice.	
	" 19		Battn marched from LECHELLE to field E of EQUANCOURT. Shelters, bivouacs hastily put up. Material found in village of FINS. Whole Battn completely settled by dinner time	
	" 20		Coys paraded 9am - 12.30. G.O.C inspected camp. Capt C.F. BALDWIN took over duties of Adjutant from Capt E.W. EDWARDS M.C. on latter proceeding to take over duties of Staff Captain 100th Brigade Handing over took place on the 19th. Warning order of 20 minutes notice received owing to heavy shelling of GAUCHE WOOD. Stand down at 10.30pm. Showers throughout day	
57c S.E.			A & B Coys at digging. Lewis Gunners of C & D on range. Battn had 1½ hours notice to move up to trenches to take over Reserve Line from Scottish Rifles X13 & 19. 19th Infy Bde attacked in front. Battn disposition 'A' right front Coy. 'B' left front Coy. 'C' support 'D' Reserve.	
	" 22		Quiet morning. Received orders to carry out relief of 1st Queens in front line in conjunction with attack on LIMERICK POST. Coy Commanders reconnoitred in afternoon, orders issued at 5.45pm. Zero hour 9.30pm. Coys late in assembling. Attack postponed till 5 o'clock when A & B Coys walked into their objectives without opposition. C in support D in reserve. Casualties 3 killed 14 wounded. Lt Daltho commanded Bly. Lt Hill A Coy	

2449 Wt. W14957/M90 750,000 1/16 J.B.C. & A. Forms/C.2118/12.

Instructions regarding War Diaries and Intelligence Summaries are contained in F. S. Regs., Part II. and the Staff Manual respectively. Title Pages will be prepared in manuscript.

WAR DIARY
or
INTELLIGENCE SUMMARY

(Erase heading not required.)

Army Form C. 2118.

Place	Date 1918	Hour	Summary of Events and Information	Remarks and references to Appendices
	Sept 23		Quiet morning, situation cleared up. Two front Coys consolidated. Attempts made to capture cross roads X22.c. Posts pushed forward to GLOUCESTER ROAD. Enemy assembled for counter attack dispersed by artillery. Ration party shelled at dump, four casualties. B Echelon shelled, 2 limbers blown up but no casualties. KRRC & Brigade on left carried out local operation, only partly successful.	
57c S.E.	" 24		Attack on our left by KRRC to clear MEUNIER TRENCH. A & B Coys assisted by pushing forward posts to GLOUCESTER ROAD. Operation not entirely successful. KRRC lost heavily. General came round in morning. Heavy shelling. Enemy counter attacked on our left. Took loop in DADOS TRENCH. Quiet afternoon. D Coy moved to fresh position to avoid shelling.	
	" 25		Exceptionally quiet morning & afternoon, wet in morning. Visibility good in evening. Aerial activity. Attempt to retake DADOS TRENCH & CROSS ROADS. B Coy co-operated but not successful. Lieut H G HILL wounded left hand. C Coy relieved D Coy early in the evening.	
	" 26		Comdg Officers conference held at BHQ. Enemy shelled at round BHQ in the morning. All Coy Commanders called for at 3.30pm. Quiet evening. D Coy relieved B Coy from the line. Quiet relief. Another attempt made on DADOS LOOP by QUEENS failed.	
	" 27		Brigade attacked along the line. Quiet morning on our sector. Hostile shelling. Working parties out. Much aerial activity. C & D Coys in front line. A in support. B Coy in reserve.	
	" 28		Very quiet morning. COs conference in afternoon. Coy Commanders came down to BHQ to receive orders. Brigade to take STONE & PIGEON trenches, 1000 yards from front line. KRRC to go through & H.L.I & WORCESTERS & cross the canal. Battn moved up to LIMERICK TRENCH during night to assembly positions.	

2449 Wt. W14957/M90 750,000 1/16 J.B.C. & A. Forms/C.2118/12.

Instructions regarding War Diaries and Intelligence Summaries are contained in F. S. Regs., Part II. and the Staff Manual respectively. Title Pages will be prepared in manuscript.

WAR DIARY
or
INTELLIGENCE SUMMARY
(Erase heading not required.)

Army Form C. 2118.

Place	Date 1918	Hour	Summary of Events and Information	Remarks and references to Appendices
	Sept 29		Zero hour 5.50. D Coy on the right, C Coy on the left. A+B Coys second wave. Weak & ineffective barrage, our men caught by intense M.G fire from the Cross Rds X22.C.6.6. After a splendid effort to work round, Coys had to withdraw to original front line having suffered heavy casualties. H.L.I advanced on left some way but obliged to withdraw leaving prisoners. Bde ordered to re-organise & hold present position. Casualties 8 Officers killed 3 wounded, about 220 of O.R killed & wounded, some wounded came in during night. Officers killed. Lieuts RANSON GLYNN. SUDBURY LAMBERT WRIGHT BENBOW & WOODWARD. Officers wounded Lts BARNARD. STARKEY & WALFORD	
	" 30		Enemy discovered to have retired. Patrols pushed out at once to W bank of Canal Whole Division moved forward. 100th Brigade occupied the final objectives of former day, no sign of enemy W of Canal, slight shelling. A+B Coys in front line C in reserve D Coy in support. Coys reorganised into [illegible] [illegible] Strong Patrols sent out at night along the front to reconnoitre the crossings. Good news continues to come in. Heavy showers during night.	

G. I. [illegible] Lt Col
Comdg 2nd Bn The Worcestershire Rgt.

2449 Wt. W14957/M90 750,000 1/16 J.B.C. & A. Forms/C.2118/12.

Report on operations in which the 2nd Bn. Worcestershire Regt. took part, between Sept. 21st & Sept. 30th.

Sept. 21st

On the morning of the 21st Sept. when the Bn. was in camp near Equancourt, orders were received to move to a position of Reserve to the 19th Inf. Bde. then holding part of the Brown Line S. of Villiers Guislain. That night the Bn. occupied those defences covering the railway in the vicinity of Vaucellet Fm.

Sept. 22nd

The Bn. was ordered to attack Limerick Post.
The 19th Inf. Bde. were already in possession of Meath Post, but were unable to clear their right to Kildare Avenue.
The operations were timed for 9.15 pm.
Preparatory orders were not received until midday when only a hurried reconnaissance of the position was possible.
The Coy. Commanders who went to Meath Post did not return until 6 pm. having been hurt by a shell splinter on their way back.
Final written orders were received at 4 pm.
Consequently it was after 6 pm. when the Company Commanders had received their final orders & could return to their Companies to explain the plan.
By 7 pm. it had settled down to a thoroughly wet night & there was no moon.

2/ Add to this the fact that those guides detailed by the 19th Inf Bde. to guide our Companies to their positions of assembly lost their way in the darkness & by 9.18 pm. our barrage came down & passed on before the attacking troops were in position. The Enemy barrage immediately fell along Thrush Valley & the sunken road our Companies suffering considerable Casualties – viz. 3 ~~officers~~ killed & 19 wounded – Bn. H.Qrs. temporally established in the sunken road by Poplar Trench was blown in, & also the Bn. Aid Post.

However the Companies were soon re-assembled & orders were issued for an advance on Limerick Post at dawn. This was carried out successfully & by 7 am. the post was occupied without opposition. The position was at once consolidated & posts pushed out in the direction of Gloster Rd.

23rd Throughout the 23rd, though little movement was observed to front, Enemy M.G. fire & Sniping became intense, especially from the direction of the cross roads –

8 More than one attempt was made to capture these Cross roads, but without success.
An attempt made by the Enemy to advance from Gloster Road was frustrated by our artillery.

Sept. 24th On the morning of the 24th at about 11.30 am the Enemy moved out of the Cross roads and attacked our troops on the right, & retook the Loop.
The Bn. formed a defensive flank along Kildare Avenue – but nothing further developed.

Sept. 25th Our right company co-operated with those troops on our right in an attempt to retake the Loop – but without success.

Sept. 26th A further attempt by British troops to capture the Loop failed.

Sept. 27th Was a quiet day on the Bn. front.

Sept. 28th The Bn. received its orders to form the right of the attack by the 10th Inf. Bde. on Stone Trench & Pigeon Trench –
The attack to begin at 5.50 am – on the morning of the 29th.

3 A

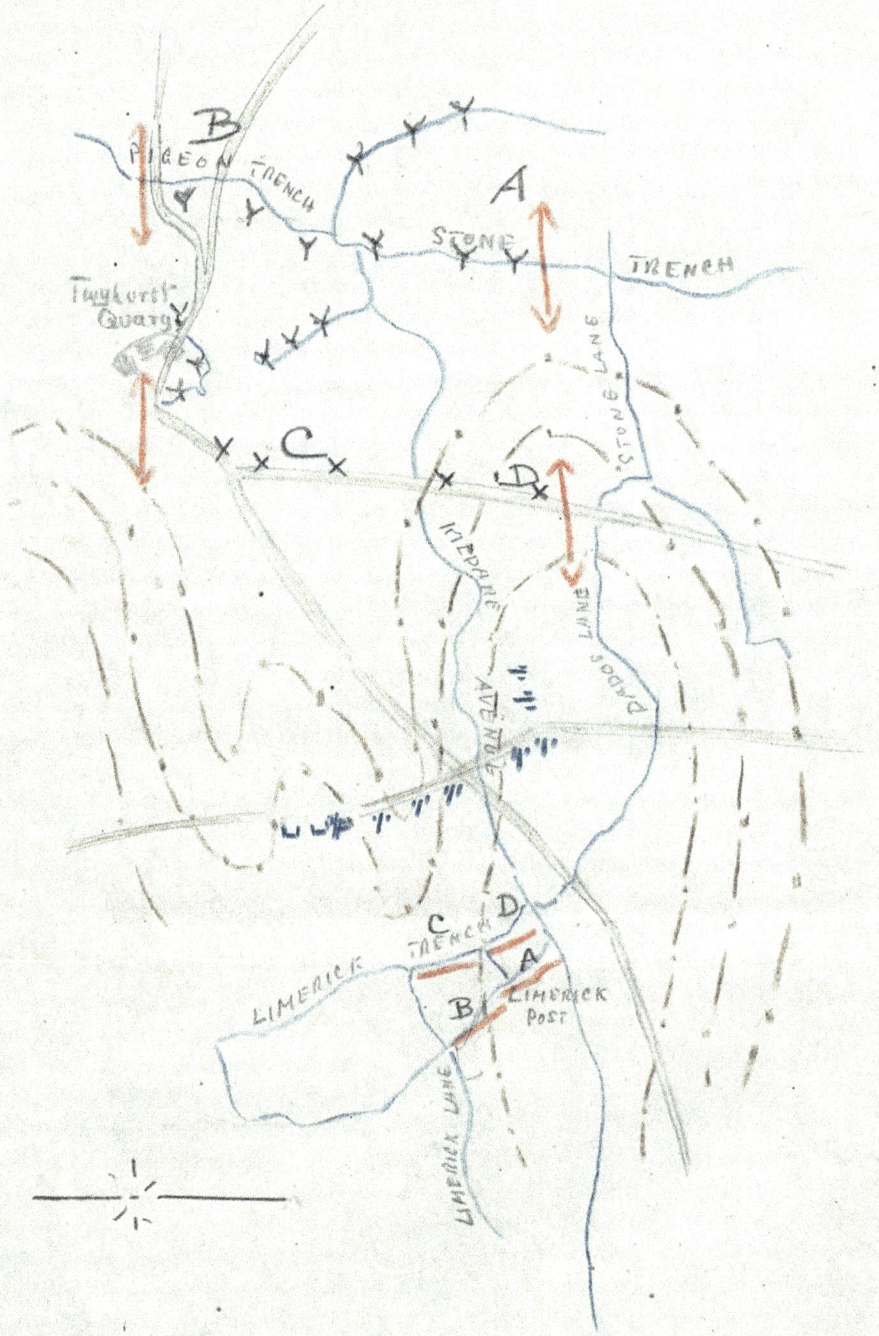

Rough Plan not to scale.

LEGENDE

Bn. Frontage (objective)

Enemy Snipers Posts

" M.G.

Rough Contour Line

Position of Assembly

C D

B A

84

The Bn. moved up to the position of assembly during the night 28/29th Sept as follows:—

D Coy right front Coy.		See attached diagram.
C Coy left " "		
A right support		
B left support		

The Coys were ordered to advance in open formation – two platoons in front, one platoon in support & one platoon in reserve –

The leading platoons to be extended those behind in diamond formation.

D & C Coys were to advance & occupy the 1st objective – viz. the sunken road marked XXXX (see diagram)

A & B Coys to pass through & occupy the final objective marked YYYY (see diagram)

This ~~[illegible]~~ involved a v. considerable alteration to the original objective for the Companies, as the divisional boundaries was altered during the night 28/29th Sept.

5

Sept. 29th At 4.am the Companies were in positions & at 5.50 am (zero hour) a.v. their artillery barrage came over & our troops went forward in the face of a withering M.G. fire.

The Artillery barrage moved so quickly that our men had to run in order to keep up with it.

The attack was brought to a stand still before it reached Gloster Road.

E. Ms & snipers posts afterwards located are shown on attached diagram.

D Company whilst its right was held at the tunnel in Kildare Avenue by a v. strong bombing block its left swung forward a little towards the cross roads. But as each party got forward they were instantly exterminated. The fate of C Coy. was no better, for as they moved obliquely down the Tangelle Valley & across the small spur which separates it from the Tangelle Ravine, caught the full blast of those Enemy M.G. posted by the cross roads, & those who escaped these were met by

6 snipers posts dug in on Ploster Road.
Here Lt. Wright M.C. was found shot
through the head, grasping a bomb in his hand, leading his platoon,
the whole of which was killed. His
leading must have been magnificent.
Close behind him & on his right
was found Lt. Lambert & his platoon
which suffered a similar fate.
On the right where D Coy's left managed
to swing up the hill side towards the
Cross roads the ground testified
to the splendid effort on the part
of its officers to lead their platoons
to their objectives. -
Not a single man of the Bn. crossed
Ploster Road.
By 7 am. fighting died down &
those who had escaped being killed or
severely wounded were finding their way
back to our original position. When the
order was received for the Bn to reorganise,
In the evening a few others unwounded
found their way back to our lines. -
During the day attempts to bring in our
wounded were immediately stopped by
Enemy M.G. & snipers. -

7 Throughout the night of 29/30th Enemy M.G. fire was active, sweeping our front line parapets. but at daybreak there were indications that the trenches in front were unoccupied. patrols were immediately sent forward who reported that there were no signs of the Enemy. Orders were at once issued for the Bdr. to move forward.

Sept 30th

By 1pm. A & B Coys have reached & occupied their original final objectives without opposition.

By Evening the Bn. had occupied the whole of the original objective. patrols were pushed out towards the Canal & advanced posts established.

The Enemy appeared to be on the Eastern side of the Canal, but not on the Western side.

8

Casualties to the Bn were as follows:–

8 officers killed { Lt. Ranson, Lt. Lambert, " Glyn, " Wright, " Sudbury, " Woodward, " Neil, " Benbow }

3 " wounded { Lt. Barnard, " Walford, " Starkie }

Approx: 80 men killed

" 150 " wounded.

Approx Total Casualties **241**

G. J. L. Stoney ? W. Colonel
Comdg 2 Worcestershire Regt

In the Field
Oct. 2nd 1918

19

Instructions regarding War Diaries and Intelligence Summaries are contained in F. S. Regs., Part II. and the Staff Manual respectively. Title Pages will be prepared in manuscript.

WAR DIARY
or
INTELLIGENCE SUMMARY

(Erase heading not required.)

Army Form C. 2118.

ORDERLY ROOM No. 3143 Date 1.11.18 2nd BATTN THE ...

1.

51

Place	Date	Hour	Summary of Events and Information	Remarks and references to Appendices
	1.10.18.		Quiet morning. Parties out burying our dead. Eight officers buried together at X 22. c. 6.6. K.R.R. chaplain officiated. Strong officers patrol went out at night to try the crossings of the canal: unable to get over owing to M.G. fire.	Map Ref. 57.C S.E.
	2.10.18.		Occasional shelling. Braces + great-coats ordered up. Burial of dead completed. Generals PINNEY + BAIRD came round trenches. Cooks came up in the evening. Enemy shelling rather heavily in the evening.	
	3.10.18.		Quiet morning. Details of relief came up in the morning; 1st Queens relieved Coys in trenches: Cameronians relieved forward posts. Relief started at 3.30 + completed at 6 o'clock. Moved back to bivouacs W. 24.	
	4.10.18		Morning spent in cleaning up &c. Companies re-organised.	
	5.10.18.		News that 19th Bde. had crossed the canal. Battalion standing by at three quarter hours notice. General PINNEY inspected the camp.	W. 24.
	6.10.18.		Minimum reserve came up with the following officers:- Capt TOUGH. M.C. Lts. CROYDON-FOWLER; WILLIAMS; LAUGHTON; DUDLEY. Relief of M.R. left before dinner. 15 O.R's reinforcements arrived in evening. Lt DAVIES: 2/Lt BULLOCK joined the battn: latter posted to D Coy: former returned to M.R. Capt SOMERS-COX + Lt MALONE left for M.R.	

Instructions regarding War Diaries and Intelligence Summaries are contained in F. S. Regs., Part II. and the Staff Manual respectively. Title pages will be prepared in manuscript.

WAR DIARY
or
INTELLIGENCE SUMMARY.
(Erase heading not required.)

2 Army Form C. 2118.

Place	Date	Hour	Summary of Events and Information	Remarks and references to Appendices
	7.10.18.		Coys under Coy. Commanders. Four platoons per Coy. reformed. Capt. TOUGH proceeded on leave. Rain in evening. Standing to at one & half hours notice	Sheet 57 S.E.
	8.10.18.		Battalion scheme cancelled. Col: Stoney to N.R. Major SYMONS takes over command. Battn. with transport moved off at 5.0.C. & marched to X16 central. Transport in TARGELLE Valley. Orders for move came in during night.	O 376 & 377.
	9.10.18		Battalion moved off at dawn. Crossed SCHELDT CANAL & halted S.14.b. Officers sent forward to reconnoitre. Moved off again at 11.30 a.m. marched to DEHERIES. O31a. Transport followed. Men marched exceptionally well, covering distance of 12 Kilos. during day. In bivouacs. B Echelon & N.R. moved up during night.	O 378 & 379.
	10.10.18		Still advancing in front. Brigade moved off at dawn in support of 98th Bde: who were passing through 19th Bde. Battn: advanced in artillery formation to LE FAYTE passing to the north of CLARY & BERTRY. H.L.I. in front. KRR's on the right. Halted at 9.30 am P4.a. First line transport came up. Officers went forward	57 B 1/40,000

T2134. Wt. W708—776. 500000. 4/15. Sir J. C. & S.

Instructions regarding War Diaries and Intelligence Summaries are contained in F. S. Regs., Part II. and the Staff Manual respectively. Title pages will be prepared in manuscript.

WAR DIARY
or
INTELLIGENCE SUMMARY.
(*Erase heading not required.*)

Army Form C. 2118.

3

Place	Date	Hour	Summary of Events and Information	Remarks and references to Appendices
	10.10.18 Contd.		to reconnoitre. 98th Bde. hold line K14 + 21 between NEUVILLY + LE CATEAU.	
	11-10-18		Standing to at 5. am. Waiting news all morning + afternoon. A + B. Coys. under Lts WALTHO + BOSWELL ordered to secure crossings of River SELLE + cover our re-construction of bridges. Brigadier's conference at 5.30 pm. Operation orders at 11.30. pm.	B.O. 380.
	12.10.18.		Headquarters, C + D Coys fell in at 0200 hrs. marched to assembly positions. Attack by 100th Bde across River SELLE. H.L.I. on the right resting on MONTAY. K.R.R's on left resting on NEUVILLY. C + D. Coys in Brigade Reserve. A + B. Coys. ordered to secure and consolidate railway when attacking forces had passed through. Attack held up on the right. K.R.R's reached their objective but fell back. Line of railway held for short period. C + D Coys. ordered to form defensive flank on the left to meet expected counter-attack. Units mixed up in sunken road but re-organised later. Attack ordered again for 1730 hrs. at the last moment cancelled.	

T2134. Wt. W708—776. 500000. 4/15. Sir J. C. & S.

Instructions regarding War Diaries and Intelligence Summaries are contained in F. S. Regs., Part II. and the Staff Manual respectively. Title pages will be prepared in manuscript.

WAR DIARY
or
INTELLIGENCE SUMMARY.
(Erase heading not required.)

4. Army Form C. 2118.

Place	Date	Hour	Summary of Events and Information	Remarks and references to Appendices
	12.10.18 (contd)		Crossings of the river secured once again & posts established east of river. Heavy shelling all day in sunken road & in the Ravine.	
	13.10.18		Wet day. Officers of the relieving unit go up line. Relief orders came out at 16. hrs. 2nd R.W.F. relieved C & D Coys. A & B in Ravine marched out independently. Relief complete by 2100 hrs. Battalion in billets at LE FAYTE. Casualties for two days:- Officers. 2nd Lt. CROYDON-FOWLER killed; 2nd Lts. DUDLEY, GARRETT; WATKIN-JONES wounded. 2 O.R's killed; 5 missing; 38 wounded.	Sh. 57 B. B.O. 352
	14.10.18		Battalion moved at 11.00 hrs to billets at CLARY. M.R rejoined. Excellent billets.	CLARY
	15.10.18		General cleaning up & baths. Fine day.	
	16.10.18		Inspection by General PINNEY. Commanding 33rd Division. Very wet morning. Court Martial at 1500 hrs; President Major SYMONS. Draft of 40. O. R's arrived.	
	17.10.18		Brigade Gas Officer inspected Box Respirators of Battalion. Coys: at disposal of Coy Commanders. Staff Ride in afternoon; Commanding Officer, Adjutant, and Coy. Commanders. Tactical problem set by General PINNEY. Very wet evening.	

Instructions regarding War Diaries and Intelligence Summaries are contained in F. S. Regs., Part II. and the Staff Manual respectively. Title pages will be prepared in manuscript.

WAR DIARY
or
INTELLIGENCE SUMMARY.
(Erase heading not required.)

5

Army Form C. 2118.

Place	Date	Hour	Summary of Events and Information	Remarks and references to Appendices
	19.10.18		Battalion Field day. Route march from billets to DEHERIES. Stopped on way to watch Whippet Tanks. At 11.00 hours Battalion moved off in Artillery formation towards CLARY, stopped in front of HURTEVENT FARM. Marched back independently. Baths in afternoon. Wet day.	
	20.10.18		Church Parade at 1100 hrs. Band marched Battn: down to Cinema. Warning order received. Conference of Coy: Commanders in afternoon.	
	21.10.18		Battn: moved off at 0845 hrs to billets at BERTRY. Capt. CROWE V.C. returned from leave. Brigade conference at 6.30 p.m. about pending operations.	
	22.10.18		Battn: paraded 0945 hr for practice in artillery formation. Operation orders during the afternoon. Battn: paraded at 2000 hrs. and marched to Railway Embankment to position of assembly. K16a. Heavy shelling during night. Attack by the 98th + 19th Bdes: at 0200 hrs with four objectives. 100th Bde to take 5th objective.	B.O. 385. Sheet 57a. BERTRY
	23.10.18		Battn: commenced to move forward at 0800 hrs. and advanced in artillery formation with left resting on MONTAY - ENGLEFIELD road. C + D front companies under Capt. HOPKINS and Lieut. LAUGHTON. B Company under Lieut. BOSWELL in support.	

Instructions regarding War Diaries and Intelligence Summaries are contained in F. S. Regs., Part II. and the Staff Manual respectively. Title Pages will be prepared in manuscript.

WAR DIARY
or
INTELLIGENCE SUMMARY
(Erase heading not required.)

Army Form C. 2118.

6.

Place	Date	Hour	Summary of Events and Information	Remarks and references to Appendices
	23-10-18 (contd)		A. Coy under Lt. Davies in reserve. Passed 1st + 2nd objectives: then a long halt at L1d. At 15. hrs moved forward again: passed 3rd objective and arrived at E of VENDEGIES WOOD: dug in + consolidated in depth.	
	24.10.18		At 0400 hrs. advance continued in support of 98th Bde. Ordered to move through 98th Bde. and continue to 5th objective. Slight delay at the start owing to units in front being held up. Order finally came through for 2nd Worcesters to advance on 150. Knoll. F.12.a whilst H.L.I. + K.R.R. worked round on flank. Worcesters to hold + attract fire for K.R.R's to attack hill. 2nd Worcesters reached their objective without opposition and consolidated as follows:- C + D. Coys along road through F6a - A7b. B Coy. Knoll 150. A. Coy. F11b. Hdqrtrs at F6.c 2.4. Patrols pushed out to try + enter village but met by M.G's, gas shelling + trench mortars. Shelling very heavy in vicinity of Hdqrtrs. Rations shelled + some of Transport gassed.	B.O. 386. Sheet 57 b.
	25.10.18.		No further advance during day. Attempt to move forward failed. O.P. established in chateau near X roads. Rations up early. Orders for attack issued verbally at K R R H.Q. at 2100 hrs. Coy. Commanders conference at 2330 hrs.	G 183.
	26.10.18		19th Bde on the left: 98th Bde on right ordered to attack ENGLE FONTAINE from Northerly + Southerly directions respectively. 100th Bde to actually mop up village and take positions on E. side of village. 2nd Worcesters responsible for village. Attack started at 0100 hrs. C + D. to move down into village B. in close support. A in reserve. Attack completely successful.	Sheet 57 b.

Instructions regarding War Diaries and Intelligence Summaries are contained in F. S. Regs., Part II. and the Staff Manual respectively. Title Pages will be prepared in manuscript.

WAR DIARY
or
INTELLIGENCE SUMMARY
(Erase heading not required.)

7.

Army Form C. 2118.

Place	Date	Hour	Summary of Events and Information	Remarks and references to Appendices
	26.10.18 (contd)		ENGLEFONTAINE captured with 500 prisoners. Companies reached their allotted objective and consolidated. Few casualties. Intermittent shelling during day. Counter-attack expected but did not materialize. Relieved by 2nd R.W.F. at 1500 hrs; very quick and good relief. Battalion moved back to billets in FOREST. Casualties 22-26. 2/Lt. BULLOCK: Killed. Lieut. LAUGHTON wounded. 4 O.R's killed. 33 O.R's wounded.	B.O. 387. Sheet 57b. FOREST.
	27.10.18		General cleaning up, baths &c. Capt. TOUGH returned from leave. 140. O.R's reinforcements joined Battn.	
	28.10.18		Conference with Coy. Commanders for reorganising. Funeral of Lieut. BULLOCK & Pte Rogers in Cemetery.	
	29.10.18		Inspection by Commanding Officer of Coys. followed by inspection of billets &. Slight gas shelling of village during night. Lieut BRYANT returned off leave.	
	30.10.18		Companies paraded in Kgd: practised attack formation. Battn started from old enemy position & advanced in open formation to first sunken road.	
	31.10.18		Inspection of Brigade by Corps Commander. Presentation of medals. March past by column of companies: 58 O.R. reinforcements arrived in afternoon. News of armistice with Turkey.	

J. I. [signature]
LIEUT-COLONEL,
COMDG. 2nd Bn. THE WORCESTERSHIRE REGT.

2449 Wt. W14957/M90 750,000 1/16 J.B.C. & A. Forms/C.2118/12.

2 Worc Regt

Army Form C. 2118.

Instructions regarding War Diaries and Intelligence Summaries are contained in F. S. Regs., Part II. and the Staff Manual respectively. Title pages will be prepared in manuscript.

WAR DIARY
or
INTELLIGENCE SUMMARY.
(Erase heading not required.)

Vol 52

Place	Date	Hour	Summary of Events and Information	Remarks and references to Appendices
	1-11-18		Companies at disposal of [illegible] Gunners with Capt. [illegible]	FOREST.
	2-11-18		[illegible] reconnaissance of [illegible] work.	
			[illegible] at 17.30 hrs.	
			[illegible] H.Q. [illegible]	
	[illegible]		[illegible] FOREST [illegible]	
			[illegible] HECQ [illegible]	
			[illegible]	
			FOREST [illegible]	
			[illegible] routes of approach [illegible]	
			[illegible]	
	[illegible]		[illegible]	
			[illegible]	
			[illegible] NORMAL [illegible] LA TETE [illegible]	
			[illegible] SARBARAS [illegible]	

2

Army Form C. 2118.

WAR DIARY
or
INTELLIGENCE SUMMARY.
(Erase heading not required.)

Instructions regarding War Diaries and Intelligence Summaries are contained in F. S. Regs., Part II. and the Staff Manual respectively. Title pages will be prepared in manuscript.

Place	Date	Hour	Summary of Events and Information	Remarks and references to Appendices
	5-11-18		[illegible] A & B Coys [illegible] forward to [illegible] any remaining enemy from SASSEGNIES. By [illegible] hrs Batt. had relieved 4th KINGS in a position along SAMBRE river & railway embankment E of SASSEGNIES. Orders issued at [illegible] C.O. [illegible] to [illegible] attack across SAMBRE, provided a bridge had been completed by [illegible] Coy. R.E. by 05-30 hrs.	
	6-11-18		Continued shelling by enemy in early morning at 05-30 hrs. All four companies crossed the river without casualties & swiftly advanced over [illegible] ground to villages of PETIT-MAUBEUGE & LEVAL both of which were captured, with small loss by 07-30 hrs. Heavy shelling by the enemy continued all day. At 13.30 hrs Battalions of 19th [illegible] passed through [illegible] continuing the advance [illegible] night.	
	7-11-18		Batt. [illegible] at [illegible] hrs at [illegible] PETIT-MAUBEUGE [illegible] [illegible] Divisional Reserve [illegible] forward to AULNOYE [illegible] [illegible] for [illegible] the situation [illegible] front of	

D. D. & L., London, E.C.
(A10266) Wt W5300/P713 750,000 2/18 Sch. 52 Forms/C2118/16

3

Army Form C. 2118.

Instructions regarding War Diaries and Intelligence Summaries are contained in F. S. Regs., Part II. and the Staff Manual respectively. Title pages will be prepared in manuscript.

WAR DIARY
or
INTELLIGENCE SUMMARY.

(*Erase heading not required.*)

Place	Date	Hour	Summary of Events and Information	Remarks and references to Appendices
	7.11.18		Division being [illegible]. Bn Echelon marched into this same village and	
			commenced billeting. At 13.15 hrs march continued to POT-DE-VIN.	
			Orders received to assemble in woods [illegible] 98th Inf Bde reaching their	
			objective – the AVESNES-MAUBEUGE road, to pass through them & to capture	
			a position [illegible] edge of wood. [illegible]	
			owing to 9th Inf Bde failing [illegible]	
			with Glasgow Highlanders.	
	8-11-18		Shortly after [illegible] hrs [illegible] 98th [illegible]	
			relieving Batt marched out [illegible] by [illegible] POT-	
			DE-VIN along yesterday's route to PETIT-MAUBEUGE where billets	
			were ready [illegible] by [illegible]	
			[illegible] operations. Lt Col J J [illegible]ADHAM D.S.O. [illegible]	
			& assumed command of Batt. [illegible]	

D. D. & L., London, E.C.
(A10266) Wt W5300/P713 750,000 2/18 Sch. 52 Forms/C2118/16

Army Form C. 2118.

Instructions regarding War Diaries and Intelligence Summaries are contained in F. S. Regs., Part II. and the Staff Manual respectively. Title pages will be prepared in manuscript.

WAR DIARY
or
INTELLIGENCE SUMMARY.
(Erase heading not required.)

Place	Date	Hour	Summary of Events and Information	Remarks and references to Appendices
	9.11.18		Commanding Officer inspected billets of the men, [illegible] transport etc in morning. In afternoon a conference attended by all officers was held at H.Q.	
	10.11.18		Sunday. Voluntary parade under 16/K.R.R.C. Chaplain. Coys using the [illegible] baths [illegible] by Qr. Master. At 15.00 hrs C.O. & 2/in C. inspected the transport of the Battn. [illegible] from LOCQUIGNOL. News received of German Emperor's abdication.	
	11-11-18		Official information received by 08.30 hrs that all hostilities would cease by 11.00 hrs & that an armistice had been signed. Coys bathing in BERLAIMONT 07.00 - 14.00 hrs. Draft of 1 Officer & 92 O.R. arrived. Orders received for move tomorrow to BERLAIMONT.	
	12-11-18.		Battalion moved after dinners to outskirts of BERLAIMONT E of River SAMBRE. Fair billets.	BERLAI-MONT.
	13.11.18		Inspection of draft by Major STOREY and inspection of billets, general cleaning up etc. [illegible]	

D. D. & L., London, E.C.
(A10266) Wt W5300/P713 750,000 2/18 Sch. 52 Forms/C2118/26

Instructions regarding War Diaries and Intelligence Summaries are contained in F. S. Regs., Part II. and the Staff Manual respectively. Title pages will be prepared in manuscript.

WAR DIARY

or

INTELLIGENCE SUMMARY.

(Erase heading not required.)

Army Form C. 2118.

Place	Date	Hour	Summary of Events and Information	Remarks and references to Appendices
	14·11·18		Route march in morning. [illegible] in afternoon.	
	15·11·18		Started from BERLAIMONT 11.00 hrs. Marched through GRAND CARRIERE and FOREST de MORMAL, reached ENGLEFONTAINE at 14.00 hrs. Packs carried on limbers, billeted near our old objective.	ENGLE [illegible]
	16·11·18		Started off again at 08-30 hrs. Marched down main road through FOREST to CLARY. Interval of one hour for dinners on the way. Same billets as 14 October.	
	17·11·18		No church parades. Company Commanders conference in morning. Lieut. MALONE rejoined. Very cold day.	
	18·11·18		Company training in morning. Football started in afternoon. Sports Committee Meeting in evening.	
	19·11·18		Route march in morning. Lecture on demobilisation in afternoon. 10 officers and 140 N.C.O's attended. Companies paid out in evening. Football in afternoon.	

D. D. & L., London, E.C.
(A10266) Wt W5300/P713 750,000 2/18 Sch. 52 Forms/C2118/16

6.

Army Form C. 2118.

WAR DIARY
or
INTELLIGENCE SUMMARY.
(Erase heading not required.)

Instructions regarding War Diaries and Intelligence Summaries are contained in F. S. Regs., Part II. and the Staff Manual respectively. Title pages will be prepared in manuscript.

Place	Date	Hour	Summary of Events and Information	Remarks and references to Appendices
	20-11-18		Company Training. Foggy weather but cold. Football in afternoon.	
	21-11-18		Route march in morning. Football in afternoon.	
	22.11.18		Brigade Thanksgiving Service at 10.00 hrs. on D Coys parade ground. March past the Divisional Commander. Billeting party under Capt. POINTON M.C. left for [illegible] area.	
	23.11.18		Capt. HOPKINS. M.C. commands Battn. on Col. BADHAM D.S.O. proceeding to England on 5 days Special Leave. Officers reconnaissance party for [illegible]. Cleaning up of billets in morning. Company Cross-Country Run. Baths in morning + afternoon.	
	24.11.18		[illegible] Paraded at 9.30 hrs in Divisional Recreational Hut. Companies collected salvage in morning.	
	25.11.18		[illegible] 20th [illegible]. Rest of Battalion salvage + Company Training.	

D. D. & L., London, E.C.
(A10266) Wt W5300/P713 750,000 2/15 Sch. 52 Forms/C2118/16

Instructions regarding War Diaries and Intelligence Summaries are contained in F. S. Regs., Part II. and the Staff Manual respectively. Title pages will be prepared in manuscript.

WAR DIARY
or
INTELLIGENCE SUMMARY.
(Erase heading not required.)

Army Form C. 2118.

Place	Date	Hour	Summary of Events and Information	Remarks and references to Appendices
	26.11.18		A & B Coys. visit aerodrome. C & D training on Salvage Area. Lecture in afternoon on Demobilization by Rev. STUART KENNEDY	
	27.11.18		Brigade Commander inspected Transport. Companies at disposal of Coy. Commanders. D Coy. visit aerodrome - Flying demonstration. Football matches in afternoon.	
	28-11-18		Company training. Company Commanders conference at 09.00 am on Demobilization Tokens.	
	29-11-18		Battalion Route march in morning. Football match v. 20 Squadron R.A.F. Lost 1-2.	
	30-11-18		Cleaning up of billets etc. Armourer Sergt-Major inspected rifles of A & B Coys. 2Lt. C. R. [illegible] ([illegible]) left Battalion.	

E L Hopkins Capt.
Comdg.
2ND BN. THE WORCESTERSHIRE REGT.

D. D. & L., London, E.C.
(A10266) Wt W5300/P713 750,000 2/16 Sch. 52 Forms/C2118/16

Instructions regarding War Diaries and Intelligence Summaries are contained in F. S. Regs., Part II. and the Staff Manual respectively. Title pages will be prepared in manuscript.

WAR DIARY
or
INTELLIGENCE SUMMARY.
(Erase heading not required.)

Army Form C. 2118.

Place	Date	Hour	Summary of Events and Information	Remarks and references to Appendices
	1.12.18		[illegible] TANNER M.C. [illegible]	[illegible]
			[illegible] Officer [illegible]	
			[illegible] of AMIENS	
	2.12.18		Usual Coy [illegible] Conference of Coy [illegible]	
	3.12.18		Battalion [illegible] march [illegible] MARETZ. C.O. [illegible]	
			Coys [illegible] Capt. BOSWELL M.C.	
			awarded D.S.O. Capt. HOPKINS M.C. [illegible] M.C. [illegible] KELLY M.C.	
	4.12.18		H.M. THE KING passed through the village of CLARY [illegible] by the	
			Battalion [illegible] the village. Capt. [illegible]	
			C.J. BALDWYN proceeded on leave to U.K.	
	5.12.18		Companies at disposal of Coy Co[illegible]	
			All officers [illegible] attended a lecture on Education [illegible]	
			Education Officer – Capt. F. de ZULUETA. Football match [illegible]	
			afternoon 16th Bn. K.R.R.C. in afternoon [illegible]	

S.53

Instructions regarding War Diaries and Intelligence Summaries are contained in F. S. Regs., Part II. and the Staff Manual respectively. Title pages will be prepared in manuscript.

WAR DIARY
or
INTELLIGENCE SUMMARY.
(Erase heading not required.)

2

Army Form C. 2118.

Place	Date	Hour	Summary of Events and Information	Remarks and references to Appendices
	6.12.18		Battalion paraded for route march under Capt. E.L. HOPKINS M.C. at 09.30 hrs marching through ELINCOURT + MARETZ. Boxing contests [illegible] weights held in afternoon.	
	7.12.18.		All Companies bathing at CLARY. Commanding Officer inspected all billets Coys preparing for move to new area. 2nd Lt ASHCROFT joined Bn for duty.	
	8.12.18		Paraded at 09.30 hrs for Divine Service under Rev. E.V. TANNER. M.C.	
	9.12.18		Battalion commenced an eight days march to VILLERS-CAMPSART area W. of AMIENS. Paraded at 09.30 hrs marched from CLARY via LIGNY-HAUCOURT-ESNES-CREVECOEUR to temporary accomodation in MASNIERES. Dinners served on the way. Divisional Commander visited the Battalion at dinner. Move [illegible]	
	10.12.18		Very rainy all day. Batt'n marched away from MASNIERES at 09.30 hrs passing through MARCOING, RIBECOURT + HAVRINCOURT + halting for the night in a wet muddy camp at HERMIES.	

D. D. & L., London, E.C.
(A10266) Wt W5300/P713 750,000 2/18 Sch. 52 Forms/C2118/16

Instructions regarding War Diaries and Intelligence Summaries are contained in F. S. Regs., Part II. and the Staff Manual respectively. Title pages will be prepared in manuscript.

WAR DIARY
or
INTELLIGENCE SUMMARY.
(Erase heading not required.)

Army Form C. 2118.

3

Place	Date	Hour	Summary of Events and Information	Remarks and references to Appendices
	11.12.18		Another wet day bad for marching. Battn. left at 09.15 hrs & marched to FAVREUIL going through DOIGNIES, BEAUMETZ & VELU, crossing the BAPAUME-CAMBRAI road. Reached FAVREUIL at 13.30 hrs & Bn. accommodated in huts	
	12.12.18		At 09.00 hrs Bn commenced march through BAPAUME down the main road through the old Somme battlefield to ALBERT. Very wet day & very muddy roads. Reached the camp at 14.00 hrs. Battn marched well.	
	13.12.18		Left camp at 09.00 hrs marched away into better country. Divisional Commander inspected the Battn as it passed by down the ALBERT-AMIENS road. A fine day and at 13.30 hrs Battn reached a hut camp on E outskirts of PONT NOYELLES.	
	14.12.18.		Bn paraded at 09.00 hrs & continued the march along the main road. Marched through AMIENS & LONGPRE. Two coys billeted in [illegible]. H.Qrs & two coys billeted in St. SAUVEUR. Colonel BADHAM assumed temporary command of 100th Infy Bde. Capt. HOPKINS M.C. took over command of the Battalion.	

D. D. & L., London, E.C.
(A10266) Wt W5300/P713 750,000 2/18 Sch. 52 Forms/C2118/16

Instructions regarding War Diaries and Intelligence Summaries are contained in F. S. Regs., Part II. and the Staff Manual respectively. Title pages will be prepared in manuscript.

WAR DIARY
or
INTELLIGENCE SUMMARY.
(Erase heading not required.)

Army Form C. 2118.

Place	Date	Hour	Summary of Events and Information	Remarks and references to Appendices
	15.12.18		Marched out of St. SAUVEUR at 09.00hrs. Bn crossed over R. Somme & passed through AILLY-BREILLY CONDRINCY. Outside BOUGAINVILLE Battn was halted by Staff Officer & ordered to proceed to St. AUBIN instead of original village BOUGAINVILLE. Battn billeted by 16.00hrs.	
	16.12.18		At 09.00hrs. Bn paraded & marched out to final destination St. MAULVIS via HORNOY FRESNEVILLE. Bad roads. Reached St. MAULVIS at 13.30hrs. Major SYMONS returned from leave & assumed command of the Battn. Good billets found.	
	17.12.18		Bn spent in resting & in cleaning up after the march. Arrangements put in hand for sports & recreation & for Xmas dinners etc. Visit from Brigade Commander. Two new officers arrived from England.	
	18.12.18		Another day of general cleaning up. Party left for England to proceed to escort the colours to the Battn consisting of Capt TOUGH M.C. Capt BOSWELL D.S.O. M.C. R.S.M. FARLEY D.C.M. R.Q.M.S. ~~[illegible]~~ EVANS M.M. & C.Q.M.S. POLLARD. Sports Committee held a meeting. 2nd Lt. DALY appointed Sports Officer. Lt SCOTT M.C. appointed Transport officer.	

D. D. & L., London, E.C.
(A10266) Wt W5300/P713 750,000 2/18 Sch. 52 Forms/C2118/16

5 Army Form C. 2118.

Instructions regarding War Diaries and Intelligence Summaries are contained in F. S. Regs., Part II. and the Staff Manual respectively. Title pages will be prepared in manuscript.

WAR DIARY
or
INTELLIGENCE SUMMARY.
(Erase heading not required.)

Place	Date	Hour	Summary of Events and Information	Remarks and references to Appendices
	19-12-18		Coys at disposal of O's C Coys for general training + steady drill.	
			Lt. Col. J.F. BADHAM proceeded on leave to U.K. Command taken by Major O.V.L. SYMONS. A mess meeting held at 17.30hrs with reference to Christmas arrangements. Classes in boxing commence.	
	20-12-18		Roll call parade at 07.30hrs. commenced. Coys at disposal of O. C. Coys for general training. Plans discussed for the rapid erection of huts etc in Battn. Area. Cross country run.	
	21-12-18		Coys under Coy. Commanders for steady drill + musketry.	
			Box respirators inspected by Gas N.C.O.	
	22-12-18		Coys under Coy. Commanders. Very wet day.	
	23-12-18		Another wet day. Company Training.	
	24-12-18		Demonstration by No 4 Platoon on Recreational Training. C Coy at Baths. Football match at 11.00hrs. v. 101st F.A. at VILLERS.	

D. D. & L., London, E.C.
(A10266) Wt W5300/P713 750,000 2/15 Sch. 52 Forms/C2118/16

19

2 Dorset Rgt

VR 52

Instructions regarding War Diaries and Intelligence Summaries are contained in F. S. Regs., Part II. and the Staff Manual respectively. Title pages will be prepared in manuscript.

WAR DIARY
or
INTELLIGENCE SUMMARY.
(*Erase heading not required.*)

Army Form C. 2118.

Place	Date	Hour	Summary of Events and Information	Remarks and references to Appendices
	25-12-18.		XMAS. DAY. Fine morning. Church Parade in Square at 10.00. Xmas dinners by platoons with exception of A. Coy. who had dinner in open.	
	26-12-18.		No parades. A. Coy bathe in morning. B. Coy in afternoon.	
	27-12-18		Company route marches. Wet day.	
	28-12-18.		Wet day. G.O.C. 33rd Division presented medal ribbons at 11.00 hrs. Inspection put off owing to wet weather. MAJOR SYMONS to Brigade.	
	29-12-18.		No church parade. Voluntary service at 10.00 hrs. Wet all day.	
	30-12-18		Horses inspected by D.A.D.V.S. and classified. Education Officer lectures A & B Coys. No. 4. Platoon give demonstration for C & D. Coys.	
	31-12-18.		Coys. under O.C. Coys. for Drill & Recreational Training. MAJOR SYMONS returns from Brigade H.Q.	

Owen Symons Major LIEUT-COLONEL,
COMDG. 2nd Bn. THE WORCESTERSHIRE REGT.

D. D. & L., London, E.C.
(A10266) Wt W5300/P713 750,000 2/18 Sch. 52 Forms/C2118/16

33

2nd Worcester

Army Form C. 2118.

Instructions regarding War Diaries and Intelligence Summaries are contained in F. S. Regs., Part II. and the Staff Manual respectively. Title pages will be prepared in manuscript.

WAR DIARY
or
INTELLIGENCE SUMMARY.
(Erase heading not required.)

18 53

Place	Date	Hour	Summary of Events and Information	Remarks and references to Appendices
	1-1-19		[illegible] about the [illegible] came through [illegible] that Colour Party had arrived at [illegible] Reception Camp	
	2-1-19		COLOURS arrived at 10.30 hrs. A Guard of Honour (composed of 25 O.R. [illegible] from each Company) under command of Capt. [illegible] M.C. met the Colour Party on [illegible] the village and escorted them into Square of St. MARTIN. Divisional Band headed the march. Battalion drawn up in [illegible] [illegible] Companies afterwards marched past the Colours. COLOURS kept in [illegible] Room.	
	3-1-19		[illegible] accompanied by transport [illegible] at 08.00 hrs and marched [illegible] STERNMONT to REAL CAMPS. [illegible] Companies marched [illegible] very few fell out.	
	4-1-19		[illegible] ALL [illegible] BOCAMONT + LONDINIERES. Billets [illegible]	
	5-1-19		[illegible] at MARTIN [illegible] 13.30 hrs. [illegible]	
	6-1-19		Cleaning up [illegible] Brigade Conference at 15.20 hrs.	
	7-1-19		[illegible] Company Commanders ~~[illegible]~~ decided [illegible]	
	8-1-19		Brigade Conference at 10.30 hrs. [illegible] supplies [illegible]	
	9-1-19		Usual [illegible] parties. [illegible]	
	10-1-19		Preparations made for receiving [illegible]	
	11-1-19		[illegible] parade [illegible] to consolidate [illegible]	

9.54

D. D. & L., London, E.C.
(A10266) Wt W5300/P713 750,000 2/16 Sch. 52 Forms/C2118/16

Instructions regarding War Diaries and Intelligence Summaries are contained in F. S. Regs., Part II. and the Staff Manual respectively. Title pages will be prepared in manuscript.

WAR DIARY
or
INTELLIGENCE SUMMARY.
(Erase heading not required.)

Army Form C. 2118.

Place	Date	Hour	Summary of Events and Information	Remarks and references to Appendices
	12-1-19		Voluntary Church Parade. Group [illegible] busy in preparations [illegible]	
	13-1-19		Fatigue parties all day.	
	14-1-19		First parties arrived at C Block. Nearly 1,000 came in.	
	15-1-19		B. Block start to function. Very wet all day.	
	16-1-19		[illegible] Battalion arrives to take over B. Block.	
	17-1-19		Battalion bathed in morning. Pay out in afternoon. 18 O.R. demobilised.	
	18-1-19		C Block very busy. 21 O.R. demobilised.	
	19-1-19		Voluntary Church Parade. Everyone busy [illegible] CAPT. [illegible] as Garrison Staff Captain.	
	20-1-19		[illegible] day. ESSEX Regt. takes over B. Block from A & B Coys: latter [illegible] to C Block.	
	21-1-19		Fine day. 2,000 pass through C Block. Lt Col. J. F. BADHAM [illegible] from leave.	
	22-1-19		Cold day. 7 O.Rs demobilised.	
	23-1-19		MAJOR O.V.L. SYMONS & CAPT. SOMERS-[illegible] 26 O.Rs & 1 Officer [illegible]	
	24-1-19		[illegible] 4 O.Rs demobilised.	
	25-1-19		Cold day. Company Commanders conference at 10.00 a.m. 10 O.Rs demobilised.	
	26-1-19		50 O.Rs per coy for Church parade. 32 O.Rs & 2 Officers demobilised.	
	27-1-19		[illegible] demobilised [illegible]	
	28-1-19		C Block passed over 3,000 men during day. [illegible] BENNETT & [illegible] left Battalion.	

D. D. & L., London, E.C.
(A10266) Wt W5300/P713 750,000 2/15 Sch. 52 Forms/C2118/16

Instructions regarding War Diaries and Intelligence Summaries are contained in F. S. Regs., Part II. and the Staff Manual respectively. Title pages will be prepared in manuscript.

WAR DIARY
or
INTELLIGENCE SUMMARY.

(Erase heading not required.)

Army Form C. 2118.

Place	Date	Hour	Summary of Events and Information	Remarks and references to Appendices
	29-1-19		Routine	
	30-1-19		Routine	
	31-1-19		Routine	

J. F. Brauham[illegible]

LIEUT-COLONEL,
COMDG. 2nd Bn. THE WORCESTERSHIRE REGT.

D. D. & L., London, E.C.
(A10266) Wt W5300/P713 750,000 2/18 Sch. 52 Forms/C2118/16

9

Instructions regarding War Diaries and Intelligence Summaries are contained in F. S. Regs., Part II. and the Staff Manual respectively. Title pages will be prepared in manuscript.

WAR DIARY
or
INTELLIGENCE SUMMARY.
(Erase heading not required.)

2 Worcester Regt

Army Form C. 2118.

8 54

Place	Date	Hour	Summary of Events and Information	Remarks and references to Appendices
MARTIN	13.2.19		C & D bathed in afternoon 4 ORs demobilised	
EGLISE	14.2.19		A & B Coys bathed in morning & blankets passed through delouser.	
			1 Officer 43 ORs demobilised	
	15.2.19		Routine	
	16.2.19		Voluntary Church Parade. 22 ORs demobilised.	
	17.2.19		Routine	
	18.2.19		Routine	
	19.2.19		Routine	
	20.2.19		Routine	
	21.2.19		Routine 3 ORs demobilised	
	22.2.19		Routine	
	23.2.19		Routine. 3 Officers went on draft conducting leave	
	24.2.19		Routine	
	25.2.19		Routine. Col Bradshaw returned from Brigade & re assumed command of Battn	
	26.2.19		4 Officers 219 ORs reinforcements from 14th Bn. arrive Capt Hopkins MC 2 Officers on draft conducting leave	

S. 54

(A9175) Wt W2358/P36 600,000 12/17 D. D. & L. Sch. 52a. Forms/C2118/15.

Instructions regarding War Diaries and Intelligence Summaries are contained in F. S. Regs., Part II. and the Staff Manual respectively. Title pages will be prepared in manuscript.

WAR DIARY
or
INTELLIGENCE SUMMARY.
(Erase heading not required.)

Army Form C. 2118.

Place	Date	Hour	Summary of Events and Information	Remarks and references to Appendices
MARTIN EGLISE.	1.2.19		Parade at 10.00 hrs of all available officers & ORs. Farewell Speech by Br Gen A W Baird on leaving the Brigade	
	2.2.19		Parade service at 10.00 hrs. A Coy go through Delouser. Lt-Col J. Bradham DSO takes over temp command of 100th Brigade. Capt Hopkins MC assumes temp command of the Battn. 33 ORs demobilised.	
	3.2.19		Routine. B Coy pass through Delouser.	
	4.2.19		Routine. 1 Officer 33 ORs demobilised.	
	5.2.19		Routine. 4 ORs demobilised	
	6.2.19		Routine.	
	7.2.19		Routine 4 ORs demobilised	
	8.2.19		Routine 31 ORs demobilised	
	9.2.19		Routine 25 ORs demobilised	
	10.2.19		Routine	
	11.2.19		6 ORs & 193 ORs arrived as reinforcements from 3rd Bn. Brigade Commander inspected draft at 15.00 hrs 14 ORs demobilised.	
	12.2.19		Routine 36 ORs demobilised	

Instructions regarding War Diaries and Intelligence Summaries are contained in F. S. Regs., Part II. and the Staff Manual respectively. Title pages will be prepared in manuscript.

WAR DIARY
or
INTELLIGENCE SUMMARY.
(Erase heading not required.)

Army Form C. 2118.

Place	Date	Hour	Summary of Events and Information	Remarks and references to Appendices
MARTIN EGLISE	24.2.19		Inspection of draft at 14.00 hrs by Commanding Officer 1 Officer 24 ORs demobilised.	
	28.2.19		Inspection of Battn huts by Commanding Officer, During Jany & Feby 12 Officers & 434 ORs were demobilised	

J. F. Badham Lieut-Col
Comdg 2nd Bn The Worcestershire Regt

(A9175) Wt W2358/P361 600,000 12/17 D. D. & L. Sch. 52a. Forms/C2118/15.

2 Worcesters

M 55

Army Form C. 2118.

Instructions regarding War Diaries and Intelligence Summaries are contained in F. S. Regs., Part II. and the Staff Manual respectively. Title pages will be prepared in manuscript.

WAR DIARY
or
INTELLIGENCE SUMMARY.
(Erase heading not required.)

Place	Date 1919	Hour	Summary of Events and Information	Remarks and references to Appendices
	Apr 1		Routine. League football match in afternoon v N.F. New Summer time	
	2		Church Parade of all available ranks. [illegible]	
	3		Brigade Conference at 10.30 hrs. Coy Commanders Conference at 5.30pm.	
	4		Routine. Conference of all officers at 5.30pm.	
	5		Routine	
	6		Routine	
	7		Draft of 4 officers & 108 ORs. arrive from 1st Bn Worcestershire Regt. Lieut Ashcroft departs on ordinary leave. [illegible] [illegible] on draft conducting leave	
	8		Routine	
	9		Voluntary Church Parade	
	10		Routine. 20 ORs demobilised	
	11		Commanding Officer proceeds to G.H.Q. for two days duty. Capt Sowton [illegible] returns from leave.	
	12		Routine. Coy Commanders Conference	
	13		Routine	

D. D. & L., London, E.C.
(10340) Wt W5300/P713 750,000 3/18 E 2688 Forms C/2118/16.

S.55

Instructions regarding War Diaries and Intelligence Summaries are contained in F. S. Regs., Part II. and the Staff Manual respectively. Title pages will be prepared in manuscript.

WAR DIARY
or
INTELLIGENCE SUMMARY.
(Erase heading not required.)

Army Form C. 2118.

Place	Date 1919	Hour	Summary of Events and Information	Remarks and references to Appendices
	Sept 14		One Platoon per Coy started training under OC Coys. Remainder of available men parade under RSM.	
	15		Platoon training.	
	16		Voluntary Church Parade	
	17		Platoon training. Demobilisation commences in B Block. Regimental farewell dinner to Capt W.A. Edwards MC. Staff Capt 100th Infy Bde, late Adjutant 2nd Bn The Worcestershire Regt	
	18		Coys parade in full marching order for inspection by Commanding Officer	
	19		Platoon training. Lt-Col J.T. Radbourne DSO to Hospital. 15 ORs demobilised. Capt E.L. Hopkins assumes command	
	20		Platoon training. Orders came in about move.	
	21		Whole morning spent in cleaning up camp. Lt Col J.T. Radbourne DSO returns from Hospital. Miss Silver "Singer of the Worcestershire Regt" gives concert in evening.	

D. D. & L., London, E.C.
(10340) Wt W5300/P713 750,000 3/18 E 2688 Forms C/2118/16.

Instructions regarding War Diaries and Intelligence Summaries are contained in F. S. Regs., Part II. and the Staff Manual respectively. Title pages will be prepared in manuscript.

WAR DIARY
or
INTELLIGENCE SUMMARY.
(Erase heading not required.)

Army Form C. 2118.

Place	Date 1919	Hour	Summary of Events and Information	Remarks and references to Appendices
	Mar		Batter moves by train to HAVRE. A & B Coys go by first train with Bn HQ & ½ Transport, moves out of ARQUES at 2000 hrs. C & D Coys, QMR & ½ Transport entrain at 2200 hrs & move off at 0330 hrs 23rd	
	23		C & B Coys arrive HAVRE (Gare des Hangars) at 0700 hrs. C & D Coys at 1200 hrs. Batter moves into huts at CINDER CITY, fairly comfortable quarters. Bad sanitary arrangements.	
	24		Coy's night duty 17 guards to find. Guard mounting at 10.30 hrs	
	25		Usual guard finding & one coy training. Br Gen GUGGISBERG came down in morning	
	26		Routine. A Coy proceeds by lorry to HARFLEUR on detachment & to find guards & escort for Depot Coy I of W.	
	27		Routine. Col Rashaw DSO proceeds to GHQ for duty. Capt E L Hopkins commanding Batter.	
	28		Routine. Capt E L Hopkins MC to hospital. Capt & Adjt C E Baldwin assumes temporary command of Batter. Capt A C Sutton MC takes over Adjutancy	

D. D. & L., London, E.C.
(20340) Wt W5300/P713 750,000 3/18 E 2688 Forms C/2118/16.

Instructions regarding War Diaries and Intelligence Summaries are contained in F. S. Regs., Part II. and the Staff Manual respectively. Title pages will be prepared in manuscript.

WAR DIARY
or
INTELLIGENCE SUMMARY.
(Erase heading not required.)

Army Form C. 2118.

Place	Date 1919	Hour	Summary of Events and Information	Remarks and references to Appendices
	Nov 29		Routine. Cadre of 1st Battn arrives. 6 officers & 43 ORs with transport.	
	30		Routine. Voluntary Church Parade.	
	1		Routine. Commanding Officer returns from G.H.Q. kit inspection. ½ D Coy at Baths.	

A C Pointon Col
for LIEUT-COLONEL,
COMDG. 2nd Bn. THE WORCESTERSHIRE REGT.

D. D. & L., London, E.C.
(10349) Wt W5300/P713 750,000 3/18 E 2688 Forms C/2118/16.

2nd Bn The Worcestershire Regt

Instructions regarding War Diaries and Intelligence Summaries are contained in F. S. Regs., Part II. and the Staff Manual respectively. Title pages will be prepared in manuscript.

WAR DIARY
or
INTELLIGENCE SUMMARY.
(Erase heading not required.)

2 Worcester R

Army Form C. 2118.

WO 56

Place	Date	Hour	Summary of Events and Information	Remarks and references to Appendices
Cinder City Le Havre	1-4-19		"B" Coy turned out early as Picket for a fire in the Docks Visit from Lt Col Whalley D.S.O. and Cadre of 3rd Battn, who are awaiting embarkation.	
—"—	2-4-19		Capt & Adjt C. F. Baldwyn proceeded on leave to U.K.	
—"—	3-4-19		Routine as usual.	
—"—	4-4-19		Routine as usual	
—"—	6-4-19		New programme of work for the Battalion	
—"—	7-4-19		Major Hopkins M.C. returned from Hospital Early morning parades commenced 10 men demobilised N.C.Os Class 14·00 hours to 15 hours	
—"—	8-4-19		Fine weather - Routine as usual - preparing to hand over to 17th Battn on our reduction to Cadre strength.	
—"—	9-4-19		11 Officers commenced their short course of training at 100th Infy Bde School.	
—"—	10-4-19		Draft of 28 O.R. arrived from 14th Battalion. C.O. attended demonstration at Brigade School Routine.	
—"—	11-4-19		An escort found to England, under Lieut Perry M.C Subscriptions collected for Worcestershire War Memorial at paying out parades.	
—"—	12-4-19		Period 07-15 – 07-45 hours spent in Barrack cleaning C.O. visited and inspected all Barrack rooms during the morning Football team played 39 Gen: Hospl winning 3-0	

S.56

D. D. & L., London, E.C.
(10340) Wt W3300/P713 750,000 3/18 E 2688 Forms/C/2118/16.

2nd Bn The Worcestershire Regt

WAR DIARY
or
INTELLIGENCE SUMMARY.
(Erase heading not required.)

Army Form C. 2118.

Instructions regarding War Diaries and Intelligence Summaries are contained in F. S. Regs., Part II. and the Staff Manual respectively. Title pages will be prepared in manuscript.

Place	Date	Hour	Summary of Events and Information	Remarks and references to Appendices
Cinder City Le Havre	13-4-19		Voluntary Church parades.	
	14-4-19		Routine. Battn has to be reduced to cadre strength by 12.00 hours tomorrow.	
			Conference of O C Coys, Q.M. & T.O. to present new arrangements and settle details of handing over.	
			"Wing Boys" concert party gave the Battn a performance in the evening.	
	15-4-19		All retainable or volunteers Officers & men of this Battn were transferred at 12.00 hours to the 17th Bn The Worcestershire Regt. under temporary command of Lt Col. Stadham, D.S.O.	
			All horses and ammunition handed over.	
			The personnel of the cadre paraded at 12.00 hours for Commanding Officers inspection. They are henceforth in readiness to move	
	16-4-19		New Orderly Room occupied by the cadre	
	17-4-19		Total subscriptions to Worcestershire War Memorial Fund announced as £ 351-13-0 "from Officers, W. Os, N C Os & men of 2/Worcestershire Regt in France April 1919".	
			Ordnance Officer arrived to inspect Battalion stores.	
	18-4-19		Routine.	
	19-4-19		Routine	
	20-4-19		Easter Sunday. Capt C. F. Baldwyn returns from leave. Voluntary Church parade. Football match in afternoon, 17th Battn team wins.	
	21-4-19		Holiday for men not doing Guards.	
	22-4-19		Routine	
	23-4-19		Routine	
	24-4-19		Routine	
	25-4-19		Routine	

D. D. & L., London, E.C.
(10340) Wt W5300/P713 750,000 3/18 E 2688 Forms C/2118/16.

2nd Bn The Worcestershire Regt

Instructions regarding War Diaries and Intelligence Summaries are contained in F. S. Regs., Part II. and the Staff Manual respectively. Title pages will be prepared in manuscript.

WAR DIARY
or
INTELLIGENCE SUMMARY.
(Erase heading not required.)

Army Form C. 2118.

Place	Date	Hour	Summary of Events and Information	Remarks and references to Appendices
Cinder City Le Havre	26-4-19		Routine	
	27-4-19		Routine	
	28-4-19		Routine	
	29-4-19		Routine	
	30-4-19		Routine	

E. L. Hopkins. Major ~~LIEUT-COLONEL~~,
COMDG. 2nd Bn. THE WORCESTERSHIRE REGT.

D. D. & L., London, E.C.
(10340) Wt W3300/P713 750,000 3/18 E 2688 Forms C/2118/16

Instructions regarding War Diaries and Intelligence Summaries are contained in F. S. Regs., Part II. and the Staff Manual respectively. Title pages will be prepared in manuscript.

WAR DIARY
or
INTELLIGENCE SUMMARY.
(Erase heading not required.)

Army Form C. 2118.

Place	Date	Hour	Summary of Events and Information	Remarks and references to Appendices
Le Havre	1/5/19		Routine	
"	2/5/19		"	
"	3/5/19		"	
"	4/5/19		"	
"	5/5/19		"	
"	6/5/19		"	
"	7/5/19		"	
"	8/5/19		Orders received to reduce personnel of Cadre to 3 Officers and 36 Other ranks.	
"	9/5/19		2/Lieut S.Mainwaring and 2/Lieut D.Powell to leave for England.	
"	10/5/19		"Special Order of the Day" issued about Cadres.	
"	11/5/19		Routine	
"	12/5/19		Routine. Hot weather.	
"	13/5/19		Routine. Cadre photographed at 16-30 hours.	
"	14/5/19		Routine.	
"	15/5/19		"	
"	16/5/19		"	
"	17/5/19		"	
"	18/5/19		"	
"	19/5/19		Wire received informing us of our destination FOVANT.	
"	20-5-19		Routine.	
"	21/5/19		Bugles presented by 10th Bn Worcestershire Regt arrived also Orderly Room box from 3rd Echelon.	
"	22/5/19		Routine	
"	23/5/19		Routine	
"	24/5/19		"	
"	25/5/19		"	
"	26/5/19		"	
"	27/5/19		"	
"	28/5/19		"	
"	29/5/19		"	
"	30/5/19		Verbal orders received for Ca[illegible] to embark on June 1st.	
"	31/5/19		Routine.	

E.J.Hopkins MAJOR ~~LIEUT-COLONEL~~
COMDG 2nd Bn THE WORCESTERSHIRE REGT

D. D. & L., London (10340) W5300/P713 750,000 3/18

www.ingramcontent.com/pod-product-compliance
Lightning Source LLC
Chambersburg PA
CBHW080900230426
43663CB00013B/2587
9781474516730